ATLANTA

A City of the Modern South

Compiled by Workers of the
Writers' Program of the Work Projects Administration
in the State of Georgia

AMERICAN GUIDE SERIES

ILLUSTRATED

Sponsored by the Board of Education
of the City of Atlanta

SMITH & DURRELL

Republished 1973
SOMERSET PUBLISHERS — a Division of Scholarly Press, Inc.
22929 Industrial Drive East, St. Clair Shores, Michigan 48080

UNIVERSITY OF GEORGIA,

State-wide Sponsor of the Georgia Writers' Project

FEDERAL WORKS AGENCY

BRIG. GEN. PHILIP B. FLEMING, *Administrator*

WORK PROJECTS ADMINISTRATION

HOWARD O. HUNTER, *Commissioner*
FLORENCE KERR, *Assistant Commissioner*
HARRY E. HARMAN, JR., *State Administrator*

Library of Congress Cataloging in Publication Data

Writers' Program. Georgia.
   Atlanta, a city of the modern South.

   Original ed. issued in series: American guide
series.
   Bibliography: p.
   1. Atlanta. 2. Atlanta—Description—Guide-books.
I. Series: American guide series.
F294.A8W8 1973   917.58'231'044   72-84460
ISBN 0-403-02200-2

Preface

IN THE minds of many American citizens, tradition is the very essence of the South. They expect to find it both as a grace and a disaster, sometimes flowering as fine living and exquisite manners, sometimes wrapped like a vine about an entire community and strangling all the best energies of progress. This picture takes into account only two aspects: on the one hand magnolias, black mammies, fried chicken, and beautiful belles; on the other cornbread with fat-back and lackadaisical farmers.

To both these preconceptions Atlanta is its own best refutation. At first sight the tourist may see no tradition at all. All the bustle and clamor of this ever-changing city seem to take no account of the past, to make no terms with anything but modern ways and rapid production. This city of big stores, of smoking factories, of handsome modern residences, is truly a city of the modern South. Yet the reader must not be misled by the subtitle of this book. Young as it is, Atlanta has a most dynamic history, swift, exciting, sometimes turbulent.

In assembling the vital facts, the Georgia Writers' Project consulted many written records and interviewed many people. The written sources were helpful. The research workers of the project pored over everything from old newspaper files to Walter G. Cooper's *The Official History of Fulton County*. The interviewing of people was more difficult—and more fascinating. In a city as young as Atlanta it was sometimes possible to find older citizens who remembered back to the exciting days of Reconstruction, and occasionally these men and women would recall comments of their parents that threw light on the very beginnings of Atlanta. The books and papers gave necessary facts; the people interviewed gave an atmosphere fresh from actual experience. They did not always remember exact dates, but by such remarks as "We children weren't allowed to play on that street," or "You didn't have to take a chaperon if there were two couples in the surrey" they imparted a living quality to their reminiscences of Atlanta's history.

v

Since the publication of Margaret Mitchell's *Gone With The Wind* and the extraordinary publicity given the city by the world premiere of the motion picture, an increasing number of people have wanted to know more about Atlanta. *Atlanta, A City of the Modern South,* compiled by the Georgia Writers' Project and sponsored by the Atlanta Board of Education, should answer many of their questions. The first part tells of the development of the city in its many phases; the second part locates and describes some of the principal points of interest; a chronology, bibliography, and index will be found in the third section. It is for both tourist and Atlanta citizen that this work has been published.

SAMUEL TUPPER, JR.,
State Supervisor
KATHRYN A. HOOK,
Project Technician

Contents

Part I: The General Background

Part II: Points of Interest

CONTENTS ix

Part III: Points of Interest in Environs

Part IV: Appendices

Illustrations

General Information

Information Service: Atlanta Chamber of Commerce, Chamber of Commerce Bldg., Pryor St. at Auburn Ave.; Atlanta Motor Club (AAA), Biltmore Hotel, 817 W. Peachtree St.; Dixie Motor Club, 309 Peachtree St., NE.; Atlanta Convention and Visitors' Bureau, Rhodes-Haverty Bldg., 134 Peachtree St., NW.; Atlanta Historical Society, Biltmore Hotel, 817 W. Peachtree St. For correct time call WAlnut 8550.

Railroad Stations: Terminal Station, Mitchell and Spring Sts., SW., for Central of Georgia Ry., Atlanta & West Point R.R., Seaboard Air Line Ry., and Southern Ry.; Union Station, 2 Forsyth St., NW., for Atlanta, Birmingham & Coast R.R., Louisville & Nashville R.R., Nashville, Chattanooga & St. Louis Ry., and Georgia R.R.; Peachtree Station, 1688 Peachtree St., NW., for Southern Ry.

Bus Station: Union Terminal, 81 Cain St., NW., for Southeastern Greyhound of Alabama, Southeastern Management Co., Atlantic Greyhound Corp., Teche Greyhound Lines, Southeastern Stages, Inc., Georgia Stages, Inc., Service Stages, Inc., Smoky Mountain Stages, Inc., Southeastern Motor Lines, Dahlonega-Atlanta Bus Line, Neel Gap Bus Line, Tennessee Coach Co., Suburban Coach Co., and Interurban Transit Lines.

Sightseeing Busses: Daily sightseeing tours from downtown hotels, the Union Bus Terminal, and the Sightseeing Bus Stand, Peachtree and Broad Sts., NW. Automobiles for hire and guides also available.

Airport: Atlanta Municipal Airport, 9.2 m. S. of city at Hapeville on US 41, for Eastern and Delta Air Lines; special bus, fare 75¢, stops at hotels, Terminal Station, and downtown ticket offices of air lines.

Taxis: 35¢ for first 2½ miles for one to five passengers; 10¢ for each additional ⅖ mile; $2.50 an hour.

Streetcars and Local Busses: 10¢; two tokens for 15¢; shoppers' busses limited to central business section, 5¢.

Traffic Regulations: Speed limit 25 m.p.h. Right turn permitted on red light after full stop; left turn on green light only. Signs by traffic lights mark intersection where no left turns are permitted. One-way streets marked by arrows. Signs indicate where parking is permitted in downtown area; parking on right of street enforced even in residential section.

Radio Stations: WSB (NBC red network, 750 kc.), Biltmore Hotel, 817 W. Peachtree St.; WGST (CBS, 920 kc.), Forsyth Bldg., Forsyth and Luckie Sts., NW.; WATL (Mutual, 1400 kc.), Henry Grady Hotel, 210 Peachtree St., NW.; WAGA (NBC blue network, 1480 kc.), Western Union Bldg., Marietta and Forsyth Sts., NW.

Theaters and Motion Picture Houses: Erlanger Theater, 583 Peachtree St., NE., for occasional Broadway successes on tour; Municipal Auditorium-Armory, Courtland and Gilmer Sts., NE., for scheduled concerts and operas; 48 motion picture houses, including 6 for Negroes.

Accommodations: About 90 hotels, including 10 for Negroes; many tourist homes. Space permits listing only the larger and better-known hotels. City Hotels: Ansley, 98 Forsyth St., NW.; Atlanta Biltmore, 817 W. Peachtree St., NE.; Atlantan, 111 Luckie St., NW.; Briarcliff, 1050 Ponce de Leon Ave., NE.; Byron, 552 W. Peachtree St., NW.; Clermont, 789 Ponce de Leon Ave., NE.; Cox-Carlton, 683 Peachtree St., NE.; Georgian Terrace, 659 Peachtree St., NE.; Hampton, 35 Houston St., NE.; Henry Grady, 210 Peachtree St., NW.; Imperial, 355 Peachtree St., NE.; Jefferson, 87 Pryor St., SW.; Kimball House, 33 Pryor St., SW.; Marion, 67 Pryor St., NE.; Piedmont, 108 Peachtree St., NW.; Robert Fulton, 114 Luckie St., NW.; Tremont, 192 Mitchell St., SW.; Winecoff, 176 Peachtree St., NW.

Environs Hotels: Candler, 150 E. Ponce de Leon Ave., Decatur; Colonial Terrace, 2140 Peachtree Rd., NW.; Hangar, Municipal Airport, Hapeville.

Negro Hotels: Mack, 548 Bedford Pl., NE.; Royal, 214 Auburn Ave., NE.; Savoy, 239 Auburn Ave., NE.

Restaurants: Arcade, 110-12 Forsyth St., NW.; Brass Rail, 138 Peachtree St., NW.; Colonnade, 2415 Piedmont Rd., NE.; Ellen Rice Tea Room, 63½ Poplar St., NW.; Frances Virginia Tea Room, Collier Bldg., Peachtree and Ellis Sts., NE.; Herren's, 84 Luckie St., NW.; Holsum Cafeteria, 181 Peachtree St., NE.; Majestic, 1026 Peachtree St., NE.; Peacock Alley, 1564 Peachtree St., NE.; Pig'n Whistle, 293 Ponde de Leon Ave., NE., and 2143 Peachtree Rd., NW.; Rector's, 620 Peachtree St., NE.; S & W Cafeteria, 189 Peachtree St., NE.; Ship Ahoy, 95 Luckie St., NW.; Tavern Tea Room, 625-27 Peachtree St., NE.; Venable's, 73 Forsyth St., NW. (*Space permits listing only some of the better-known restaurants. All the larger hotels have coffee shops and dining rooms, and there are modern restaurants in all sections of the city.*)

Dining and Dancing: Empire Room, Biltmore Hotel, 817 W. Peachtree St.; Herren's Evergreen Farm (*open during summer only*), US 23; Paradise Room, Henry Grady Hotel, 210 Peachtree St., NW., floor show; Rainbow Roof, Ansley Hotel, 98 Forsyth St., NW., floor show; Wisteria Garden, 172½ Peachtree St., NW.

Baseball Games: Ponce de Leon Park, 650 Ponce de Leon Ave., NE., Southern League (Atlanta Crackers); Rose Bowl Field (Georgia Tech), Fifth St., NE.; Hermance Stadium (Oglethorpe University), Peachtree Rd., NE.

Football Games: Grant Field (Georgia Tech), North Ave. and Techwood Dr., NW.; Hermance Stadium (Oglethorpe University), Peachtree Rd., NE.; Ponce de Leon Park, 650 Ponce de Leon Ave., NE., for high school games.

Recreational Facilities

Amusement Park: Lakewood Park, Lakewood Ave., SE. (*open May 1-Oct. 5; bowling alley and roller rink open year round*), 370.9 acres; lake for boating, race track, midway, roller rink, bowling alley, exhibition buildings for Southeastern Fair.

County Parks: Adams Park, Cascade Rd., SW., 168 acres; golf course, swimming pool, lighted tennis courts, softball diamond, playgrounds, picnic grills, bridle paths, lake for fishing, community house with branch library. Georgia Botanical Garden, Gordon Rd., SW., 459 acres. North Fulton Park, Powers Ferry Rd., NW., 320 acres; golf course, polo field, stables and bridle paths, tennis courts, swimming pool, lake for canoeing and fishing, archery range, picnic grills and shelters.

Municipal Parks: Cochran Park (Oakland City), Holderness St., SW.; swimming pool, tennis courts, playgrounds. Grant Park, S. Boulevard and Atlanta Ave., SE., 144 acres; swimming pool, lake for boating, tennis courts, baseball and softball diamonds, pony ring, playgrounds, picnic grounds, greenhouses, zoo, Cyclorama of the Battle of Atlanta. Maddox Park, Bankhead Ave., NW.; swimming pool, tennis courts, playgrounds. Mozley Park, Mozley Dr., SW.; swimming pool, tennis courts, basketball courts, baseball and softball diamonds, playgrounds. Piedmont Park, Piedmont Ave. and 14th St., NE., 185 acres; golf course, swimming pool, lake stocked with fish, tennis courts, baseball and softball diamonds, picnic grounds, pony ring, playgrounds. Washington Park (Negro), Lena and Ollie Sts., NW.; swimming pool, tennis courts, playgrounds, baseball and softball diamonds, picnic grounds.

Bowling: Blick's Bowling Center, top floor Belle Isle Garage, 20 Houston St., NE. Blick's Lucky Strike Bowling Alley, 671 Peach-

tree St., NE.   Speedway Bowling Alley, 693 Marietta St., NW.
(*Only centrally located alleys listed.*)

Golf: Adams Park Golf Course (county-operated), Cascade Rd.,
SW., 18 holes. Asa G. Candler Park Golf Course (city-operated),
McLendon Ave. at Mason Ave., NE., 9 holes. Black Rock Club,
Campbellton Rd., SW., 18 holes. Bobby Jones Golf Course (city-
operated), Memorial Dr., NW., 18 holes. College Park Golf Course,
W. Harvard Ave., College Park, 9 holes. Dixie Lakes Golf Course
(county-operated), 16 m. SW. on US 29, 9 holes. Forrest Hills Golf
Course, Columbia Dr., Decatur, 9 holes. James L. Key Golf Course
(city-operated), Kalb St., SE., 9 holes. John A. White Golf Course
(city-operated), Huff Rd. at Cascade Ave., SW., 9 holes. North
Fulton Park Golf Course (county-operated), Powers Ferry Rd., NW.,
18 holes. Piedmont Park Golf Course (city-operated), Boulevard at
Tenth St., NE., 9 holes. New Lincoln Golf Course (Negro), Simpson
and Hightower Rds., NW., 9 holes.

Riding: Adams Park, Cascade Rd., SW. North Fulton Park, Powers
Ferry Rd., NW. Pine Hill Stables, W. Wieuca Rd., NW. Pinetop
Stables, W. Wieuca Rd., NW. Roxboro Riding Club, Powers Ferry
Rd., NW. Simmons Riding Academy, Candler Rd., NE.

Roller Skating: Atlanta Skating Casino, 31 North Ave., NE. Lakewood Roller Rink, Inc., Lakewood Park, Lakewood Ave., SE. Roller-
drome, 634 Penn Ave., NE.

Swimming: Pools in all *Municipal Parks* and *County Parks*. Black
Rock Club, Campbellton Rd., SW. Briarcliff Gardens, 1260 Briar-
cliff Rd., NE. Mooney's Lake, Morosgo Dr., NE. Venetian Athletic
Club, Nelson's Ferry Rd., Decatur. YMCA, 145 Luckie St., NW.
YWCA, 37 Auburn Ave., NE. YMCA (Negro), 22 Butler St., NE.

Tennis: See *Municipal Parks* and *County Parks*.

Churches

(Only the larger churches of most denominations are listed.)

Assembly of God: Tabernacle, 311 Capitol Ave., SE.

Baptist: Druid Hills, 1085 Ponce de Leon Ave., NE.; First, 754 Peachtree St., NE.; Second-Ponce de Leon, 2715 Peachtree Rd., NE.; Tabernacle, 152 Luckie St., NW.

Christian and Missionary Alliance: Atlanta Gospel Tabernacle, 850 Euclid Ave., NE.

Church of Christ: Moreland Avenue, 671 Moreland Ave., SE.; West End, 580 Hopkins St., SW.

Church of Christ, Scientist: First, 1235 Peachtree St., NE.

Church of God: Hemphill Avenue, 869 Hemphill Ave., NW.

Congregational: Central, 180 Ponce de Leon Ave., NE.

Disciples of Christ: First Christian, 200 Pryor St., SW.; Peachtree Christian, 1580 Peachtree St., NW.

Episcopal: All Saints', 634 West Peachtree St., NW.; Cathedral of St. Philip, 2744 Peachtree Rd., NE.; St. Luke's 435 Peachtree St., NE.

Evangelical and Reformed: St. John's, 836 Euclid Ave., NE.

Evangelical Lutheran: Grace, 914 Cherokee Ave., SE.

Foursquare Gospel: Foursquare Gospel Church, 31 Trinity Ave., SW.

Jewish: Congregation Ahavath Achim, 346 Washington St., SW.; Temple, 1589 Peachtree, NW.

Lutheran: United Lutheran Church of the Redeemer, 731 Peachtree St., NE.

Methodist: Druid Hills, 675 Seminole Ave., NE.; First, 360 Peachtree St., NE.; Glenn Memorial, 1976 North Decatur Rd., NE.; St. Mark's, 781 Peachtree St., NE.; Trinity, 565 Washington St., SW.; Wesley Memorial, 63 Auburn Ave., NE.

Mormon: Church of Jesus Christ of Latter-day Saints, 605 Boulevard, NE.

Nazarene: First, 123 Moreland Ave., SE.

Orthodox: Greek Orthodox Church of the Annunciation, 522 Pryor St., SW.; Syrian, 233 Central Place, SE.

Pentecostal: Apostolic Assembly Pentecostal Tabernacle, 476 Washington St., SW.

Presbyterian: Central, 201 Washington St., SW.; Druid Hills, 1026 Ponce de Leon Ave., NE.; First, 1328 Peachtree St., NE.; North Avenue, 607 Peachtree St., NE.; Westminster, 493 Ponce de Leon Ave., NE.

Primitive Baptist: Bethany, 171 Moreland Ave., SE.

Roman Catholic: Church of Christ the King, 2699 Peachtree Rd., NE.; Immaculate Conception, 152 Central Ave., SW.; Sacred Heart, 335 Ivy St., NE.

Salvation Army: Temple Corps, 54 Ellis St., NE.

Seventh-day Adventist: Beverly Road Church, Beverly and Peachtree Rds., NE.

Unitarian-Universalist: Unitarian-Universalist Church, 669 West Peachtree St., NE.

NEGRO CHURCHES

Baptist: Friendship, 435 Mitchell St., SW.; Liberty, 395 Chamberlain St., SE.; Wheat Street, 359 Auburn Ave., NE.

Congregational: First, 104 Houston St., NE.; Rush Memorial, 150 Chestnut St., SW.

Episcopal: St. Paul's, 135 Ashby St., NW.

Methodist: Big Bethel, 220 Auburn Ave., NE.; St. Paul's, 453 McDaniel St., SW.; Warren Memorial, 741 Greensferry Ave., SW.

Presbyterian: Radcliffe Memorial, 297 Houston St., NE.

Roman Catholic: Our Lady of Lourdes, 29 Boulevard, NE.

Seventh-day Adventist: Second, 105 Ashby St., SW.

Calendar of Annual Events

FEBRUARY

No fixed date   Southeastern Golden Gloves Boxing Tournament.

No fixed date   MacDowell Festival.

MARCH

No fixed date   Georgia Federation of Music Clubs Contest.

APRIL

No fixed date   Atlanta Garden Club Association Flower Show.

No fixed date   Opening Southern Baseball Association Season.

No fixed date   Grand Opera Season.

No fixed date (Biennial)   Young Artists' and Student Musicians' Contest.

Easter   Interdenominational Sunrise Service.

No fixed date   Dogwood Festival and Garden Tours.

Twenty-sixth   Confederate Memorial Day Exercises.

Twenty-eighth   Reunion of Irish Horse Traders.

MAY

Eighth through tenth   Horse Show.

No fixed date   Music Week.

No fixed date   State Marble Tournament.

No fixed date   Uncle Remus May Festival.

JULY

Fourth   Automobile Races at Lakewood.

Week of Fourth   Southeastern Chess Tournament.

No fixed date   Soap Box Derby.

AUGUST

Second Friday   Sacred Harp Singers' Southeastern Convention.

SEPTEMBER

Labor Day   Automobile Races at Lakewood.

No fixed date   Georgia Old Time Fiddlers' Association Convention.

No fixed date   Dog Show.

OCTOBER

First Week   Southeastern Fair.

Opening Georgia Tech Football Season.

Second Week   DeKalb County Harvest Festival.

No fixed date   Opening of All-Star Concert Series.

NOVEMBER

No fixed date   Cat Show.

DECEMBER

Ninth   Joel Chandler Harris Memorial Service.

No fixed date   Roller Derby.

Part One

THE GENERAL BACKGROUND

Atlanta
A City of the Modern South

NONE of the railway approaches to Atlanta gives a just introduction to the city. A newcomer entering the outskirts can scarcely believe that a thriving business section and handsome residences lie somewhere beyond the barricade of factories and grimy warehouses. Yet in a moment the downtown skyline towers suddenly in the smoky heavens, and in another half hour, perhaps, he is being driven past estates as imposing as any in the modern South. On the other hand, he could live here for months and see nothing more inspiring than rows of houses indistinguishable from those of any other city. He may see avenues of mansions or dreary back streets, pleasant cottages or tumbledown Negro shanties. Wealth and poverty, beauty and drabness—Atlanta has them all.

The newcomer may believe he has caught its intrinsic spirit when he turns east from the Terminal Station into the bustling downtown section built about the flagpole at Five Points and cut in half by Peachtree Street, Atlanta's principal thoroughfare. Here is a city of angular corners, of narrow, irregular streets crowded with traffic, of smoke, of hurrying figures, of high buildings forming a jagged and beautiful skyline, of darkly shadowed entrances and towers catching the sun, of soot-blackened granite and shining plate glass, of old walls crumbling while, to the clatter of riveters, new walls spring up toward the sky.

Atlanta has almost everything except age. Only a century has passed since the first railroad builders dug and hammered the town into being, and through its years of tumultuous history it has grown into a city too rapidly to look well to its monuments. In order to find the landmarks of Atlanta's earliest history, it is necessary to go down below the downtown streets into a dark underground, eternally roaring with the noise of the railroad trains that gave birth to the settlement. Here, encased in a protecting fence of crossties, stands the "zero milepost," set up in 1842 to mark the eastern terminus of the Western & Atlantic Railroad. In this region the pioneers cleared

3

the brush and built rough shanties. Now the forest paths have been hidden by cobblestones and steel rails gleaming in every direction, and the five viaducts overhead hum with the echo of passing trains. Under the sheds passengers get on and off trains to an intermittent accompaniment of other noises, the thud of mail sacks being thrown to the platform, the creak of wheels as the baggage carts are pushed by men in overalls, and the trainmen's recurrent call of "All aboard!"

Up to the level of Peachtree Street again and east of Five Points is another section that is old—for this vigorous and youthful city. This area, encircling the Capitol for several blocks, was the heart of fashionable Atlanta until the middle 1880's when commerce broke into the lines of handsome Victorian dwellings. These houses, looming spacious behind their green lawns, were mostly erected after the Greek Revival period and they bore the more romantic ornamentation of a later day: ironwork, cupolas, bay windows, and turrets with pointed roofs. Many of these still survive, but shabbily as cheap lodging houses. Nevertheless, the neighborhood about Capitol Square still has a measure of its old dignity because of many large trees and some of the older churches that stoutly hold their ground. Here also are some of the older synagogues, and occasionally a rabbi, bearded, a black skull-cap set upon his gray locks, walks by with gravely folded hands. The kosher markets along Washington Street and Capitol Avenue are thronged with Jewish housewives in aprons and shawls, dark faces glowing and hands gesturing volubly as they fill their baskets with fish, chickens, and vegetables. Scarcely less animated are the Greek peddlers with their pushcarts heaped with peanuts or rich fruits, laughing and bickering along the pavements. Despite the imposing mass of the Capitol and the tanks and smokestacks of factories farther eastward, this section belongs neither to the law-maker nor the industrialist. It belongs rather to the little foreign groups that have found their way to this city—Greek, Syrian, and Italian.

Some of the residential sections have an air that is completely unexpected. Only a few minutes' drive from the Terminal Station is West End, whose oak-shaded sidewalks and roomy, balustraded frame houses suggest a small Southern town of the turn of the century. Much of this atmosphere of neighborly gossip and front porch rockers may be caught in other suburbs or near-by towns, College Park, Hapeville, or Decatur. Nearer the hub of the city this spirit may seem to be dead, but sometimes it has only gone from the front porch to the garden in the back yard. In every part of the city the garden is an important element of family life, for Atlanta has many days of warmth and sunshine. Although rainfall is abundant, there is no long rainy season, and even the cold snaps of winter are varied by many mild days.

Druid Hills, which in spring is crowded with motorists viewing its many white-blossoming dogwood trees, is handsome all the year with shrubbery, sloping lawns, terraced formal gardens, and fine houses, many of which are roofed with red or green tiles. Still more luxurious estates are found in the area northwest of Peachtree Street near Buckhead; few cities can show more sumptuous homes than some of those along Pace's Ferry Road or in the newer Blackland and Tuxedo Park developments. Less pretentious but very attractive and smartly kept dwellings are found in such subdivisions as Garden Hills or Morningside, or the more centrally located Ansley Park, a residential labyrinth of streets intricately curving and intersecting.

Despite outward appearances, the many quarters of the city are neither isolated from nor independent of each other. Such busy little commercial centers as those around Tenth Street, Buckhead, or Little Five Points may seem to offer everything the housewife could need, but as likely as not she will choose to do her shopping farther from her home. Even the manufacturing town of East Point or the industrial villages of Scottdale or the Exposition Mills are not self-sufficing units but integral parts of the metropolitan area.

Atlanta's large Negro population, though segregated, is scattered all over town in large or small pockets. The most populous business thoroughfare is Decatur Street, running eastward between rows of pawnshops with crowded windows, restaurants emitting the sharp smell of frying fish, and clothing stores with suits and overcoats hung over ropes along the pavements. Here the scene is full of animation and there is an eternal symphony of gay noises—the crack of rifles in the shooting galleries, the wooden clatter of balls in the poolrooms, the thin, fast music of sidewalk phonographs, and always the voices, loud but musical.

Auburn Avenue is a far quieter Negro business district of decorous hotels and office buildings. There are evidences of still greater refinement along Ashby Street and in the vicinity of Atlanta University, where many of the more prosperous Negroes maintain attractive homes. Atlanta is the world's largest center for Negro education, and the colleges are constantly taking a more important place in municipal life. Perhaps no other Southern city shows so great a divergence, not only economic but educational and social, in the condition of its Negro citizens. The university set and their friends maintain a good living standard for themselves and work toward the improvement of their race. But the poorer Negroes live squalidly along their own streets which appear abruptly in all parts of the city; here the ramshackle wooden shanties and rooming houses are crowded with many families and the streets are noisy with the cries of little ragged brown children.

A city so large, so scattered, and so diverse in its many components lends itself only with difficulty to general statement. A few such comments can be made, of course, but they must be advanced cautiously and with due regard for dissimilar points of view. For example, national publications have frequently singled out Atlanta women for their beauty and smart clothes, but other observers flatly declare that the girls here are no prettier than American girls anywhere. The question of amusements is another case in point. Many a traveling salesman stranded here without acquaintances complains that there are no night clubs, no regular theatrical performances, and no outstanding restaurants, and that there is nothing to do but go to one motion picture after another. Yet girls of debutante age visiting here during the gay winter season declare that 24 hours are not enough for all the luncheons, dinners, teas, and dances that are showered down so lavishly. There is always an abundance of club life for both the dancers and the golf and tennis crowd. In a few sets there is more entertaining in the club than in the home, but most Atlanta hostesses come into their own most truly and graciously in their own households and at their own tables. There is comparatively little entertaining at the hotels, which are essentially commercial.

Indeed, one of the few just generalizations that can be made is that Atlanta is a predominantly commercial city. Although it is the State capital, it is too large to be dominated by legislative and judicial functions. It is the same with educational affairs: Georgia Tech, Emory, Oglethorpe, Agnes Scott, and Atlanta University are exceedingly important to several large groups without making Atlanta a college town. Nor does industry predominate, although Atlanta wealth is derived from sources ranging from cotton goods to bottled drinks. It is business that takes first place.

Any newcomer feels this enveloping importance of commerce as soon as he enters a large office in the Hurt Building, the Candler Building, the William-Oliver Building, or any of the national banks. He becomes aware of an electric quickness in the tempo; officials and clerks, though cordial, are not inclined to waste time. There is little of the leisurely personal touch that is characteristic of business conferences in smaller Southern communities. Atlanta offices are conducted with the method and manner of the metropolitan East. It is the same with the shops. Stock, equipment, and decorations are smartly modern, and buying is brisk.

Since Atlanta is the Southeastern center for distribution offices of large national concerns, there is a constantly shifting population of salesmen and district managers. These men and their families, settling briefly in hotels and apartment houses, seldom stay long enough to become a permanent part of the city. Atlanta businessmen still form the essential nucleus. Many of the names that were prominent in the commercial life of pioneer Atlanta are still prominent, even though the stores and offices that bear them are frequently owned by New York firms. Although Atlanta's geographical situation is deep in the South, busy train and airplane service ties it closely to the big cities of the Eastern Seaboard and draws it into the orbit of national commerce.

From its earliest settlement, this community has pushed its development by vigorous enterprise. Not aristocratic cotton planters but energetic railroad men gave it life, and it was this spirit of dogged survival that brought recovery and increased power after the town had been burned by General Sherman's destroying forces. And this spirit still animates Atlanta.

There is an abundant enthusiasm for music and the other arts; there is plenty of graciousness and gentility. But in the final analysis these qualities are less salient than those that twentieth-century language designates as drive or punch. Atlanta is alert and aggressive— a true city of the Modern South.

History

ATLANTA'S early history resounds with the ring of iron spikes driven against shining new rails, the clang of locomotive bells and the hoarse voices of whistles, the clattering of wagons over rutted roads, the bawling of teamsters and laborers, and the carousing of gamblers, with an occasional shot sharpening the cacophony. Only a few miles removed from cultured plantation life, this frontier town was settled around a railroad terminus that was conceived in economic stress.

After Eli Whitney's invention of the gin in 1793, there was an increasing tendency among Southern planters to sacrifice food crops and livestock to the cultivation of cotton. Cotton brought money, whereas food could be bought; but transportation of Western meat and grain to Georgia's principal cotton section, necessitating travel over several different water routes and hauling over bad roads, was slow and expensive. River traffic was uncertain since increasing settlement and cultivation along the banks had clogged the channels, and land travel was impossible when heavy rains slimed the red-clay roads. The conviction grew that railroads were the only solution to the problem, and in 1826 Hamilton Fulton, State chief engineer, and Wilson Lumpkin went so far as to survey a route from the Tennessee River to the South Atlantic seaboard. Finally in December 1836, the State legislature created the Western & Atlantic Railroad to run from the Tennessee River to the southeastern bank of the Chattahoochee River and continue to "some point," defined in an amendment the next year, "not exceeding eight miles, as shall be most eligible for the running of branch roads to Athens, Madison, Milledgeville, Forsyth, and Columbus."

Growth of the little settlement around the terminus was sure to come, for it formed a gateway to the hardly accessible inlands on the south and an egress for commerce to the north and west. Georgians on the whole, however, had little faith in its development. Even as late as 1847, just before it became the City of Atlanta, the townspeople

8

themselves were dubious of its future. At that time Colonel Stephen H. Long, chief engineer of the State railway, predicted that after completion of the railroads the town would dwindle to little more than a crossroads store and a blacksmith shop.

There are few records concerning the site before transportation to the cotton belt became of vital concern. It is known that during the Revolution there was a Cherokee Indian town, The Standing Peachtree, on the south bank of the Chattahoochee River approximately seven miles from the present Five Points, and it was reported that the remaining land south of the river had been won by the Creeks from the Cherokees in a succession of ball games. According to Revolutionary War records of August 1, 1782, a secret agent was commissioned to investigate rumors of friction between these two tribes near the town. It is from The Standing Peachtree that Peachtree Creek and Atlanta's famous Peachtree Street get their names. One version of the name's origin states that the Indians met under a "pitch tree" at the spot for games and conferences and used pitch from the tree to caulk their canoes; another declares that it was derived from a large peach tree growing on a near-by Indian mound (near the present pumping station). In 1813, during the Creek War, Lieutenant George R. Gilmer with 22 white recruits was sent to establish a fort near the site, which, by his own statement, was between 30 and 40 miles beyond the frontiers of the State. After he left, an important Indian trading post was established at the spot, which was crisscrossed by numerous Indian trails. In 1821 the legislature authorized that rentals of land in Fayette County be paid at The Standing Peachtree, and the earliest postal records indicate that the place was a post office in 1826. The first ferryman on the Chattahoochee River, J.M.C. Montgomery, was postmaster.

According to Henry Stringfellow, who came astride an Indian pony from Alabama over the Etowah Trail, the present Alabama Street was a primitive footpath in 1820. Scattered over the region were small corn patches, the only agricultural efforts of the Indians, who subsisted principally by fishing in the Chattahoochee and hunting in the canebrakes along its banks and in the near-by "jungles." For four years Stringfellow lived among the Indians. Here he joined in a green corn dance held upon the return of a hunting party, and on the footpath he witnessed an internecine battle between factions of the Creeks, who had split after the signing of the Treaty of 1821, in which the section was ceded to the Federal Government.

Six miles east of the spot a white settlement was incorporated in 1823 as the town of Decatur and seat of the year-old DeKalb County. Between that time and 1836, Charner Humphries established his Whitehall Tavern two and a half miles southwest of Five Points.

The inn was the only overnight accommodation for travelers from south Georgia to Tennessee and was a voting precinct as well. Near the inn musters of the DeKalb County militia districts were held, followed by considerable merrymaking. The road to Whitehall was later straightened and became Whitehall Street.

Although three public roads ran through the site of the future railroad terminus, the immediate vicinity was a wilderness and there were few travelers other than Indians going on hunting expeditions or passing through to the trading post at The Standing Peachtree. When "General" Abbott Hall Brisbane, assistant surveyor to Colonel Long, came to the site in 1837, the only inhabitant he found was Hardy Ivy, who was the first settler in the section that is now downtown Atlanta. Ivy, a farmer, had contracted to pay "in produce as he could spare it" for 200 acres of land in Canebrake, as the wooded section was then known. He had erected his hewn-log cabin near the present corner of Ivy Street and Auburn Avenue, and his bones, it is said, lie beneath the hard-packed ground of a parking lot just west of Ivy Street.

In the summer or early fall of 1837 Brisbane drove the stake, probably under the present Broad Street viaduct, marking the southeastern terminus of the projected railroad. Actual construction of the, road was not begun until 1838, but a few settlers moved immediately to the designated terminus in order to take advantage of the potential commercial and land benefits. Interest aroused in the site by the legislative act flagged from time to time as the exhaustion of funds for the Western & Atlantic deterred progress on the road, and for several years the population fluctuated markedly. By the fall of 1839 there were in the village only a few impoverished families living in dirt-floored shanties, an old woman and her daughter, and John Thrasher, the village's first merchant and the grading contractor for the Monroe Railroad (Macon & Western) branch. Affected by the Nation-wide depression, the stock of that road dropped to ten cents on the dollar. "Cousin John" Thrasher, who was paid partly in the stock for work on the Monroe embankment (near the present Terminal Station), took his holding to McDonough and traded it for a gold watch, a carriage, and merchandise for his commissary. In July 1841, after selling his land for four dollars an acre, he abandoned his store and disgustedly shook the red dust of the terminus from his high-heeled boots for, as he thought, all time.

The prospect of completion of the Western & Atlantic line to Marietta, however, apparently inspired the sale of real estate at a public auction in 1842. On Christmas eve the engine *Florida,* brought the 65 miles from Madison on a 16-mule-drawn wagon, was set up and started near the Whitehall Street crossing on its trip over the virgin track. An excited crowd of 500 from Decatur and the surrounding section gathered in the village, which now consisted of about 6 houses huddled at the present site of Five Points, and cheered the train on its way to Marietta, 22 miles distant.

After completion of the track to Marietta, some of the settlers who had moved away returned and the new ones began moving in. This renewal of interest seemed unjustified in 1843 when growth of the town was halted again by suspension of work on the Western & Atlantic because of financial difficulties that led to an unsuccessful attempt to sell the road for $1,000,000. For some months into 1844 the population consisted chiefly of unemployed railroad hands, many of whom whiled away their time drinking and gambling.

Despite such hindrances to development, on December 23, 1843, the State legislature chartered the town under the name of Marthasville in honor of the daughter of ex-Governor Wilson Lumpkin, who earlier had done much to further State interest in railroads. Under the charter a five-man board of commissioners governed the town.

There were then in Marthasville two stores, the Western & Atlantic Railroad office (which also housed the engineers), a hotel, and approximately a dozen dwellings. The hotel had been literally moved into the settlement the previous year from Boltonville across the river on two flat cars drawn by a slowly moving locomotive. About fifteen acres had been cleared, including five that had been given to the state for the railroad yards. There were four highways meeting at the site of Five Points, Whitehall-Peachtree and Marietta-Decatur Roads, of which perhaps Marietta was the most thickly settled. The latter part of 1844 brought the establishment of a tread sawmill and several stores. In 1845 the town built its first lockup on Pryor Street near Alabama Street. It was a one-room structure twelve feet square on the outside, with walls three logs thick, and the key that fitted the enormous lock was eight inches long and weighed a quarter of a pound. But the lack of foundations enabled prisoners to burrow their way out or tip over the structure and thus make their escape. In the triangle near the present junction of Houston and Pryor Streets a small building was erected by private subscriptions to be used as school, church, and Sunday school. Such activity and a gradual increase in population inspired the Reverend Joseph Baker to undertake the publication of a weekly newspaper, the *Luminary*. It was unpopular, however, because of its emphasis on spiritual rather than topical affairs.

The same year the board of commissioners appealed to the legislature for a city charter to change the name to Atlanta and provide for a surveyed street system. Because many of the townspeople opposed the change on the grounds that it would increase taxes, the charter was

not granted, but an act was passed in December changing the name of
the town to Atlanta and making it headquarters for the voting precinct
that had been at the Whitehall Tavern. Suggestion of the name is
generally credited to J. Edgar Thomson, then chief engineer of the
Georgia Railroad. His ingenious derivation was ". . . the terminus
of the Western & Atlantic Railroad—masculine Atlantic, feminine
Atlanta." With no systematic layout of the streets, the townspeople
continued to build haphazardly along the cowpaths and in whatever
manner suited their personal whims. When the charter was finally
granted, it was too late to straighten the streets already lined with
buildings.

Impetus to growth of the town had been given by the arrival, on
September 15, of the first through train over the newly completed
branch of the Georgia Railroad from Madison, opening the market
to Augusta. In 1846 the Macon & Western branch opened transportation between Macon and Atlanta. The town now had three railroads terminating at the State Square, which was the five acres of
Land Lot 77 given to the State by Samuel Mitchell, of Zebulon, for
railroad shops. The land around the square had been divided by
Mitchell into 17 town lots, most of which had been sold by the first
of the year. In April he had deeded to the Macon & Western for a
station site a block adjoining the State Square and bounded by Alabama,
Whitehall, Pryor, and the tracks. Soon afterward his remaining land
was surveyed and subdivided into blocks with intervening streets, which
were given to the city. Three adjacent tracts, Land Lots 51, 52, and
78, were similarly developed by their owners.

Active real estate development stimulated growth in other lines.
Two short-lived newspapers began publication in that year; and in the
one following two schools were opened, making a total of four in
operation. At this time, when the estimated population was 300, the
town was extended banking facilities by the Georgia Railroad agent
to sell exchange on Augusta, Atlanta's chief market. E.Y. Clarke, an
early historian, says that the year 1847 saw the erection of a block
of brick buildings and cites among "other evidences of coming municipal
greatness" the razor strap man who daily perched upon a stump near
the corner of Whitehall and Alabama Streets and hawked his wares to
passers-by. So voluminous was the cotton trade at this time that it
was often impossible to weigh all the staple on the day it was brought
in. Long lines of cotton-loaded wagons drawn by oxen and four-
and six-mule teams lumbered daily into the town and departed filled
with commodities of the Atlanta merchants.

Government by the commissioners had been merely nominal, and
the rough elements of the population had been quick to take advantage.
Any attempt of the board to collect a tax or enforce a law had been

occasion for derisive laughter. A large part of the citizenry was composed of railroad laborers and floaters who violently opposed all measures of municipal law. These people lived in two villages on the outskirts of the city, Snake Nation and Slab Town, the latter so named because its impoverished inhabitants constructed their huts of slabs salvaged from the near-by crosstie sawmill. A third disreputable section, Murrell's Row, just off Decatur Street, was named for a bandit who roved the Southern States. Here laws were ignored, cockfights were held in the back yards, gambling went on day and night; shouting, loud quarreling, and shooting often shattered the quiet of the nights, and respectable citizens were afraid to venture near the spot after dark.

The charter of the City of Atlanta, as granted by the legislature on December 29, 1847, provided for government by a mayor and six councilmen. The first election, in which all 215 voters of the town's estimated population of 500 participated, was held on Kile's corner exactly one month later. The new city government made an effort to curb the rampant lawlessness. During the first two months numerous disorderly conduct cases were tried in the mayor's court and fines imposed for these and other infractions of the law, such as draying without licenses and shooting within the city limits. Laws were passed prohibiting the transaction of business on Sunday. To prevent disease threatened by the low living standards of most of the inhabitants, a board of health was appointed during the summer. The active city council in June decided on regular semimonthly meetings and special meetings as necessary. Since there was no permanent gathering place, the Committee on Horse Racks was made responsible for setting up the bell before each session at the site selected so that the councilmen might locate the meeting place by following its sound. This duty eventually devolved upon the marshal and deputy marshal, who in the early fall were each fined five dollars for failure to move the bell. In November the council was forced to dismiss the city clerk for refusal to report the receipts of his office. So strenuous were the efforts to enforce the laws that even Mayor Moses W. Formwalt had a disorderly conduct case lodged against him, presumably because of his saloon which was popular with rough characters.

With improved civic conditions and a constantly increasing population, the church people, who attended nonsectarian services in the "triangle" building, felt the need for organization of their own denominational groups. Methodist, Baptist, Presbyterian, Episcopal, and Catholic churches were organized in 1848, and all except the Presbyterians erected their buildings in that year and the one following. The Presbyterians, under the leadership of Dr. J.S. Wilson, who had served as minister in the triangle church since its erection in 1845, continued for a time to hold their services there.

Supported by church circles as the candidate most likely to work beneficial reforms, Dr. B.F. Bomar was elected mayor in 1849. Bomar's administration levied a property tax of three-tenths of one per cent and, in line with the precedent set by Formwalt, deposited fines for disorderly conduct and other violations in the city treasury. Nevertheless in April of that year, because of irregular tax receipts, the city was compelled to float a $500 bond issue, its first, to cover operating expenses. A petition had been made for the straightening of Whitehall Street and, for the sake of economy, Bomar sentenced city prisoners to dig up stumps on the street, the number in proportion to the seriousness of the offense. A 20-foot plank road was constructed on a portion of the street, and plank sidewalks, 8 feet wide, were built as they could be afforded. A temporary hospital was established, and the *Atlanta Intelligencer,* the first Atlanta paper to attain any degree of permanency, began publication. In this year also the Western & Atlantic Railroad was completed to Chattanooga, Tennessee, affording the growing city a wider market.

Although to the orderly element of the populace Formwalt's administration had seemed inadequate, it probably had accomplished all that was possible in that short period after 12 years of almost no municipal discipline. The next two administrations introduced no new reforms calculated to show quick results. The 1850 council did, presumably in desperation, require that each person obtaining a business license post a bond of $200 as a guaranty that no violation of city ordinances would be tolerated on the premises. This council also built a new calaboose, larger and stronger than the first but still too small; in order to imprison new offenders, those who had been confined for the longest period of time were taken out, given a strapping, and released. But these elementary measures could not alter Atlanta's reputation as a wide-open frontier town, where there was said to be one saloon for approximately every 50 inhabitants. Desirable potential settlers were frightened away, and many inhabitants threatened to move unless drastic changes were effected.

Late in 1850 the conservative citizens took a more vigorous stand and formed themselves into the Moral, or Orderly, Party, receiving the full support of the *Atlanta Intelligencer.* The opposing group, of which the gamblers and drinking faction were members, was called the Rowdy, or Disorderly, Party. After a lively fight the Moral Party won the election, and the new mayor, Jonathan Norcross, immediately began to wage an intensive campaign against crime and lawlessness.

In defiance, the Rowdy Party staged an attempt at a "reign of terror." One member, when arraigned before the mayor and council for disorderly conduct, refused to make any defense but whipped out a long knife and brandished it threateningly. The sheriff struck down the knife with his walking stick, but in the melee that followed the prisoner escaped. Two nights later the Rowdy Party placed a cannon loaded with dirt and powder in front of Norcross' store on Peachtree Street and warned the mayor to resign or have his store blown up. The mayor assembled a volunteer police force of 100 armed men which surrounded the party headquarters on Murrell's Row about midnight and, breaking in, arrested 20 of the men. The leaders were locked in the calaboose and released later only upon their promise to leave town. A group of the volunteer police later raided Snake Nation and Slab Town, ran the inhabitants from their homes, crashed in walls, and burned some of the shacks. Prostitutes were scuttled out of the vicinity in wagons and warned never to return.

Although the mass criminal element had been routed, for the next ten years the city officials were deluged by complaints of citizens against their neighbors. Council proceedings were filled with such items as that of December 1857, "Hogpens still giving trouble," and of July 23, 1858, when council was petitioned to require the "owners of cows and cattle to have the same Stabled at night. As there are many of the Citizens of the City who are greatly annoyed by Cows lying around their gates and Lots. . . ." The marshal was harried by the problem of keeping the streets cleared of the bodies of hogs killed by the heavy wagon traffic. Young rowdies rolled barrels containing squealing pigs down the Alabama Street hill and, when the marshal rode up to stop them, tied firecrackers to his horse's tail. Brothels were declared a nuisance and a fine of $50 was set. Hotel owners were fined for throwing garbage into the streets, and laws were passed against the blocking of sidewalk traffic in front of Whitehall Street stores during auctions. But little heed was paid to these laws.

As late as 1850 the schools had met with little success and many of the early teachers had moved away. Since only a few of the citizens were slaveholders, the children were often kept at home to help with the chores about the gardens and livestock. In 1851, however, several teachers felt that times were propitious for the opening of more schools and in that year several schools and academies, one high school, and a music school were opened. In 1853 the first free school, financed from the State poor school fund, was opened, and in 1858 an ill-starred movement for a city public school was begun.

The town was now more than four times the size of Decatur, and a movement was initiated to make Atlanta a county seat. Forthwith in 1853 the legislature created from half the DeKalb County territory the County of Fulton, named presumably for Hamilton

Fulton. At about this time the ambitious citizenry also made an unsuccessful attempt to have the State capital transferred to Atlanta, Mayor John F. Mims resigning in order to lead the campaign.

Early settlement had been made to the north of the tracks and some houses were being built along Peachtree Street, but expansion was chiefly to the south. Business houses were concentrated along Whitehall and Alabama Streets, Market (Broad) Street was the center of the market district, residences extended out Pryor Street to Garnett Street, and small frame houses occupied the space between Alabama and Mitchell Streets.

During the 1850's the city developed rapidly. Banks were established; the Athenaeum, the city's first theater, and Parr's Hall provided entertainment by stock companies; a local dramatic club was organized; a concert hall was opened; the Fulton Brass and String Band provided music for parties; and a five-acre fair ground (Fair Street) was bought and offered for the use of the Southern Central Agricultural Association. Fraternal societies were formed, as well as the military Gate City Guards and Atlanta Grays. Other churches were erected and there was vigorous business and residential building. Streets and sidewalks were paved, and a gas plant was built, the streets being lighted by gas on Christmas night, 1855. A city hall, a market house, and fire stations were constructed, and a fire engine was bought. Atlanta Fire Company Number One was chartered by the legislature. Mechanics Fire Company Number Two was organized, and, after a fire in which several lives were lost for lack of ladders, the Atlanta Hook and Ladder Company was formed. By the end of the decade the city had still another fire company, Tallulah Fire Company Number Three. The Atlanta & West Point Railroad was completed to Alabama and two other railroads, the Atlanta & Charlotte Air Line and the Georgia Western, were chartered. By April 1, 1859, the city had a population of almost 10,000, and the assessed value of its real estate was $2,760,000.

Atlanta citizens had given little thought to the slavery question beyond becoming aroused in 1857 to the extent of sending military and financial aid to Kansas when that territory became a source of conflict between slave-holding and abolitionist settlers. But by 1860 Atlanta was feeling strongly the tension between North and South. In January merchants met and decided on cessation of trade with Northern wholesale merchants who were abolitionists. By April feeling ran so high that a meeting was held to consider secession from the Union to join Mexico under the leadership of Juarez, but conservative opposition defeated this enterprise. Nevertheless, sentiment mounted with the passage of time. Because of the answers Stephen A. Douglas gave here at a public meeting on October 30 to questions regarding the right of secession, the public was infuriated and the *Intelligencer,* mouthpiece of the secessionists, bitterly attacked him. The next day the Fulton County Minute Men organized to be ready for the fight against abolitionist domination and named a correspondence committee to maintain contact with similar organizations throughout the South. Secession meetings were held every few days during December, and on the 22d Atlanta celebrated South Carolina's break from the Union with an all-day program, beginning with a sunrise salute of 15 guns and terminating with a torchlight parade and the burning in effigy of Abraham Lincoln before the Planters' Hotel. Fulton County delegates to the State secession convention were elected on January 2, 1861.

Under the stress of the war, building activities ceased and some businesses were crippled, but the city soon began to hum with war industries. There was a steady influx of people, some fleeing from the stand of war, others employed by the Confederacy in the manufacture of war implements, medicine, and machinery for making arms and ammunition. On June 3 an important convention of Southern bankers was held here to consider measures of financial co-operation with the Confederate Government. The city was placed under martial law on August 11, 1862, by order of General Braxton Bragg, and Mayor James M. Calhoun was appointed civil governor of the city. Atlanta then became a large hospitalization center as well as headquarters for quartermasters and commissaries. All available large buildings, including the medical college, several hotels, and schools, were converted into hospitals.

As an inland city of the Deep South, Atlanta had had little fear of actual bombardment, despite the knowledge that its five railroads and many war manufactories made it the goal of Northern troops determined to cripple the Confederate Army by cutting off its main source of supply. As a local preparedness measure, however, in May 1864, all males between the ages of 16 and 65 were registered at the courthouse on Washington Street and equipped with arms. But even then, with the fighting only 100 miles away, Atlanta people were not gravely apprehensive since the enemy had been driven from the State at Chickamauga the preceding fall. General William T. Sherman, however, had his eyes on Atlanta, "the citadel of the Confederacy," and by means of his semicircular flanking movements to the rear of the exhausted Southern troops had progressed in a few weeks as far as Kennesaw Mountain, only 22 miles distant, from where the first faint sounds of firing were heard in the city.

The contending forces pushed on to the Chattahoochee River, the Northern line like a giant whip that continually curved around and snapped at the heels of the Confederates, turning them ever southward. By July 9 Sherman's 23d Corps (of the Army of the Ohio) had crossed the river near Soap Creek, entrenching close by, and that night General Joseph E. Johnston with his Confederates crossed near Bolton, camping northeast of the crossing. On the night of the 17th Johnston received President Davis' order relieving him of the command and giving it to General John B. Hood, who completed Johnston's pre-arranged alignment of the troops north and east between the Federal trenches and the city. The Home Guard and "Joe Brown's Malish," 10,000 men between the ages of 16 and 65, had been dispatched to guard the river crossings, where they skirmished with small groups crossing the river.

By flanking maneuvers all the Federal companies, 106,000 strong, had crossed by the 17th and on the 18th were spread out fanwise from the mouth of Peachtree Creek to Decatur. Just beyond Decatur they wrecked several miles of the Georgia Railroad tracks. On the 19th, while Hood, with a total force of 47,000 men, was forming his battle line facing Peachtree Creek, General George H. Thomas was crossing the creek with his Army of the Cumberland. The attack of William J. Hardee and Alexander P. Stewart, planned by Hood for one o'clock on the afternoon of the 20th while Thomas was still crossing, was delayed by a shift to the right over thickly wooded terrain. By four o'clock Thomas had reached the south bank and flung up light breastworks.

The Confederates attacked at five main points along Thomas' line, which stretched out Collier Road from Peachtree to Howell Mill Road. About half-past four General W.B. Bate's men swooped down Clear Creek Valley east of Peachtree and charged up the slopes of Brookwood Hills to battle furiously with General John Newton's 4th Corps forces. General W.H.T. Walker advanced up Peachtree Road and assaulted Newton's corps on the front and right. The fighting quickly spread westward. General George Maney struck the front of General W.T. Ward's division just west of Peachtree Road. General W.W. Loring advanced on John W. Geary's line and, when Colonel Benjamin Harrison's men fired into his right, his left wing drove between the lines of Geary and A.S. Williams, pushing Harrison's brigade back to the creek. With the assistance of other Union forces, however, Harrison's line was quickly replaced. General E.C. Walthall attacked General Williams between Northside Drive and Howell Mill Road, but the Confederates made no gains, and just before dark Bate made another sally without success. After five hours' fighting, a division of artillery that Thomas placed just east of the bridge raked the valley, forcing the Confederates to retire.

Estimated casualty figures for the Battle of Peachtree Creek are 5,000 Confederates and 2,000 Federals. Among those killed was Brigadier General C.H. Stevens, one of Walker's commanders. Three shells fell within the city, the first killing a little girl at the corner of Ivy and Ellis Streets.

At about six o'clock in the evening General Hardee was ordered to send P.R. Cleburne's division, which he was holding in reserve, to the aid of General Joseph Wheeler, who was losing ground under fire from J.B. McPherson's forces between the city and Decatur. It was not until daybreak of the 21st that Cleburne relieved Wheeler at Bald Hill (Leggett's Hill near the corner of Memorial Drive and Moreland Avenue), where his men had retreated at sundown. Wheeler's orders were to extend his line to the right, but while the changes in position were taking place two Federal divisions assaulted the Confederates and drove them off the hill, which M.D. Leggett was ordered to hold as a strategic point for firing on the Confederate States Navy rolling mills. Light skirmishing in this vicinity continued throughout the day. During the day the Confederate soldiers north of the city reconstructed fortifications at the northern corners of the inner defense lines, and in the night they moved back closer to the city.

That night Hardee's corps, under orders from Hood, moved by a circuitous route through the southern part of the city to steal up behind McPherson's forces in the Leggett's Hill section. Hardee's men were to attack McPherson's rear at daybreak of the 22d while B.F. Cheatham's corps assaulted the front with the aid of Wheeler, in the hope of pushing the Union troops back to the creek. The plan was not realized because Hardee's battle-tired men were slow in traveling the 15 miles to their destination and it was noon before they were ready to attack. Meanwhile, most of the Federals, starting as early as three o'clock in the morning, had moved up to the abandoned outer defense trenches. Wholesale shifting of both the enemy and defending troops created restless anxiety among the citizens, and in midmorning curious groups repaired to the housetops to watch developments.

The Battle of Atlanta began about noon when the divisions of Walker and Bate, under Hardee, broke into a clearing north of Glenwood Avenue and ran into T.W. Sweeney's division of the 16th Corps, just after it had turned from Clay Street into Fair Street (Memorial Drive). The intrepid Hardee, who had expected to come up back of McPherson's 17th Corps, gave quick orders to left face, and the fierce battle that then ensued raged for more than two hours.

Meanwhile, Cleburne's and Maney's troops had engaged those of Giles A. Smith's 17th Corps division at Glenwood and Flat Shoals Avenue. Charging the Federal breastworks, the Confederates captured the 16th Iowa Regiment, the 2d Illinois Battery, and Murray's Battery. The hard-pressed Federals fled their trenches, through the woods and up the slopes of Leggett's Hill, where they aligned themselves to the east of Leggett's forces, filling the gap between them and

the 16th Corps. The Confederates gave chase, making the air ring
with the piercing rebel yell. Reinforced by Stevenson's division of
Cheatham's Corps, which Hood ordered to the spot from Grant Park,
they charged up the slopes, fell back and charged again, until the hill-
top was a mass of grappling humanity.

General H. Wangelin's brigade was brought in to assist the 16th
and 17th Corps in holding the hill. The Confederate line was reinforced by T.C. Hindman's and H.D. Clayton's divisions of Cheatham's Corps, which marched out just north of the Georgia Railroad
to engage the 15th Corps. The fighting had spread to the west and
north of the railroad into the present Inman Park. A.M. Mani-
gault's brigade, assisted by the brigades of Sharp, Brown, and Reynolds,
split the Federal line near the Troup Hurt house (close to DeKalb
Avenue), and captured Battery A, 1st Illinois. Pushing past the
house, they also captured DeGress's battery of five 20-pound Parrott
guns, which they turned upon the enemy but were forced to leave in
place because the Federals stationed north of the site shelled the horses.
Federal infantry and artillery reinforcements hurried to repair the
gaping line, and the Confederates were stopped by the fresher and
greater strength of the opposing forces. The battle was over by dark,
but near Leggett's Hill there was intermittent rifle fire all during the
night.

During the battle young boys just entering their teens, old men,
convalescents, refugees, and soldiers in the city on leave, grasping any
article that might be used as a weapon, rallied to the aid of the Southern soldiers. The slaughter was terrific and, since there was no way
of counting the dead not on Hood's roster, authorities believe that all
casualty figures given are vastly underestimated. Computed losses,
including the wounded and captured, vary from 6,000 to 10,000 Confederates, and from 4,000 to 7,000 Federals. The Confederate general
Walker and the Union general McPherson were among those killed.
Although the Federals were not driven back to the creek, Hood
reported that his men had been greatly encouraged by "the partial
success of the day."

There were light skirmishes but no more real battles until 11:30
in the morning of July 28 at Ezra Church. Four divisions of Confederate infantry, led by Generals Stewart and S.D. Lee, attacked
the right flank of General John A. Logan's Army of the Tennessee
as it moved southwest of the city toward the Atlanta & West Point
and the Macon & Western Railroads. The vastly outnumbered Confederates desperately fought Logan's men, who hastily flung up impro-
vised breastworks of logs and of benches dragged from within the
church. Again the attacking Confederates fought chiefly in the open
and lost heavily. Generals Stewart, Brown, Loring, and Johnson were

wounded, and about sundown General Walthall gave the command to cease fighting. Estimated losses were between 2,700 and 5,000 Confederates and 650 Federals killed and wounded. No definite advantage was gained by either side.

The Federals then settled down to a steady bombardment of the city, but the firmly entrenched Confederates successfully resisted all attempts to break through the lines. On August 6 when Federal troops drew too close to the railroads (near Lee Street), Bate's Confederate division made two furious sallies against General G.W. Schofield's line, scattering the forces, capturing two stands of colors, and killing and wounding 800 men.

Damage to the city and the loss of civilian life mounted as bombs and Minié balls rained down. Although water was scarce, every householder was required to keep a ladder and two buckets of water in readiness in the event an exploding shell set fire to his house. At strategic points around the city were stationed large guns, deafening in their response to the booming of the enemy's immense siege guns. The air was thick with smoke and the stinging smell of burnt powder, the streets were gashed with great shell holes, and houses were demolished. All during the day and night women, children, and aged men scrambled in and out of bombproof dugouts in back yards or scurried to and from warehouse basements. Hood says, "The ninth was made memorable by the most furious cannonade which the city sustained during the siege."

Privation and disease added to the suffering within the city. Confederate money was almost valueless, and typhoid fever struck down soldiers and noncombatants alike. There were numerous fires other than those caused by bursting shell, usually at night, and the volunteer firemen, detailed to guard duty on the streets, worked under difficulty because the Federals made targets of the fires.

During August the Federals concentrated most of their forces around the defenses that protected the two railroads to the southwest, but after the disastrous affair of the 6th they made no further advances toward the tracks. By the end of the month the Northerners had relinquished hope of penetrating the city lines, and, skirting the firing trenches, they moved southward to cut the railroads farther down and to draw Hood's forces from the city. Sherman, however, left his 20th Corps at Atlanta to protect the captured Western & Atlantic Railroad, which, repaired by his men, brought a daily average of 145 cars of supplies to the Federals.

On the 29th the Union forces wrecked the Atlanta & West Point Railroad at Red Oak and Fairburn. Two days later the Battle of Jonesboro was lost by the Confederates, and with the cutting of the Macon & Western Railroad the city was isolated from outside supplies and military reinforcements. On the next day six Federal divisions completely routed Cleburne's forces at Jonesboro and forced their retreat to Lovejoy Station.

Hood's only recourse was to try to divert Sherman from the stricken city. His troops began marching from Atlanta that afternoon, and he himself moved out at five o'clock toward Lovejoy Station. With the order to evacuate, the commissary warehouse was opened to the people, who, after months of short rations, hurried eagerly to their homes loaded with flour, syrup, sugar, and hams.

The hours after midnight were long remembered. The city rocked with blasts and rumblings of earthquake dimensions, while crowds of tired, bedraggled soldiers from the trenches streamed through the streets, pushing south to join Hood. Five engines, a train of ordnance stores, and 80 cars of ammunition, together with Confederate warehouses, were dynamited and kindled by Hood's rear guard before it marched out.

After a sleepless night the citizens waited apprehensively in the defenseless city, but the Federals remained quiet in their bivouacks. No messenger came from outside, and finally at nine o'clock on the morning of September 2, when the tension became intolerable, Mayor James M. Calhoun gathered together a few of the citizens. The group carrying a white flag and unarmed—one man having removed four pistols from his person at the mayor's suggestion that they disarm—rode three miles out Marietta Street to the Federal lines, where Mayor Calhoun formally surrendered the city.

Almost immediately the troops began marching in, and between that time and the 7th approximately 80,000 soldiers filed into the small city. Wallace P. Reed, an Atlanta historian, records: "At first the soldiers took what they wanted, but in the main they behaved tolerably well." The sutlers moved in with their supplies of everything from dry goods to the latest novels. A depot of quartermaster's stores was opened. Officers established their headquarters in some of the larger homes. The work of building new fortification lines was begun, and other measures were taken to prepare for defense in the event the Confederates tried to recapture the city. Fine residences were torn down and the materials used to build cabins for soldiers, tents were set up, and the city rapidly assumed the appearance of a gigantic army camp. Indeed it was Sherman's plan to make it one, and on September 4 he issued his order for evacuation by the citizens.

Because the railroads to the south of the city were a tangle of twisted rails, he wrote General Hood on the 7th outlining a plan of evacuation for southbound refugees and proposing a two-day truce at Rough and Ready. Hood agreed, at the same time protesting the inhumanity of driving innocent people from their homes. Five days later 1,565 white citizens with 79 loyal Negro servants were transported in wagons by Northern soldiers to Rough and Ready with trunks, bedding, and light furniture. One hundred men, stationed there by Hood, assisted them on to the railroad at Lovejoy Station. From there many of them went to Exile Camp, near Dawson, until they could return home. The other refugees fled to the north by the Western & Atlantic, chiefly to Tennessee and Kentucky, while most of the Negroes, whose numbers had been supplemented by those who had come great distances to camp around Sherman's lines during the siege, remained with the Federal troops. About 50 white families, presumably Union sympathizers and foreigners, also were allowed to remain during the 75 days of Sherman's occupation.

It was during this time that the Federal general, abandoning his pursuit of the elusive Hood through northwest Georgia, decided to destroy Atlanta and march to the sea, cutting the Confederacy in two with a broad path of desolation. On November 14 torches were applied simultaneously in various parts of the city and the more substantial buildings were blown up by gunpowder. One of the Federal officers writing to his wife, said, ". . . all the pictures and verbal descriptions of hell I have ever seen never gave me half so vivid an idea of it as did this flame-wrapped city tonight. Gate City of the South, farewell." While flames crackled and buildings crumbled around them Sherman was serenaded by one of his bands, and he said afterwards that he could never hear the "Miserere" from *Il Trovatore* without remembering that night. The next day he moved his troops out of the burning city on his destructive way to the coast.

Almost immediately some of the citizens began returning, and early in December the Confederates reoccupied the ruined city with Colonel Luther J. Glenn in command. On the 7th a city election was held, and Calhoun was re-elected mayor.

Within the city limits only 400 of 3,800 buildings were left standing, and of 500 on the outskirts only 100 remained. An unexplained mystery causing conjecture and no little suspicion among the loyal Southerners was the selection of buildings to escape destruction by Sherman's men. In widely separated districts groups of houses were unscathed by the flames that reduced most of the city to ashes, and one entire business block was left untouched. The returning citizens set to work at once, men, women, and even children putting their hands to the construction of houses. Shanties were built with brick and boards salvaged from the ruins, but many of the homes were makeshift—discarded army tents, old freight cars, and, in some cases, scraps of old tin roofing nailed to rickety wooden framework. Some of the people boarded in the remaining private homes until they could erect more comfortable shelters. Almost all the commercial buildings had been wrecked, and during the hurried rebuilding a number of small structures were moved intact to Whitehall Street by some merchants, while others set up business in hastily erected shanties.

As late as Christmas many of the streets, piled with debris, were impassable. Dogs, abandoned by their refugee owners, foraged in droves at night and slept during the day under the roofs of flattened houses on the edge of town. So terribly ravaged was the section that there were no birds even when spring came. Food and fuel were scarce and, since Confederate money was almost valueless, few could afford the commodities that were available. There was dreadful suffering during the cold winters of 1864 and 1865. People scoured the battlefields for lead bullets, which they sold to buy food. Persimmon seeds were pierced for buttons, old clothes were raveled and rewoven, corn shuck hats and wooden-soled shoes were made, diced side meat was used for lard, and barter and trade took the place of cash transactions. A smallpox epidemic aggravated conditions in 1865 and 1866. Beggars roamed everywhere, but by 1866 the church congregations were able to hold fairs for the benefit of the most impoverished citizens.

Mounds and ridges of bare red earth on the outskirts of the city were tragic reminders of the real price of war. In this year the Atlanta Memorial Association was organized, and the bodies of soldiers were removed from their temporary graves and reinterred in Oakland Cemetery and in the Marietta cemetery. The date General Johnston surrendered the territory east of the Chattahoochee River to Sherman, April 26, was set aside for Memorial Day, which was first celebrated in 1867.

On May 4, 1865, Colonel Glenn turned over the city to the Federal leader Colonel B.B. Eggleston. On the 16th the United States flag was raised formally in front of Eggleston's headquarters and lowered to half-mast because of Lincoln's death.

The majority of the citizens were willing to accept quietly the irremediable circumstances. This attitude undoubtedly was aided by Mayor Calhoun, who stated at a public meeting held June 24 that he had never favored secession and that his greatest wish was to return to the Union. In this attitude he was supported by other leaders in the city who were sympathetic to the Union. Resolutions adopted at the meeting expressed hope for early resumption of the State's former relations and function in the Union and voted confidence in President Andrew Johnson's administration.

With the passage of the Sherman Reconstruction Bill in February 1867, over President Johnson's veto, the tone set by Calhoun changed to discord. A large group of citizens favored violent opposition, another was resigned to submission, and a third claimed to uphold President Johnson but adopted an attitude of watchful waiting. After the supplemental bill was passed by the House also over the President's veto, the city was in an uproar, and a public meeting was called for the morning of March 4. The newspapers, fearing the consequences of too outspoken opposition, advised the utmost caution in action and speech. The gathering listened in tacit disapproval to the submissive resolutions drafted by pro-Union Colonel Henry P. Farrow and his committee, but there was cheering and handclapping after the reading of Colonel Luther Glenn's resolutions, which were conservative without being subservient. The crowd stamped and shouted its approval when Colonel T.C. Howard suggested that the Glenn resolutions be adopted, with an amendment designating the Reconstruction Bill as "harsh, cruel and unjust . . . degrading to the bitterest and last degree as it sinks us below the legal status of our former slaves, surrenders the control and policy of the Southern States to the blacks. . . ." Because of the confusion the meeting was dismissed, but Colonel Farrow announced that an adjournment meeting would be held that night for further consideration of his resolutions. At the latter meeting ex-Governor Brown made an eloquent plea for the Farrow resolutions, which were formally adopted.

A few months later the city government, strangely enough, adopted a proposal to appropriate ten acres for a city park to be the site of a monument to Abraham Lincoln. J.L. Dunning, local president of the Lincoln Memorial Association, made the request of council and stipulated that the association would erect the monument at a cost of approximately $1,000,000. The wise council, doubting the ability of the association to raise the amount, considered adoption as the best means of keeping the matter from the ears of the already aroused public. Nothing more was heard of the monument.

A large delegation of the submissionists welcomed General John Pope, commander of the Third Military District set up by the Sherman law, when he arrived at the station on March 31, 1867. A reception was held for him that night, and a banquet was given at the National Hotel on his return from Montgomery on April 11, when Atlanta was made headquarters for the district. This cordial treatment overwhelmed the brevet general, who had expected, at best, complete indifference from all. The first impression made by Pope was an agreeable one; he arrived in civilian clothes and was courteous to everyone he met. The rigorous laws imposed on the South by Congress, however, made it impossible for any administrator of the military government to please the victims of their penalties. Then, too, Pope made the mistake of allowing himself to be surrounded by unprincipled politicians and trucklers who hoped to profit through the association. It was only a short time before the people were calling for his removal.

Ex-Governor Joseph E. Brown, the outstanding leader of the State conformist group, made a number of speeches in the city, for the most part pursuing his usual theme of strict submission to the military measures. Emphasizing the advantages to be gained thereby, he stressed the futility of the State's pending appeal to the United States Supreme Court. The many non-conformists were strong in their resentment of the harsh laws and scornfully rejected Brown's proffered sops but lacked an effective leader of their own.

Then, in the summer of 1867, Benjamin Hill mounted the other oratorical stump in Atlanta and swayed the masses with his brilliant speeches. He was followed by Robert Toombs, fierily eloquent on his return from exile. Now having leaders to mold them, the non-conformists in October organized themselves into the Conservative Party, "anti-convention, anti-reconstruction, anti-radical." Representatives from Clayton, Cobb, and Fulton Counties met in Atlanta on November 23, four days after Pope's order for the State constitutional convention, and appointed delegates to the State Conservative convention to be held in Macon. On December 9 the constitutional convention met in the Atlanta City Hall. At the first day's meeting there were 22 Negro delegates and 108 white, many of whom were carpetbaggers and scalawags.

During the convention's holiday recess General Pope was removed by President Johnson, who was sympathetic to complaints against Pope and his carpetbagger advisers. It was hoped that this would intimidate the convention, but the hope was vain; the President's views availed nothing against Congress, and the convention had the support of the radical Congressional leaders. The expenses were excessive, and on January 13 General George G. Meade, who had replaced Pope on the 7th, issued his order removing the Democratic governor Jenkins and State treasurer Jones from office for their refusal to pay the exorbitant claim for expenses of the convention. The public was incensed and the Atlanta press was vituperative.

The convention adjourned on March 11 after choosing Rufus B. Bullock Republican gubernatorial nominee. The election was held April 20-23, the Fulton County polling taking place at the courthouse, which was surrounded by Federal soldiers. As voters filed in to the polling place, the soldiers marched in and stood about it with fixed bayonets. Dr. J.F. Alexander, one of the two managers the county ordinary was permitted to appoint, placed his hands over the ballot box, said "No ballots shall be put in this box except over my dead body until those soldiers are removed," and delayed the voting until the soldiers were withdrawn. Fulton County gave the Democratic nominee General John B. Gordon, of Atlanta, a majority of votes, but Bullock was elected by the Negro vote over the State. Many Conservative citizens, refusing to take the amnesty oath, did not vote either on the governorship or on the ratification of the new constitution, which contained a provision for a change in the capital site.

Atlanta as the new capital was the scene of the shameful fiasco that was Bullock's administration. In the city hall on July 4 convened the legislature described by Claude G. Bowers in *The Tragic Era* as "a cross between a gambling den and a colored camp-meeting." Here on the 21st the Fourteenth Amendment was ratified, and on the next day the dignity of Bullock's inaugural ceremony was shattered by an audacious voice in the rear of the hall crying, "Go it, niggers!" Here in September Negro legislators were ejected by the Conservative Democrats with the aid of some of the Republicans and radical Democrats who had become disgusted with the behavior of the Negro members. In the temporary capitol at the corner of Marietta and Forsyth Streets, in January of 1870, twenty-four white legislators were excluded arbitrarily by a Federal military commission, and 31 Negroes were seated. In February the Fifteenth Amendment was ratified.

The military trial of prisoners arrested in connection with the Ashburn murder in Columbus, an alleged political crime committed shortly after adjournment of the constitutional convention, was held at McPherson Barracks, near Atlanta, for three weeks beginning June 30, 1868. There was strong public indignation over the arrest, confinement, and brutal treatment of a number of innocent white and black persons. As a member of the prosecuting counsel ex-Governor Brown became even more unpopular and was the target of invectives hurled by speakers at a political rally in Atlanta. On July 23, 1868, twenty thousand Democrats sweltered for five hours under a bush arbor erected on Alabama Street as they listened to the fiery speeches of such men as Benjamin Hill, Robert Toombs, and Howell Cobb. The famous Bush Arbor Meeting initiated the campaign to end the carpetbagger rule in Georgia. And, while the Democrats worked to throw off radical Republican domination, the administration with its "million-dollar legislature" unwittingly furthered their cause by extravagant corruption. The depleted State treasury could not long support a government whose committee expenses included such items as the one for "50 gallons of whisky, 15 gallons of sherry, 7,100 cigars and 57 dozen lemons."

Probably Atlanta was the only place in the State to receive any benefits from the wanton extravagance. Bullock's semiofficial agent, H.I. Kimball, lavishly dispensed the State funds. A Northern promoter connected with many enterprises including the Tennessee Car Company and a number of Georgia railroads, he secured legislative authorization of apparently legitimate schemes that brought profit to him and his associates at the taxpayers' expense. He had bought the unfinished opera house at Forsyth and Marietta Streets and completed it, leasing it to the city for Atlanta's first capitol and installing, in 1868, on the first floor a $10,000 post office. He sold the building to the State at a good profit in 1870, and in that same year he constructed with $300,000 of State-endorsed railroad bonds the elaborate Kimball House. Here he and Bullock spent thousands in wining and dining military officers, legislators, and their friends.

Undermined by its own rottenness, the radical Republican regime in Georgia passed out of existence when the Democrats won the election in December 1871. In anticipation of this outcome and the resulting investigation, Bullock had left the State three months earlier.

Meanwhile, the city was being reconstructed in a manner more acceptable to the citizens. The noise of foundries and machine shops sounded together with the sawing and hammering of construction. Four of the railroads were operating again by the fall of 1865 and the Georgia road was being repaired. On March 3, 1866, the legislature extended the city limits to a distance of one and a half miles in each direction. The gas works were repaired and the streets again lighted on September 15. By the end of that year there were 250 business structures, most of which were brick; the assessed value of real estate was $7,000,000 and the amount of trade was $4,500,000. The city census showed a population of 10,940 white people and 9,288 Negroes, almost double that at the beginning of the war.

Among this relatively large population there was some demand for a library in the city, and in 1867 the first library was opened in a rented room by the Young Men's Library Association. The library and the lecture course it sponsored, which brought Henry Stanley, Thomas Nelson Page, and other well-known lecturers of the day, proved popular. An extension course was offered in the form of lectures by various members of the University of Georgia faculty, and an art school was also sponsored by the library.

Important steps in education were taken in 1869, and indeed it was time. Negro schools had been opened by the Freedmen's Bureau after the war, but the only white schools in the city were privately operated and beyond reach of most of the citizens. In September a committee of councilmen and citizens investigated educational needs and made plans for a city school system. Two years later the schools opened, and by the end of the term approximately 4,000 students were being taught by 56 teachers in the two high and various grammar schools. Rapid strides were made in the establishment of institutions of higher education. Atlanta University for Negroes was opened in 1865 and before 1885 five other Negro colleges began to function. The Southern Medical College was organized from the Atlanta Medical College in 1879, the Southern Dental College was established in 1887, and the Georgia School of Technology was opened in 1888.

As early as 1869 building costs had dropped sufficiently for Atlanta to start construction on a grand scale. Included in the buildings erected in 1870 were the DeGive Opera House, the Kimball House, and the $70,000 James residence, purchased in October for the governor's mansion. About 400 buildings were constructed in the following year. Building activity continued into 1873 accompanied by expanding mercantile and industrial operations, and in that year the Atlanta Manufacturers' Association was formed.

A chamber of commerce, which had been organized in 1860, had given serious attention to the problem of freight rate equity, but with the advent of the war this organization turned to more urgent questions, particularly that of direct trade with Europe. Disbanded during 1861, it was replaced in 1866 by the board of trade, which held daily meetings until 1871 when it was reorganized as the chamber of commerce.

A street railway, enfranchised first in 1866 and again in 1869 to separate private interests, finally became a reality in 1871. In that year two citizens bought the franchise and put into operation the city's first horsecar line on Whitehall from Five Points to West End. During the same period the general assembly was persuaded to revise the city charter to permit municipal ownership of a waterworks. A board of water commissioners was elected and the job was let to a construction company in the next year. Four years later the works at the South River reservoir (Lakewood Park) was in operation, and running water in many sections replaced the street-corner pumps and wells that had theretofore provided the water supply.

A natural aftermath of the post-war inflation was the depression of 1873, bringing cessation of construction, price reductions in real estate, and general business slackness. None of the banks failed, although one of the largest suspended operations for a short time. The Atlanta & Charlotte Air Line Railroad, kept alive through the war by Jonathan Norcross who had resumed construction in 1869, first began operation in September of the panic year. The city's financial condition became alarming, affected as it was by the extravagance of the Bullock government, the depression, and the liberality of the Constitution of 1868 in permitting "towns and cities to aid public enterprises and to incur indebtedness, without constitutional limitations." In November 153 citizens petitioned the council for a city charter revision, which was subsequently drafted, to require maintenance of the annual 'expense at a figure below that of the income and incumbrance of one-fourth of the real estate tax for reduction of outstanding debts. The charter was amended accordingly by the legislature in 1874, when

the estimated population was 30,869. The city's financial status began
to improve. With the abatement of the depression building revived
in 1875, improvements on real estate for the year amounted to
$1,000,000, and ground was broken in August for the erection of the
U.S. post office, to cost $275,000.

Federal soldiers were withdrawn after the national election of
1876, and, with the lifting of the military heel for the first time in
ten years, Atlanta experienced a sensation of complete release. Because
the capital site had been determined during Reconstruction in an election under military supervision, another vote on that question was
demanded. The vote, taken in 1877, confirmed the selection of Atlanta
as the capital. In September of that year President Rutherford B.
Hayes, on a good will visit, was given a cordial reception by the city.

In the urgency of rebuilding there was little time for social activities, nor was there money to pay for them. During the Reconstruction Era Bullock, the Kimball brothers, and their cliques entertained
extravagantly, but most of the impoverished citizens had little inclina-
tion for gaiety. From 1873 to 1876, however, the carnival given each
January by the Twelfth Night Mystic Brotherhood considerably enlivened the city. This event was similar to the New Orleans Mardi
Gras and featured a long parade of elaborate floats, which were chem-
ically lighted and displayed brilliant "transparencies." The parades
were followed by pageants, the crowning of Rex and his queen, and a
large ball at DeGive's Opera House. In 1878 the time was shifted
to October, during the fair, and in the next two years even more spectacular celebrations were given by the Mystic Owls, evidently the
successor to the Twelfth Night Brotherhood. The festival was discontinued after that, but the prosperous 1880's brought increasingly elaborate entertaining that for years made Atlanta the gay social center of
the State.

By 1880 commercial growth was measured in great strides. The
railroads made the city an advantageous distributing point; it was a
focus for the distribution of flour and canned meat from the Middle
West, grain from Tennessee, Kentucky, and the upper Mississippi
valley, and guano from Peru. The dry goods jobbing trade annually
brought more than $1,000,000. Iron foundries and rolling mills and
brick manufactories did capacity business. At this time, when the
inhabitants numbered 37,409, the manufactured products for the year
were valued at $13,074,037. Auctions were still popular. A Northern
visitor the previous year reported "on certain days you will hear the
beating of triangles, and have your attention attracted to the red flag
of the curbstone auctioneer. . . . Public buildings in Atlanta are not
imposing . . . more like a western town. . . . There are banks and
boards of trade, and business exchanges . . . modern conveniences from

artificial ice to a Turkish bath. . . ." That same year, 1879, had
brought the installation of the first telephone exchange.

The city was being served by five volunteer fire companies and a
hook and ladder brigade. In 1866 the first steam engine was purchased; two others were bought in 1871. Ten years later an electric
fire alarm system was installed, and in 1882 the city organized a paid
fire department and bought the equipment of the volunteer companies
for $12,110. An electric light and power company was organized the
following year and the city had its first electric lights in 1885.

A great step in expansion of the cotton industry, so vital to continued development of the city, was the World's Fair and Great International Cotton Exposition held at Oglethorpe Park in 1881. H.I.
Kimball secured it for Atlanta through his friend Edward Atkinson,
a Boston economist who suggested an international conference to discuss needed improvements in the culture and processing of cotton. The
first world's fair in the South, it opened October 5 with a long parade
to the grounds, where addresses were delivered by nationally known
men. All the States and seven foreign countries were represented in
the 1,113 exhibits, which were viewed by approximately 350,000 persons from all parts of the country. When the fair closed December 31,
a local stock company bought the grounds, covering 20 acres, and set
up a cotton mill in the main building.

At this time Atlanta was the booming metropolis of the New South.
Here the departure from the leisurely ways of Southern tradition was
hastened by a group of vigorous young men led by Henry W. Grady,
who with an inspired pen and voice cried for work, industrial development, money, and national good will. Cheap labor and natural
resources were exploited to success. Northern manufacturers attending
the fair saw for themselves, and Atlanta as the capital of this movement felt most strongly the effects that were experienced in some
measure by the whole South.

As the trading center of the Southeast, the city was a hub for many
sectional promotional conferences and events, one of the most significant of which was the Piedmont Exposition in October 1887. This
exposition of products of the Piedmont States purposed to establish a
closer co-operation between agriculture and industry and attracted an
attendance of more than 200,000. President and Mrs. Cleveland were
among the notable visitors and were elaborately entertained during
their 24-hour stay in the city.

This prosperous period made the problem of saloons more acute.
In 1888 there began one of the most heated prohibition campaigns ever
waged in the city. Mayor John T. Glenn in his inaugural address in
1889 tried to quell the storm: "Bar-rooms never built a city nor did
fanaticism ever nurse one into greatness, and their war over Atlanta

should cease . . . we have no right to prohibit it [liquor traffic], but it is our solemn duty to control it. . . ." This control was eventually exercised by imposing high license fees, limiting the hours of sale, forbidding the use of screens in front of saloons, prohibiting sale on legal holidays and election days, and forbidding minors to enter bar-rooms.

The water question became of increasing importance with the rapid growth in population, which, more than 65,000 in 1889, was considerably increased by the acquisition of West End in January 1892. The artesian well at Five Points had proved a failure, its water having been condemned by the board of health. The city was fast outgrowing the supply afforded by the South River reservoir, and the fire department was hampered by the poor water flow. Mayor Glenn in 1889 had determined to have a permanent works built on the Chattahoochee River to give the growing city an unlimited water source. Although bonds were voted, the opposition of council delayed the plan, and it was not until 1893 that the new works, completed at a cost of $821,069.74, was put in operation.

The severe pinch of the Nation-wide financial panic of the early 1890's slowed progress only temporarily. By 1895 the city had recovered sufficiently to stage, with the aid of a Government appropriation, the Cotton States and International Exposition. This fair, held at Piedmont Park from September 18 through December 31, featured a complete picture of the industries and resources of the ten cotton States and was designed to promote commerce with the Latin-American countries, as well as trade and manufacture within the United States. The Negroes had a building, and Booker T. Washington was one of the speakers on opening day. Visitors streamed in and out of the city, President Cleveland and his cabinet members led the list of the distinguished, and on Governor's Day there were 20 governors in the city. Total attendance was more than a million.

During the Spanish-American War Atlanta was the site of a training camp. The close of the war was celebrated by a peace jubilee featuring a notable military spectacle and attended by President and Mrs. McKinley, cabinet members and their wives, and many army and naval officers.

Atlanta, which had been reduced to a shambles 36 years earlier, began the new century with an extraordinary record of growth. The population of 89,872 represented an increase of almost 700 per cent during that brief period. The city now had 22 public schools, 8 fire stations, large mercantile establishments, manufactories, and banks; the real and personal property values were $53,177,717. At this time the Whitehall Street viaduct was constructed, and the city presented a $25,000 site to the Government for the erection of a Federal penitentiary.

In 1891 an electric street railway system had supplanted the "dummy engine" streetcars, popularly called "steam cars." In 1902 several years' warfare between the Atlanta Consolidated Street Railway Company and the Atlanta Rapid Transit Company reached a crisis. The former, which was the larger company, was suing the city on the claim that violation of its right-of-way was permitted in the rival company's franchise. Their franchises were expensive, for a number of mayors had urged heavy charges for utility franchises in order to prevent a private monopoly before municipal ownership could be effected. The suit was settled in favor of the larger company, but on the day after the settlement the city was appalled to learn that the two companies had merged. Keen competition had resulted in a 2½-cent fare by one of the companies, but immediately after the merger all fares were raised and schedules reduced. The protesting citizens and mayor were helpless against the monopolization of the streetcar lines. Electric, steam-heat, and street railway services were combined under the name of the Georgia Railway and Electric Company in 1902; a trolley line was extended to College Park in the same year, to Hapeville in 1906, and to Buckhead in 1907. The city then had 161 miles of tracks.

Atlanta received front-page publicity throughout the Nation in 1906 when a bitter race riot occurred. During a political campaign the preceding year, the waning Populist Party, in a desperate stand against the Democrats, had made flattering appeals for the Negro vote in the State. As a result of this attention there was some display of boldness and insolence by the lower Negro element; in November 1905, reports of Negro attacks on white women began to circulate in and around the city. Newspapers exploited the reports in headline and editorial. Rusty Row, a Negro section stretching for several blocks from Five Points along Decatur Street, was made up of gambling dives, saloons, rowdy eating places, and thinly disguised brothels. Here drunken Negroes fought in the street and knifings and murders were frequent. Investigating committees, bewildered by the flagrant immorality and the obscene pictures of white women on the walls, did not know how to begin reforms. No definite action other than an occasional police raid was taken until Saturday, September 22, 1906. Increasing reports of Negro assaults on white women reached a crux that afternoon when news of four such attacks, occurring too late for the newspapers, was spread by word of mouth.

At nine-thirty that night a crowd of 5,000 people converged at Five Points and swept down on Rusty Row, breaking plate-glass windows, overturning carriages and wagons, and unmercifully attacking every Negro in its path. A personal plea by Mayor James A. Woodward, who rushed to the scene, was unavailing, and 300 policemen were unable to cope with the mob; finally the firemen turned powerful streams of water on the crowd and swept it from the section. The frenzied mob then spread out through the downtown area. Hotels and restaurants barred entrances to protect Negro employees, but some Negroes, feeling insecure behind the barricaded doors and windows, escaped by back apertures and ran along the roof tops, eventually falling into the hands of the mob. Trolley wires were cut and Negro passengers forcibly removed from cars; ambulances taking the wounded to hospitals were stopped and Negroes dragged out. The mobs spread out into the residential districts, and householders were able to protect their servants only with guns and pistols. The State militia, unable to cover the entire city, stationed itself in the wrecked business area to prevent looting. Some of the routed inhabitants of Rusty Row banded together and began to attack white people. On Butler Street they fired more than 100 shots at a streetcar loaded with white passengers.

At two o'clock in the morning a heavy rain scattered the crowds, but outbreaks continued through Tuesday noon. On that day 25 citizens met in the council chamber and arranged for a law and order meeting at the courthouse. A relief committee administered $5,423 that had been subscribed for the care of the victims and their families. Although the accounts of the numbers killed and injured varied fantastically, the committee reported that in all 2 whites and 10 Negroes were killed and 10 whites and 60 Negroes injured. Prominent white men spoke in Negro pulpits over the city, and a racial tolerance group was formed.

This organization was the only one of its kind in the city until 1919, when the Commission on Interracial Co-operation, a national society, was organized in Atlanta. With its board of both whites and blacks, the commission has been the means of maintaining good will among the races and promoting Negro welfare. Trouble threatened again in 1930 when the "Black Shirts" took action against the employment of Negroes while numerous white people were out of work. Although there was no violence, this movement resulted in some displacement of Negroes by whites; in one week Atlanta hotels replaced 100 Negro bellboys with white ones. Other associations that have been of value in the uplift of the Negro and the promotion of better racial understanding are the Atlanta Negro Chamber of Commerce and local branches of the National Association for the Advancement of Colored People and the National Urban League.

More undesirable publicity for the city was started in 1913, when the bruised and assaulted body of 14-year-old Mary Phagan was found in the basement of an Atlanta pencil factory. After a number of arrests, Leo Frank, the Jewish superintendent of the plant, was indicted and sentenced to hang on October 10. The newspapers gave the affair sensational publicity. Thomas E. Watson's *Jeffersonian* in 1914 and

1915 inflamed public opinion and agitated racial prejudice until the case became a major issue in political campaigns. Suspected intimidation of the court and jury because of mass sentiment influenced the granting of appeals to higher courts. New trials, during which Frank was sentenced twice again to hang, and subsequent litigation stayed execution until Governor John M. Slaton on June 21, 1915, the day before his term expired, commuted the sentence to life imprisonment. The following day martial law was declared in order to protect Governor Slaton, hitherto one of the State's most popular governors, and soldiers were ordered to guard his house. His assassination was attempted at the capitol, and that night an armed mob of 5,000 bore down on his home, wounding 16 of the guards before order could be restored. There had been much activity outside the State to save Frank, but the commutation of his sentence aroused strong feeling throughout the Nation. Slaton left the State and later the country for a protracted stay.

On August 16 a lynching party of 25 overcame the warden and guards at the State Prison Farm and took Frank to the outskirts of Marietta, Mary Phagan's home, where his body was found the next morning hanging from a limb. A hysterical mob of several thousands gathered and was restrained from tearing the body to pieces only by the courageous speech of a Marietta judge. Authorities were forced by threats to display the body at an Atlanta morgue where a morbid 15,000 viewed it. The ballad "Little Mary Phagan" was composed around this tragedy.

Atlanta long had been termed "the City of Conventions," and as it grew in enterprise the annual number of conventions increased. One of the most important was the meeting of the Southern Commercial Congress in 1911, when 2,000 delegates were addressed by President Taft, Colonel Theodore Roosevelt, and Woodrow Wilson, then Governor of New Jersey. In the same year the peace jubilee and Old Guard celebration, featuring the unveiling of the Old Guard Peace Monument at Piedmont Park, gathered 1,500 military visitors. This event commemorated the good will tour of the Gate City Guard in October 1879 through the North and East and was the second of Atlanta's peace jubilees.

Three years later, however, the city was feeling again the effects of war, though indirectly. The European conflict drastically affected the cotton trade, middling cotton dropping from 12¢ to approximately 6¢, and movement of the crop was blocked. The result in Atlanta was a general business depression. Bankers, businessmen, and chamber of commerce members conferred on the best means of meeting the emergency and were instrumental in effecting the adoption of a cotton warehouse receipt that could be used as collateral in making loans. As a further measure of relief, Georgia farmers were urged to cultivate food products.

A stimulus to this movement was the large cattle show held by the Southeastern Fair Association as its first exhibit in 1915. The city leased Lakewood Park, site of the old waterworks, to the association, which was organized at the initiation of the Chamber of Commerce the previous year. The terms of the transaction were that 80 per cent of the association's profits be spent on the park. Buildings were erected, the race track constructed, and a streetcar line extended to the grounds. More than $1,000,000 were later spent on improvements, and the site has had increased popularity as a summer amusement park and a center for racing, skating, and aquatic events.

In 1914 the city had secured the Sixth District Federal Reserve Bank. Financial conditions began to improve in 1915, bank clearings in the city at the end of 1916 exceeded $1,000,000,000, and business expanded rapidly.

In January 1917, General Leonard Wood selected a site for the establishment of Camp Gordon, a cantonment where approximately 55,000 men were trained. In 1918 the War Department made it a replacement camp, and a total of 250,000 soldiers passed through it during the World War and the period preceding demobilization in December 1919. During construction of the camp, a special local war tax was imposed to pay for piping water to the site, and after the quartering of troops there a large bond issue was necessary to enlarge the waterworks.

During this time the Federal Government was spending approximately $25,000,000 annually in the vicinity of Atlanta, using all available labor in the erection of plants and the camp. On May 21, 1917, when private building was at a virtual standstill, the city was victim of a disastrous fire which, beginning in a Negro house off Decatur Street, swept out Jackson Street and Boulevard and across to Ponce de Leon. The local companies were assisted by those from other cities and 1,000 soldiers from Fort McPherson. But, in spite of dynamiting and the use of every known means of fire fighting, 2,000 homes were destroyed. The loss was estimated at $5,000,000 and approximately 10,000 people were rendered homeless. This disaster, at a time when the city was crowded with new people attracted by the camp and many war industries, made housing a serious problem until 1920 when labor was available for private building.

In 1941 Camp Gordon, abandoned for many years, became a veritable ant hill of activity. Men worked night and day constructing a large airport and a 2,000-bed cantonment hospital. The airport is a reserve training station for preliminary instruction of naval and marine corps aviators. Atlanta has been made 4th zone headquarters of the

History

RHODES MEMORIAL HALL, GEORGIA DEPARTMENT OF ARCHIVES AND HISTORY

"HOWELL'S MILL," FROM A WATER-COLOR DRAWING BY WILBUR KURTZ

"WHITEHALL TAVERN," FROM A WATER-COLOR DRAWING BY WILBUR KURTZ

"THE FIRST POST OFFICE OF ATLANTA," (THEN MARTHASVILLE), FROM A
WATER-COLOR DRAWING BY WILBUR KURTZ

"THE ARRIVAL OF THE FLORIDA AT THE TERMINUS," FROM A WATER-COLOR
DRAWING BY WILBUR KURTZ

BALTIMORE BLOCK

THE KIMBALL HOUSE, ATLANTA'S OLDEST EXISTING HOTEL

CHURCH OF THE IMMACULATE CONCEPTION, OLDEST EXISTING CHURCH
IN THE CITY

VIVIEN LEIGH AT THE WORLD PREMIERE OF "GONE WITH THE WIND"

SECTION OF THE CYCLORAMA OF THE BATTLE OF ATLANTA

UNFINISHED CONFEDERATE MEMORIAL ON STONE MOUNTAIN

THE OLD HUFF RESIDENCE, HOUSE OF THREE FLAGS

CONFEDERATE ORDNANCE ON SITE OF FORT WALKER, GRANT PARK

United States Quartermaster Corps, and a $15,000,000 supply depot is being constructed.

In 1921, the tax rate, which had been lowered to 1¼ per cent in 1897, was raised to 1½ per cent to meet increased operating expenses. In addition it was necessary to float a bond issue for improvements in the amount of $8,500,000. With the proceeds sewers were laid, streets were widened, and the Spring Street viaduct was constructed and opened to traffic in December 1923. Widening and extension of the streets leading to the viaduct immediately followed. Further construction of viaducts and schools, erection of a new city hall, and the expansion of the waterworks and sewer system were permitted by an $8,000,000 bond issue floated in 1926, when the population was 249,000. In the 1936 and 1940 elections a proposed issue of $4,000,000 for needed improvements on the schools and city hospitals failed because, although a large majority of favoring votes were cast, the total of 19,357 votes necessary for passage was not attained.

Atlanta had woman suffrage before it became a national prerogative. In May 1919, a group of women appealed to the Atlanta City Democratic Executive Committee to permit the participation of women in the city primary. The request was granted, and the Central Committee of Women Citizens was organized and canvassed the city, persuading 4,000 women, in all wards of the city, to register and vote in September. In November of that year the name of the organization was changed to the Atlanta Women Voters' League and has become officially the Atlanta League of Women Voters, now affiliated with the national league. This organization augments the valuable work of several local clubs that strive to acquaint all eligible voters with the issues involved and to stimulate active participation in elections.

The first scandal within the ranks of the city government came in the fall of 1929, when charges of bribery were made against a city official. An investigation led to the indictment of 26 persons, 15 of whom subsequently were convicted and received sentences.

Law enforcement has been of great importance in recent city elections. From late in the 1920's through the middle of the 1930's there was widespread agitation over poorly managed traffic, careless driving, and inefficient police service. The hotel operators charged the police chief with negligence and failure to co-operate in the fight against vice and crime, and labor leaders preferred charges against him for drinking and cursing while on duty; policemen were charged with "grafting and mooching" and with writing "bug" numbers. The grand jury investigation of the department led to no tangible improvements. In 1937 William B. Hartsfield, who promised reorganization of the police and detective departments, was elected to the office of mayor. During his regime there was marked improvement in law enforcement services and the general functioning of the city government. In 1939 the city closed its books with a cash surplus of $772,270.65, the largest in its history. Proceeds from liquor store bonds and taxes after the repeal of prohibition in 1938 were helpful in making this surplus possible.

Cultural activities assumed popular and important proportions in the twentieth century. In 1904 the newly formed Atlanta Art Association began bringing exhibits to the city and encouraging annual exhibitions of local work. Twenty-two years later the High Museum of Art was opened and in the following year the art school was begun. Beginning in 1910 the Metropolitan Opera Company gave performances in Atlanta each spring until 1931. As the only city south of Baltimore to have annual performances by this company, Atlanta was always thronged with out-of-State visitors during opera week. With the coming of the depression this event was discontinued, and Atlanta did not see the Metropolitan artists in opera again until the first Dogwood Festival in the spring of 1936, when the performance of three grand operas was a feature of the festivities. In the meantime the city had contented itself with the presentations of the Atlanta Philharmonic Orchestra and the All-Star Concert Series, which each fall and winter brings notable artists. The citizens enthusiastically welcomed a revival of the Metropolitan Opera season in April 1940, at which time the Dogwood Festival also was revived. During the winter months famous actors are presented by road companies in popular Broadway plays. Leading lecturers are brought to the city each year by Agnes Scott College, Emory University, and the civic clubs.

To counteract the threatened loss of citizens and business during the Florida real estate boom, the Forward Atlanta Movement was organized by the Chamber of Commerce in October 1925. The appeal of low wages and fine natural resources was again presented to the East and Middle West. An intensive campaign, costing $822,000, for the importation of new manufactories and commercial concerns was waged and in something over four years brought to the city 762 new enterprises, employing 20,286 persons and paying annual wages and salaries to the amount of $34,500,000.

In marked contrast to these booming years were the early 1930's when the city, with the whole country, felt the effects of the depression. Unemployment, which had presented no serious problem except for a brief period after the World War, became serious indeed. In 1932 a mass demonstration of a thousand unemployed blacks and whites led to the courthouse by Angelo Herndon, a Negro Communist, protested the inadequacy of relief measures. In 1933 the CWA brought some alleviation and kindred agencies, the PWA, FERA, and WPA have continued to do so. The housing agencies have replaced hundreds of unsightly shacks with eight attractive developments, five for

Negroes and three for white people, that offer low-income groups full utility services and the most modern in structural design at moderate rents. In addition the city has received many benefits through the various construction, education, and community service projects. There is a growing tendency in the city to get away from the exploitation of employees which was begun 60 years ago when there was need of industrial expansion at any cost. Initiated by the short-lived NRA measures in 1932, this trend has been accelerated by the Wages and Hours Law, and Atlanta industry in its co-operation is increasingly exceeding the requirements.

The city's importance as a county seat was heightened in 1932 with the merging of Campbell and Milton Counties and the Roswell area of Cobb County into Fulton County. This acquisition more than doubled the area of Fulton and increased its population by more than 18,000 persons.

Atlanta, for so large a city, has had few calamitous fires. The efficient fire department in April 1936 was awarded national honors in fire prevention. But in the next year and a half the city had its two most disastrous fires in 20 years. In the fall of 1936 three people lost their lives in a flame-gutted studio building in the downtown section, and in May 1938, twenty-seven persons perished when the old Terminal Hotel was burned to the ground.

One of the Nation's ranking aviation, communication, and insurance centers, the city in 1940 had a population of 302,538. The railroads that gave the city birth and have fed it to almost prodigious growth are responsible for its commercial prosperity and its establishment as the outstanding convention center of the Southeast. In 1939, 495 conventions brought 134,000 delegates to the city, more than double the number in 1935.

The tides of conventions and tourists have increased since publication of Margaret Mitchell's historical novel, *Gone With the Wind,* in 1936. Owing to phenomenal popularity of the book, international interest has been aroused in the history of the city that rose so rapidly from the ruins of Sherman's making. One of the greatest celebrations to be held here in the twentieth century was the festival attending the premiere of Metro-Goldwyn-Mayer's vivid picturization of the book in December 1939. Hundreds of visitors streamed up and down Peachtree Street, a few of them searching, in all seriousness, for the site of "Aunt Pittypat's" house, others conjecturing as to the spot Scarlett O'Hara would have chosen for the erection of her "chalet" with the scrollwork trim. Thousands lined the streets for two hours in a cold, gusty wind awaiting the arrival of the stars, only to catch a kaleidoscopic view of furs, red roses, and bared masculine heads as the delayed parade streaked past. Crowds blocked the streets around the Georgian

Terrace Hotel to see the actors and hear brief speeches of welcome from the mayor, the governor, and other prominent men. A public ball, at which men and women danced in costumes of the 1860's, was given at the auditorium that night and featured entertainment typical of the Old South.

The night of the premiere crowds packed the streets around the theater, on the façade of which a concrete, large-columned portico with Greek pediment had been superimposed. Giant magnolias flanked the pillars, and multicolored flowers bloomed in the garden that extended into the street. Spotlights played over the theater front, the people thronging the streets, dotting surrounding roof-tops, and peering out of near-by office windows. In the theater, approximately three blocks from the site of the State Square park that served as an outdoor hospital in 1864, Atlantans saw the picture. They compared the primitiveness of the pictured Peachtree Street and Five Points with their present appearance and were proud.

FOR the first few years of its existence the little settlement called the terminus was governed by no law other than the common law of the State, and only a rough frontier order prevailed among the pioneer settlers and railroad builders. A local government was established on December 23, 1843, when by legislative enactment the settlement was incorporated as the town of Marthasville and five commissioners were appointed to administer civic affairs. The charter conferred full corporate jurisdiction on the commission, which was to be elected annually by the qualified voters, but this body proved ineffectual because responsibility was divided and no means were provided for enforcing ordinances. The duties of peace officer probably were shifted from one commissioner to another as convenience dictated, for there is no mention of a marshal at this time. The commissioners were reminded emphatically from time to time by the few property owners of the settlement that they did not want any additional taxes imposed.

In 1847 the city of Atlanta was incorporated under a document which, although called an incorporating act amendatory to that of 1843, was in effect a new charter. This act changed the very character of the town's government from a commission form to a mayor and council type. From its inception until 1874, when a revised charter was adopted, the act of 1847 was greatly altered by the addition of 29 amendments, but the changes made did not alter the basic form of government under which Atlanta now operates—that of mayor and council.

The mayor and council were given authority to pass ordinances within constitutional limitations, levy and collect taxes, and impose fines for violation of ordinances. They were also empowered to elect a clerk, treasurer, marshal, and tax collector, and fix their duties and bonds. The salaries were small—only $20 annually for each of the six councilmen and $200 for the mayor. The mayor was given no strictly exclusive powers except the appointment of standing commit-

41

tees, which had no administrative authority and could only present recommendations to council. The mayor had the deciding vote in the event of a tie at council meetings but no veto power. All the specific duties assigned to him could be performed by a councilman or group of councilmen in his absence.

Early judiciary functions were simple. As there was no charter provision for the trial of State offenses committed within the city, the mayor and council in their individual capacities were made ministerial officers of the State in so far as they were empowered to issue warrants against criminal offenders and imprison them in the town jail until they could be tried in a State court. The only city tribunal was the mayor's court, which had jurisdiction over civic matters only. In 1856 a city court was established but it was abolished the following year, and the mayor's court continued to function until 1871, when a recorder's court was established to handle violations of city ordinances and a city court was set up with jurisdiction over civil and misdemeanor cases.

The charter of 1847 recognized the need for a stricter enforcement of law and specifically provided that "The marshal shall have full power and authority to call to his aid any and all of the white male citizens of said city capable of bearing arms." Three years later this provision had to be invoked to quell a riot by a lawless gang that had threatened the peace of the community for several years. In 1852 a supplementary peace force, known as the patrol, was organized. The city was divided into three districts, and in each of these a patrol captain and three patrolmen appointed by the mayor and council operated in 30-day shifts, apparently without remuneration. In 1853 a night force consisting of a chief and two assistants was installed and equipped with "dark lantern and rabble," the rabble apparently being a kind of riot stick. Added to their other duties was that of a fire watchman, and they were instructed to give the alarm when a fire broke out by rushing to the nearest engine house and ringing the bell. Temporary additions to the force were made from time to time, but crime control in these early days depended largely upon the leading citizens who were deputized by the marshal when an emergency arose. In 1858 the police force was removed from the general supervision of the mayor and council and put under the direct administration of a police committee of council, a step that was to lead finally to the organization of a distinct police department.

A volunteer fire company was organized in 1854, and later other companies were incorporated, but they worked independently until 1860. At that time representatives of the various companies met and elected a chief and two assistants to co-ordinate and direct the work of the several companies. During the War between the States the fire companies not only protected the city from the ravages of fire but also served as home militia companies, known as the fire brigade. So efficiently did the volunteer companies serve the city that it was not until 1882 that the charter was amended to provide for a paid fire department under the supervision of a board of firemasters.

Executive powers were broadened as the prosperous 1850's brought a firmer sense of financial security. An unwise provision of 1860 permitted the mayor and council to subscribe stock in private corporations at their discretion, and, confident of railroad development as a means of creating wealth, the city government subscribed $600,000 to the capital stock of two railroads seeking to enter the city. At the same time most of a $47,000 bond was outstanding. Then the orderly process of civic development was disrupted by war. When Atlanta was placed under martial law in 1862, the mayor was appointed civil governor of the city and the police force was organized into a military company. Heavy expenditures for defense and a greatly reduced tax income had already undermined the city's credit before the defeat of the Confederate States brought complete collapse to the treasury. The city was forced to borrow money where it could and, in desperation, even issued two-year scrip and bonds in order to meet current expenses, notwithstanding the highest tax rate (2 per cent) in Atlanta's history.

By 1869, through the efforts of a wise finance committee, who assumed personal responsibility for losses, the city had partly recovered, but the rapid growth in population following the war made the need for improvements and the expansion of services urgent. This meant an increase from year to year in the bonded indebtedness and floating debt until they exceeded the limit imposed by State law. During the panic of 1873-75 the balance in the treasury was insufficient to meet the interest due on the city's debts, and more loans had to be negotiated. When the unsound character of such financing caused interest rates to reach a peak of 18 per cent on small loans, civic leaders were finally stirred to action, which resulted in the adoption of a new charter.

The charter of 1874 embodied a much stronger definition of powers, although it preserved the fundamental structure of the city government. Probably the most important change was the reorganization of council itself into a bicameral body; in addition to the two councilmen elected from each of the city wards, three aldermen were elected from the city at large. The term of aldermanic service was fixed at three years, only one alderman being elected each year. The alderman serving his last year acted as mayor pro tem and as presiding officer of the general council. The bicameral council was created principally to safeguard the treasury by having the two bodies act as a check upon one another when voting upon ordinances concerning municipal finance. In all questions of increased indebtedness for the city or the expenditure of revenue, the two bodies acted separately; on all other resolutions or ordinances they acted together.

The new charter made the mayor a real factor in city government by conferring on him the right of veto and revision. For the first time he was made responsible not only for the execution of all city laws but charged with the duty of revising such ordinances as authorized expenditure beyond a certain fixed amount and of auditing all accounts against the city before payment was made. In this prerogative the mayor's office became distinctly administrative, and the tendency in all subsequent legislation has been to broaden his responsibilities.

By 1874 the population of Atlanta had grown to approximately 35,000, and consequently the administration of the city's affairs was becoming increasingly complicated. The charter further recognized the need for diffusing the executive power by establishing two distinct boards, a board of water commissioners and a board of commissioners of police, and vesting them with the supervisory powers later given to all city departments. This distribution of work through boards or departments did not decentralize responsibility, however, for the mayor and council retained disciplinary control over all departmental personnel through the power of dismissal for cause, whether the officers were elected by the people or appointed by the mayor and council.

The charter of 1874 also imposed strict legal limitations on the expenditure of municipal funds and on incurring indebtedness. It prohibited the mayor and council from issuing bonds in any amount without first submitting the issue to a vote of the people, restricted all expenditures to the annual income, and permitted borrowing only to meet payments due on the floating debt. By careful management and a slight increase in the tax rate the city government was able to supply the funds needed for current expenses and at the same time reduce the floating debt. By 1877, the year that the new State constitution limited bond issues by municipalities to 7 per cent of their taxable property, the city's credit had been restored and the interest rate on loans had dropped to 7 per cent. Further efforts to assure the city's financial stability resulted in an amendment in 1879 to provide a sinking fund adequate to meet the interest on outstanding bonds and floating indebtedness. So far had public sentiment swung in the direction of retrenchment that in 1884 the charter was again amended to prohibit the mayor and council from contracting any loans whatsoever, but the impracticability of this measure was soon apparent, and the amendment was repealed in 1887. While executive borrowing power was still limited by legal controls, it was made flexible enough to be adjusted to current tax values and civic emergencies. Two years later the office of comptroller was created to act as the city accounting department.

The Board of Commissioners of Police created by the new charter was composed of five men, none of whom was a member of council. Unlike the old police committee, which was supervisory, this body was vested with full administrative power to direct and control the police department. All appointments to the force, including the chief of police, and all suspensions and removals were in its hands, and its decisions were final. Also conferred on the board was the power to summon witnesses and records and to punish for refusal to testify or produce records.

This system proved satisfactory, and under it many improvements were inaugurated despite the handicap of inadequate finances. Patrol wagons were introduced in 1886 and telephone service was installed in 1891. A strong effort to sever the department from politics was made in 1905 when the fixed term of police employment was abolished and a tenure system established. A pension system was adopted in 1910.

Revisions were made from time to time. In 1900 the mayor was made ex officio member of the police board, and in 1904 the chairman of the police committee of council was added, but the most extensive changes were made in 1913, when the name of the board was changed to the Board of Public Safety and the city fire department was also put under its direction. The chief of police was granted the privilege of nominating all his officers and men, subject to approval of the board, but this led to repeated charges of favoritism. Finally, in 1922, the Board of Public Safety was abolished, and authority was divided between the head of the department and the police committee of council.

The Criminal Court of Atlanta was created by the Georgia Legislature on September 6, 1891, and took over all the criminal work of the city court, leaving to the latter its civil jurisdiction. The judge was appointed by the governor until an amendment in 1898 made both the offices of judge and solicitor elective by the qualified voters. The territorial jurisdiction of this court was broadened in 1935, when it became the Criminal Court of Fulton County.

From 1874 until 1913 about 60 amendments were added to the charter of Atlanta. Although some of these amendments were discarded after they had served their purpose, enough were retained to make the charter such a patchwork that it was sometimes difficult to determine what the law actually was. In 1911 a new charter was proposed, providing for a commission type of government, but it was rejected by the voters as constituting too radical a change in the form of administration. The charter of 1913, really a sweeping revision of the old charter, made no striking departure from traditional form but introduced numerous specific changes.

The most fundamental change was a further decentralization of administrative power through the creation of more city departments. Direct control over these departments was vested in charter boards, which were composed of one member from each city ward appointed by the mayor and general council. Each board appointed a chief over its department, who in turn nominated all subordinate officers and working forces, subject to the confirmation of the board. While the duties of these boards were regulated by ordinance and each was given full authority over its department, the final responsibility still rested with the mayor and council through appointive and supervisory powers. The mayor and chairman of the council committee corresponding to the department were ex officio members of the various boards and thereby remained in close contact with departmental activities. The determination of the electorate to keep control over the city's officials is indicated by the introduction of the initiative, referendum, and recall and the provision that such officials as the comptroller and the city attorney be elected by the people.

There was some reaction from departmentalization in the amendment of 1922 which abolished the boards of police, health, waterworks, and parks and transferred their authority to the committees of general council corresponding to these boards. On the whole, this change was not an improvement, especially in regard to the police department. There was a noticeable retrogression in police service, a trend that continued until late in the 1930's when decided improvements were made through the determined efforts of the administration.

Atlanta still retains the sound financial policies adopted in 1874, although some changes in operation have been made. In 1933 a budget commission was established, which is composed of the mayor, comptroller, chairman of the finance committee, and two other members of the general council elected by that body. The city has no floating debt and its bonded indebtedness is 3.9 per cent of its assessed ad valorem tax values, slightly in excess of one-half of that allowed by the general law of the State. In 1940 the sinking fund amounted to $824,450.22, and the treasury carried a cash balance of $750,000. Twenty-year serial bonds sold in 1939 at $2\frac{1}{8}$ per cent interest, while $500,000 in short-term paper was secured at the very low interest rate of 1 per cent.

Several changes have been made in the courts in the Atlanta area during recent years. In 1935 the old city court that was established in 1871 was abolished and all its pending business transferred to the Superior Court of Fulton County. Effective on April 1, 1939, the two divisions of the municipal court were changed in name to the Civil Court of Fulton County and the Civil Court of DeKalb County.

Except for the early lamp-lighting days, Atlanta has never owned its lighting system, although it was a considerable stockholder in the first gas lighting company, which was organized in 1855. But, since the days of the street wells as a source of water supply, the city has retained complete ownership of the water system. The present system has a daily capacity of 40,000,000 gallons and a maximum capacity of 55,000,000 gallons, a supply sufficient to furnish a city much larger than Atlanta.

The laws governing the city are set forth in a code which includes the charter and a large number of ordinances, as well as many statutes. No compilation of the code has been made since 1924, but a supplement was published in 1936. Atlanta still derives its corporate powers from the charter of 1847, although the changes effected in 1874 and again in 1913 were so broad that the revised documents are referred to as new charters.

As the city expanded, new wards were added until the number reached 13 in 1929, with two councilmen and one alderman for each ward. In 1935, however, the number of wards was reduced by law to 6, and consequently only 12 councilmen and 6 aldermen now compose the general council. The mayor, who is elected for a term of 4 years, appoints from council the committees that supervise the business of the city government. This power of appointment and the veto constitute the mayor's main source of influence despite the fact that he is nominally the chief executive and a voting member of all committees. Consequently, the committee system gives Atlanta a highly decentralized type of government.

The Governments of Atlanta and Fulton County, prepared by T.H. Reed and published by the Atlanta Chamber of Commerce in 1938, presents a complete survey of the city's government and makes recommendations for changes, particularly with reference to centralizing authority and combining the functions of many city and county departments. The reactions of the citizens to these recommendations are somewhat divided, and few major changes have yet been made as a result of the report.

Transportation

L̲o̲n̲g̲ before this territory was settled by white people, the ridge along which Atlanta's well-known Peachtree Street now runs was already worn by an Indian trail leading to a trading post on the banks of the Chattahoochee River. Scattered pioneer families of the early nineteenth century, who settled in the heavily wooded areas north of the present city, were often affrighted by the sight of the bucks racing their horses madly to the post, waving their hands and emitting ear-splitting yells while their black hair whipped in the wind.

During the 1820's the intrepid Methodist circuit riders blazed new trails through the area, and when campgrounds were established near Sandy Springs, Lawrenceville, and Ben Hill, the connecting trails were widened into wagon routes. Afoot, on horseback, and in mule- or ox-drawn wagons, the God-fearing pioneers made their way along roads gutted by winter freshets and choked with rotted vegetation.

In 1836 plans were announced for a State railroad to be built through the mountains of north Georgia, the southern terminus to be in this area. Various railroads in the lower part of the State planned to extend their lines to connect with this road, and a stake was driven at the present site of Atlanta to mark the proposed junction of the tracks. The arrival of lumberjacks, wood haulers, and railroad workmen attracted merchants, and soon this place, which was known simply as the terminus, developed into a trading center. Five roads, leading from Decatur, Marietta, McDonough, Whitehall Inn, and The Standing Peachtree, traversed the area, and short branch roads ran from these to the junction. Mrs. Willis Carlisle, who came to the terminus in 1841, says that the town was then a veritable wilderness and that she and her husband followed strange paths in search of a house, only to find the trails winding up at some spring or an uninhabitable shack abandoned by railroad hands. The stagecoach driven by Tom Shivers passed back and forth every other day from Decatur to Marietta, and, says Mrs. Carlisle, "this event was an oasis in the desert of our lives, for it was the only thing that broke the terrible monotony."

Other factors, however, soon broke the monotony more sharply. By 1842 the tracks of the Western & Atlantic Railroad were completed to Marietta and people were eager to see their first train, but the only engine available was in Madison, Georgia, 65 miles away, and there was no connecting track. Undaunted, the railroad engineers constructed a massive 6-wheeled wagon to which were harnessed 16 mules. This unwieldy juggernaut was pulled and pushed laboriously through uncleared paths all the way to Madison. Fights with farmers occurred on the way, for some rural folk opposed the spread of railroads and did everything possible to obstruct the building of tracks. In Madison the engine and two little "passenger boxes" were hauled aboard the creaking vehicle and the return journey was begun. Families for miles around came in their wagons and accompanied the procession to the terminus where the entire population of the settlement, swelled by visitors from as far away as the north Georgia mountains, had gathered for the occasion. There were no real streets yet; the settlement was "just a wide place in the road." Horses, mules, and oxen were tethered to stakes driven in open ground and wagons were parked in shallow openings of the brush. People climbed fences and trees to view the arrival of the train. Many wild tales had been circulated concerning the "iron horses." Some people believed it was dangerous to stand near the tracks, as it was said that the suction of the passing train would draw one to death beneath the wheels. Others believed that engines squirted scalding water, and it was common knowledge that the boilers were always exploding.

When the locomotive was set upon the tracks it looked harmless enough and the people crowded close. An excursion to Marietta had been planned to celebrate the opening of the new State road, and those invited to make the trial trip formed a gay and excited group as they waited for the train to pull away from the rough plank shed at the terminus. Rebecca Latimer Felton, the first woman Senator in the United States, was only seven when she accompanied her parents on this excursion trip, but she recalled the exciting incident later in her book of memoirs *Country Life in Georgia*. Of the big ball given in Marietta in honor of the occasion, she said: "The joyful folks danced all night. There were relays of fiddlers to keep the tunes going. I remember I thought I had been awake all the time because the music and the calling of dance figures and the dancers' feet seemed to be going on until daylight in the morning."

After this successful run the people in the vicinity of the terminus awaited with eager anticipation the completion of the State road and the extension of other railroads to connect with the Western & Atlantic

tracks. On September 15, 1845, the first through train from Augusta
pulled into Atlanta, as the town was now known, over the Georgia
Railroad tracks, and the following year the Macon & Western's first
train arrived from Monroe.

Despite its growing prominence as a railroad center, few seriously
thought the settlement would ever be other than a mere wood station,
and no consideration was given to community planning. True, property for a depot had been donated to the State railroad, and this plot,
known as State Square, was the block bounded by the present Pryor,
Decatur, and Alabama Streets and Central Avenue. Also the adjacent
lot to the west was given to the Macon & Western Railroad as a site
for its depot. Landowners built wherever they pleased and, as a result,
the eroded scars that served as streets radiated from the State Square
in haphazard fashion like the warped spokes of a wheel. In 1849,
the road which led to Whitehall Inn out near the junction of the
Sandtown and Newnan roads (now Gordon and Lee Streets) was
straightened and named Whitehall Street. Pryor Street was laid out
in the same year and named in honor of Allen Pryor, the surveyor.
Alabama Street was at that time little more than a red clay ditch,
but it was so named because of its westerly direction and because the
early settlers were proud of boasting that some day it would reach
"clear to Alabama." Business houses had concentrated along Whitehall, Alabama, and Mitchell Streets, thoroughfares that were difficult
of passage and dangerous, for newspapers of the day state that they
were pitted by great holes, some of which were 15 feet wide and 18 feet
deep.

The movement of wagons and carriages through the town was accomplished with difficulty. Heavier vehicles constantly mired down
and "going to town" was more a matter of a walk than a ride. Drivers
often had to pull their wagons up on the dirt sidewalks to avoid the
deeper puddles of the streets, and thus the sidewalks became so rutted
that they were hardly distinguishable from the streets. Even those
who rode horseback fared little better, for their mounts often stumbled
and threw the riders into the mud or red dust. Many storekeepers,
in consideration for their customers, laid boardwalks in front of their
shops. By the late 1850's several of the sidewalks nearest the railroads
were so paved and a few of the streets had been surfaced with a double
layer of crushed rock.

The roads leading into town were equally difficult of passage, but,
despite transportation obstacles, brisk trade was developing with the
surrounding territory. Long wagon trains, heavily laden with produce
and sometimes drawn by as many as six mules or oxen, pulled into
Atlanta and struggled through the quagmires to the market place on
Marietta Street. In 1856 the city purchased 3,000 shares of stock

in a company organized to build a bridge over the Chattahoochee River, thus stimulating trade with Cobb County.

A year later connecting lines of the Western & Atlantic Railroad were completed to Memphis, Tennessee, on the northwest and to Charleston, South Carolina, on the east. A group of Atlanta citizens joined the mayor of Memphis and his party when they passed through the city on their way to Charleston to mingle the waters of the Mississippi River with those of the Atlantic Ocean. At the commemorative banquet held in Charleston the group from Atlanta was toasted as coming from "The Gate City," an apt phrase which immediately took hold and did much to advertise Atlanta as the distribution center of the South. In the same year the city bought $100,000 worth of stock in the Georgia Air Line Railroad which was to run to Charlotte, North Carolina. An additional purchase of $100,000 was made the following year. In 1860 the city invested $300,000 in the stock of the Georgia Western Railroad.

At the outbreak of the War between the States Atlanta was the most important railway center in the South, with four major railroads radiating from the city. The Federal forces, realizing that the capture of Atlanta would seriously cripple the entire Confederacy, made it a goal for their drives. Their aim was achieved in 1864 when General Sherman left the city a shambles before marching to the sea.

Returning families could bring but few household furnishings over the virtually impassable roads, which had been rutted by the passage of heavy gun carriages and blasted by shell. Most bridges being destroyed, it was necessary to wade creeks or unharness the horses and walk them across the few remaining bridges. The wagons were then pulled and pushed across the flimsy structures.

Conditions were even worse inside the city, where the wreckage of buildings littered the streets. One member of the family usually ran ahead of the returning wagon, searching for a passage through the debris. One man, O.H. Jones, took advantage of the situation to establish livery stables near the City Hall. With his stock of powerful stallions he took over much of the business of moving the belongings of private families. To the public he rented "rockaways," a type of carriage very popular because its lightness and high narrow wheels rendered it unlikely to get stuck in the mud.

Even several years after the close of the war little had been done toward repairing the highways and streets. Miss Sarah Huff tells in her memoirs of the difficulties travelers experienced in approaching the city over the Marietta Road. Great pits on this road, as on all others, often made it necessary for drivers to lead their horses up onto the dirt "sidewalks," much to the chagrin of pedestrians. One ingenious vehicle, known as the slide, came into usage about this time.

It was very much like a sled, with side runners connected by crosspieces. Occasionally the runners were fashioned out of discarded railroad rails. Pulled by a horse, these sleds negotiated the muddy roads with infinitely greater ease than wagons.

The opposing armies had cleared many paths through the wooded areas surrounding Atlanta, and, through constant usage, these paths became roads. One of the most important was the line of General Joseph E. Johnston's retreat. In 1866, when Atlanta's cattle and mule market had its beginning, cattle were driven afoot from Tennessee and the north Georgia hills along this line. The route today is virtually the same as that followed by US 41.

In 1871 the officials of the five railroads running into the city jointly rebuilt the Union Station on State Square. But the city was growing in all directions and its increase in size made necessary some means of city transportation. Accordingly, the Atlanta Street Railway Company, which had been incorporated in 1866, completed its organization and built the first street railway line in the city, extending from the railroad crossing on Whitehall Street to Camp's Spring in what is now known as the suburb of West End. The early cars, mounted on cast-iron tracks and pulled by two mules, looked not unlike the "Toonerville Trolley" of comic-strip fame. The car barn was on Exchange Place where the Atlanta Theater now stands, and the stables were at the corner of Ivy and Gilmer Streets. The horsecars immediately proved so profitable that a second line began operating out Marietta Street in January 1872. In May of the same year the Decatur Street line to Oakland Cemetery began service. The Peachtree Street line began running as far as Ponce de Leon Circle in August and, two years later, was extended to Ponce de Leon Springs where the Sears Roebuck store now stands.

By 1880 the Peachtree line had been extended to the present Piedmont Park section, and a new route had been opened out Alabama Street to McDonough Street. During the next two years two new companies, the Gate City Railway and the Metropolitan Street Railway, were organized and lines were put in operation through the eastern part of the city to Ponce de Leon Springs and west to West View Cemetery.

In 1888 two innovations in street transit were introduced by newly formed companies. Early in the year Aaron Haas began the operation of steam cars, popularly known as "dummies" because the steam engines were hidden in the ordinary street car superstructure. Some south side lines were leased from the Metropolitan Street Railway Company and the steam cars, actually small trains, began operating over these routes. The citizens of Atlanta considered these steam cars not only practical conveyances but entertainment vehicles, and a "ride on the dummies" became a most popular form of amusement. Such joy rides, however, were not without hazard; the motor-driven vehicles were capable of much faster speeds than the old horse-drawn cars and the dummies often leapt the tracks.

Only a few months after the introduction of the steam cars, Joel Hurt began operating the first electric cars out Edgewood Avenue to Inman Park. In the same year the famed "nine-mile circle" was established, an electric line running from Peachtree out Houston and Hilliard Streets to Highland and Virginia Avenues and back to town over Boulevard. This new means of transportation became immediately popular and a ride over the nine-mile circle was regarded as the city's prime entertainment feature. Such streetcar tours were even advertised as being soothing to tired and frayed nerves.

But it was actually a noisy era with the rattle of three kinds of streetcars—horse, steam, and electric—the shrieking of train whistles, the rumble of heavy wagons, and the clatter of horses' hoofs over the cobblestone pavements. Even so, Miss Sarah Huff recalls with nostalgic longing "the merry bells of the horsecars ringing traffic warnings" through the dignified residential districts. Many a noted citizen, such as Joel Chandler Harris, Frank L. Stanton, Jonathan Norcross, and George W. Adair, had their favorite places in the streetcars, and riders who boarded the cars at points up the line tacitly understood that these seats were not to be taken or were to be relinquished if these gentlemen boarded the cars at their accustomed stops.

The decade of the nineties was a period of great expansion in all of Atlanta's transportation facilities. In 1890 two new street railway systems were organized. The Consolidated Street Railway Company, headed by Joel Hurt, took over all existing lines and equipped them for electric cars. The second system was the Atlanta, West End & McPherson Barracks Railway Company. The following year this system changed its name to the Atlanta Traction Company and a new company, the Collins Park and Beltline, was organized. In 1892 still a fourth company, the Atlanta City Railway, was formed. Two years later both the Atlanta Traction Company and the Atlanta City Railway went into receivership and were taken over by the Atlanta Railway Company, which was organized in 1895.

The paving of Atlanta's streets had kept pace in most instances with the extension of the streetcar lines. Crushed rock, Belgian blocks, and cobblestones were the most popular surfaces. Sidewalks were laid with bricks in herring-bone fashion. The work of grade separation had begun in 1891 on a comprehensive scale with the erection of the Forsyth Street viaduct. There followed in rapid succession the building of eight bridges, underpasses, and viaducts.

Several new railroads came into Atlanta during the nineties, and the city became general headquarters for a number of terminal companies. Early in the decade the Southern Railway System had absorbed many of the smaller companies. By the turn of the century the number of railway systems maintaining offices in Atlanta had risen to 44, and more than one third of all the freight entering the State was unloaded in the city. In 1904 the Terminal Station was erected to accommodate the trains of six big railroads.

During the first ten years of the 1900's, ten more grade separation projects were brought to completion and the city had 84 miles of paved streets and 268 miles of brick sidewalks. In 1902 all street railways were consolidated under the name of the Georgia Railway & Electric Company. In 1908 this organization took over the Georgia Power Company, which had been formed two years previously, and became the nucleus of the present company.

Despite this bustling expansion the era was not without its elegance. In his book *Chip Off My Shoulder* Thomas Stokes describes the flow of traffic past his West End home in the early 1900's. "There was constant activity. The streetcars lumbered along the incline past the house every few minutes and against the Belgian block pavement the horses beat their tattoo, now slow and regular as they pulled a heavy wagon up the incline . . . now gay and ecstatic . . . as blooded steeds proudly drew fine equipages, linked two and two. The coachman sat stiff and erect. The plumes of the women waved a feathery trail behind. It was a splendid sight."

"Constant activity" was to take on new meaning, however, and the elegance of leisure was doomed to suffer extinction by the automobile. The first "horseless carriage" to appear on the city's streets had been purchased in 1897 by J.W. Alexander. The vehicle, known as a loco-steamer, was propelled by a steam motor and was described as being "as contrary a critter as was ever endowed with cranks and other complications." Mr. Alexander's most sensational exploit was the attempt of a one-day round-trip to East Point, six miles south of Atlanta. Scoffers prophesied that he would never make it. They were right. About three miles out of town a particularly stubborn red mule disputed the right of way with Mr. Alexander's coughing contraption. The stage of angry glaring was quickly passed and the mule took the offensive with a well-placed kick which decided the encounter by depositing Mr. Alexander and his loco-steamer in a gully.

This triumph of the mule over the machine was but the last spiteful gesture of a defeated era. Shortly after the turn of the century, the automobile, while by no means commonplace, had ceased to be a sensation. One type of motive power followed another in quick succession and, in a very few years, steam-, electric-, and gasoline-powered automobiles were rolling along Atlanta's streets. When it became evident that the horseless carriage was here to stay, Atlanta's variety of street pavings gave way to the smoother and more durable asphalt. This repaving, at first a slow process, was hastened and made more comprehensive by the Florida boom of the 1920's. At that time the State constructed many new highways through Georgia, and Atlanta financed the paving of many thoroughfares through the city lest tourists choose other routes. New streets were cut through several sections of the city to relieve traffic congestion and one major elevated artery, the Spring Street viaduct, was opened.

During this period another medium of transportation arose to compete with the street railway system. This was the distracting fleet of "jitneys" or model-T Fords overloaded with commuters who were willing to put up with a great deal of discomfort to take advantage of the five-cent fare. At one time these jitneys reached a peak of 363 cars. In 1924 they were abolished by a city law which declared them to be an unsafe and unfair means of competition. This left an unrivaled field for the Georgia Power Company which, it is generally conceded, has provided Atlanta with the best street railway service in the country. The company maintains a fleet of feeder, shoppers' special, and express busses to supplement the electric streetcars and, in 1940, introduced the modern streamlined trackless trolley.

Interstate bus lines, which started running into Atlanta late in the 1920's and were considered only supplementary to train service, are now a major factor of travel. In 15 years the bus traffic has outgrown three depots, and a fourth station, the largest in the South, has recently been opened. This depot serves more than 200 daily busses operating on the 15 lines which enter the city.

Atlanta's two railway stations, the Union and the Terminal, serve the 15 main lines of 8 major railway systems running 110 passenger trains in and out of the city daily. A third station at Brookwood is maintained by the Southern Railway System for the convenience of north Atlanta residents.

As far back as 1910 Atlanta had an aerial exposition featuring "a whole flock of the new-fangled air machines." City leaders were as quick to recognize the growing importance of air travel as the early settlers had been to grasp the significance of the railroads. Many individuals, having bought their own private planes, urged the establishment of a graded landing field. In 1925 the city leased the Candler race track and converted it into an airport. In 1929 the property was purchased outright and extensive improvements made. Candler Field now ranks third in the Nation's air passenger service and eighth in volume of air mail. It is on the routes of eight major passenger lines, and in 1939 handled 99,800 commercial passengers.

Commerce and Industry

THE railroads made Atlanta. The same strokes that hammered spikes into crossties beat the breath of life into the newborn town, and the city's present eminence depends upon the hundreds of trains pulsing in and out daily via the steel arteries reaching into the body of the Nation. Atlanta is essentially a city of commerce.

The settlement became a small trading center soon after the stake was driven in 1837 to designate the proposed junction of the various existing railroads with a State line extending to Tennessee. In 1839 John Thrasher, expecting an immediate influx of railroad workers, erected a general store which was the first commercial venture of the community. But the building of the railroads did not go forward as rapidly as had been anticipated, so, in 1841, Thrasher closed his establishment and moved away from the terminus. But his action was too hasty, for the following year the road was completed from the little junction to Marietta.

The first industrial venture, a horse-powered sawmill established by Jonathan Norcross, fared better. When the tracks of the Georgia Railroad neared the town in 1844, Norcross began fashioning construction timbers for roadbeds and bridges and rough slabs for workmen's huts. The little community grew rapidly and before the year was out numbered among its enterprises a grocery store, a general emporium, and, in deference to the femininity of pioneer wives, a bonnet shop.

Early in 1845 a cabinet shop and coffin factory was opened, and on September 15 of that year the first train pulled into town over the Georgia Railroad from Madison. A year later, when the Macon & Western's first train arrived from Monroe, Atlanta's commercial life had definitely begun. Cotton, then as now, was the leading product of the State, and the railroads quickly made Atlanta an important distribution point for this staple. Warehouses were erected for storing the cotton until sold, when it was transferred to the port city of Savannah or to inland manufacturing centers. Farmers brought or shipped their crops and livestock to town and an extensive barter trade developed. Cloth was exchanged for corn and shoes for syrup, and thus it happened that all early retail stores, regardless of their specializations, also carried groceries and produce.

William N. White gives a graphic picture of Atlanta's commerce and industry in 1847, the eventful year of its incorporation. "The city," he wrote, "now contains 2,500 inhabitants; thirty large stores; two hotels; three newspapers; 187 buildings have been put up this summer within eight months and more are in progress. . . . The cotton picking season has just commenced and it comes in at the rate of 50 or 60 wagon loads a day. This is nothing to what it will be in December, and it will continue until spring; like the butter up north it is brought here to market from places 100 miles distant. Grain and all such supplies come down from the Cherokee country. . . . Business here is increasing daily. Several thousand dollars worth per diem are purchased of cotton, corn, wheat, etc. New stores are continually being opened . . . there is no product of Georgia which cannot be conveyed to Atlanta in three days time." The stores to which White referred housed such businesses as clothing and drygoods, jewelry, machine shops, wagon-works, groceries, and banking.

Real estate was being promoted extensively, White reporting that: "I have been out looking at lots at various prices, from $20 to $400 per lot all within the limits of the city. On Whitehall Street a lot 20x40 feet would be worth twice that sum . . . one can hardly make money as fast as property rises in this place."

Diversification of industry was furthered by Richard Peters, who erected a gristmill in 1848. Since his was the only such mill in the vicinity, it was often necessary for the pioneers to wait long hours before their corn or wheat could be ground, and a visit to the mill was often made an all-day occasion. Women would bring their knitting and settle themselves comfortably under shade trees where they could keep a watchful eye on the children; the men would gather in little groups and discuss crops and politics while awaiting their turn at the stone.

By 1850 street peddlers were being licensed, and at one meeting in that year the city council passed an ordinance regulating the practice whereby slaves sold farm produce and merchandise for their masters on the streets of the city.

This decade of the fifties was commercially and industrially significant. The tracks of the Western & Atlantic had been extended to Chattanooga, thereby opening new market areas. Banks, tanneries, shoe shops, gins, and factories for the manufacture of furniture, carriages, and freight cars were erected. But the arbitrary freight rates imposed by the railroads operated in such a manner as to affect adversely the Atlanta trade. Business men of older Southern cities, jealous of Atlanta's progress, used the influence of their controlling interest in the railroads to see that goods shipped to Atlanta from Northern cities cost the local merchants about 100 per cent more than other Southern cities were required to pay. This same disparity in rates applied to freight shipped from Atlanta to other points in the South. In further discrimination against the growing city, railroad schedules were so timed that trains arrived in Atlanta at late hours of the night with no stopover privileges. The resulting loss to Atlanta merchants was estimated as being in excess of $400,000 during the period from 1853 through 1858. Local merchants, owning no controlling interest in the railroads, were powerless to alleviate these transportation difficulties, and the condition was not improved until long after the War between the States.

Still, the town grew. New banks were organized, and factories manufacturing farm implements and construction materials were erected. Luxury industries established during the fifties included those for the manufacture of cigars, soda waters, candies, and cakes. In 1855 a gas plant was built, and on Christmas night of that year Atlanta's first gas lights were turned on.

The growth of the town, though amazingly rapid, had been basically sound, and its strategic location and excellent climate were two permanent advantages. Consequently, by 1860 Atlanta had surpassed almost all other Southeastern cities as a financial, industrial, and commercial center. So great had been the city's progress that even the outbreak of the War between the States did not immediately slow its momentum. On the contrary, Atlanta burst into a new frenzy of activity. Many established factories secured contracts with the Confederate Government for the manufacture of ordnance supplies, and new plants were built for the purpose. Shifts worked day and night turning out tents, pistols, swords, harness, saddles, and shoes. Rolling mills were quickly built for the manufacture of heavy guns, cannon, steel rails, and railway car equipment. Goods brought through the Union blockade were sold in Atlanta stores, and the city was crowded by foreigners who came in to offer their technical advice on the manufacture of military equipment. In 1862 the city became the South's largest army supply base and, because of its increasing military importance, was placed under martial law. As the war advanced, wealthy plantation owners of the vicinity, feeling that the city offered more security, brought their families to Atlanta and established residence. Business boomed, but the pinch of war was beginning to be felt in the rise of commodity prices. Then, in 1864, came General Sherman, to lay siege and capture the town and to raze it by fire before beginning his relentless march to the sea. All but 400 of Atlanta's 3,800 houses and commercial buildings were destroyed.

Reconstruction, however, was rapid. Temporary shelters were quickly erected to store the goods which canny merchants were collecting, and as soon as the less damaged buildings were repaired, a business on a small scale began. Federal soldiers and carpetbaggers jammed the streets, and many new names appeared on Atlanta storefronts. The rebuilding of old railroad lines and the beginning of new ones hastened the city's resumption of its commercial leadership. By 1870 Atlanta's population, which had numbered only 12,000 in 1864, had risen to 22,000.

The decade of the seventies was one of great expansion. Northern money poured into town, banks were reopened, and, as an indication of the growing size of the town, the horsecars of the first street railway made their appearance. The business census of 1875 listed 7 banks, 1 bond broker, 17 cotton brokers, and 63 life and fire insurance agents, showing that the city's position in finance was equal to its commercial and industrial supremacy. In the same year a count showed 32 boot and shoemakers, 7 carriage and wagon factories and dealers, 13 wholesale drug companies, 10 wholesale dry-goods firms, 8 flour mills, 5 foundries, and 7 furniture factories and dealers. A score of trains sped to and from Atlanta daily, bringing in raw materials and taking out finished products.

The decade of the eighties was notable for the International Cotton Exposition which was held in 1881, calling the Nation's attention to Atlanta's prestige in Southern commerce and industry. Scores of huge buildings were erected and thousands of exhibits were displayed. The exposition afforded the city great publicity and attracted from other sections of the country much money which was immediately invested in Atlanta enterprises. One direct result of the exposition was the establishment of the Exposition Cotton Mills in 1882. The main building of the exposition was converted into a factory which employed five hundred workers operating thirty thousand spindles and seven hundred and fifty looms.

During this period and until the turn of the century, Atlanta's industries very nearly eclipsed its importance as a commercial center. The development of steam power brought about a great urbanization of industry. The building of factories near waterways was no longer necessary; it was sufficient that they be located near railroads making available a large coal supply and affording easy distribution of products. Atlanta exactly filled these requirements, with the result that during the decade about 20 new factories were built for the manufacture of farm implements, cottonseed oil products, construction materials, textiles, furniture, glass, pianos, and all sorts of machinery. Also during the eighties, Atlanta's livestock market, which had its beginnings before the war, expanded to become the greatest mule market in the Nation. This was the era of patent medicines, and several companies began the manufacture of these bottled panaceas in Atlanta.

The year 1886 was significant for the beginning of a soft drink venture that has carried the name of Atlanta around the world. In May of that year J.S. Pemberton, a manufacturing chemist, perfected his formula for a soft drink and sold it under the trademark "Coca-Cola." The following year he disposed of two-thirds interest in the business to George Lowndes and Willis Venable, who dispensed the drink from the soda fountain of Jacobs Drug Store at Five Points. Asa G. Candler, a wholesale druggist, purchased controlling interest in the business in April 1888, and soon organized the Coca-Cola Company for the manufacture and promotion of the beverage. In Coca-Cola's meteoric rise to popularity Candler and his associates amassed a fortune. In 1919 the Candlers sold their interest, and the purchasers reorganized and expanded the business to such an extent that the product is now sold in more than 70 countries.

During the nineties several new railroads were extended into Atlanta, and a number of terminal companies made the city their headquarters. By the end of the decade 44 railroads maintained Atlanta offices, and more than one third of all the freight entering the State was unloaded in the city.

The outstanding event of the decade was the Cotton States and International Exposition of 1895. This display surpassed even the former exposition of 1881 and again served to advertise to the world that, although it was an inland city, Atlanta was one of the Nation's pivotal transportation centers. The response was immediate; national manufacturing and financial corporations established branch offices in the city, and it was during this decade that Atlanta's first skyscrapers were erected.

With the turn of the century the development of long-distance transmission of electric power drew industries away from urban areas. Consequently, during the first decade of the 1900's there was a lessening of the number of factories established in the Atlanta area. But what the city lost in manufactories was more than compensated for by the concentration of branch offices of national concerns. Virtually all Southeastern sales of nationally distributed goods were made through Atlanta district offices, resulting in a great increase in the city's bank clearings, postal receipts, and freight handlings. Almost all of the present railroads had been established, and Atlanta became nationally recognized as the commercial and financial center of the South.

During the decade of 1910 Atlanta became increasingly conscious of its metropolitan potentialities, and many factors combined to bring them to realization. Building had lagged considerably behind population and it now became necessary to erect new residences and business houses. The Healey, Hurt, and Transportation (now Western Union) Buildings, three of the city's first modern office structures, were erected. Two large department stores were constructed, and among the new hotels were the Ansley, Winecoff, Imperial, and Cecil (now the Atlantan). Two automobile assembly plants were located in the city, those of the Ford and Hanson Motor Companies. Recognition of Atlanta's financial leadership was signified by the establishment of the bank of the Sixth Federal Reserve District in the city.

In 1917 a devastating fire destroyed more than 60 city blocks with a property loss of $5,000,000. This created a serious housing problem as, by this time, the country had entered the World War and all available labor in the city was employed in building barracks at Fort McPherson and Camp Gordon. Not for several years could the burned area be rebuilt. But at the cantonments there was great construction activity, local industries were receiving large war orders, and workers were well paid.

The impetus of lavish spending created by the war carried the city on a wave of prosperity well into the twenties. Civic leaders began publicity drives to "put Atlanta on the map," and these drives reached a climax in the middle of the decade when the city experienced its greatest expansion in the growth of office buildings, banks, stores, real estate developments, street mileage, and population. This expansion was largely due to the activity of the Forward Atlanta Commission, organized by the Chamber of Commerce. During the four-year period ending in 1929, the commission spent almost $1,000,000 advertising Atlanta on a Nation-wide scale. Full-page advertisements were bought in leading trade and commercial magazines and papers, and thousands of pamphlets were sent to industrial leaders throughout the country. The effects of the campaign are still operative, but an immediate result was the establishment of many new concerns in the Atlanta area. It was also during this decade that many large Atlanta business houses became affiliated with Northern concerns and, through mergers, numbers of chain stores began to appear in the city.

During the early thirties Atlanta experienced its share of the Nation-wide depression. Many businesses failed, stores closed, and the proportion of unemployed mounted. Some concerns survived the trying years by merging with larger organizations. Many small specialty shops opened, hoping to succeed where more conservative general firms had failed. The majority of them, however, were but short-lived. For about two years there were so many vacant stores in downtown Atlanta that the Chamber of Commerce undertook a program urging the remaining business houses to rent the vacant store windows for a display of their goods, thereby enabling the city literally to "keep up its front."

With the instigation of various Federal Government emergency bureaus, buying power increased and business slowly revived. Extensive slum clearance projects were financed and many public improvements were made with Federal funds in Atlanta. By the end of the decade a fair amount of business stability was evident and private concerns again were willing to invest large sums in the expansion of building and production.

The impetus given commerce and industry by the building program of the national defense agencies began to be felt in 1940, when many orders for materials were placed with Atlanta firms. On the site of Camp Gordon, World War cantonment, the army began the construction of the Lawson General Hospital, and the navy started the building of an aviation base for the preliminary training of its fliers and those of the marine corps. During the following year the army bought 1,500 acres of land, 9 miles southeast of Atlanta on State 42, and undertook the erection of 14 large concrete warehouses, costing between ten and fifteen million dollars. At these storehouses, which will be called the Atlanta General Depot, supplies will be bought and stored for the signal, medical, quartermaster, and engineering corps and other branches of the army. All three of the defense projects are to serve the entire southeastern part of the United States.

The Nation-wide speed-up of industry finds Atlanta admirably equipped with facilities to maintain its commercial leadership. Its pre-eminence as a transportation center is assured by the 15 main lines of 8 railroad systems, by 8 major airlines, and by 75 highway freight lines operating over a network of paved roads radiating in all directions. Atlanta's railway express shipments are more per capita than those of any other city in the Nation. The city ranks as the third largest telegraph center in the world, eighth among cities of the United States in airmail volume, thirteenth in bank clearings ($3,009,375,000 in 1939), eighteenth in postal receipts, and fourth in the amount of fire insurance premiums cleared annually.

Atlanta's location is such that a population of 14,500,000 lives within a radius of 300 miles of the city. This easy accessibility to the consumer accounts for the more than 2,500 branch factories, warehouses, and division offices which are located in the city. For the same reason Atlanta is an ideal gathering point for Southeastern sales forces, and, in 1939, 495 conventions were held in the city with an attendance of 134,000 delegates. In Atlanta and its environs are about 900 factories manufacturing more than 1,500 commodities, the more important being textiles, food products, paper containers, drugs and chemicals, and furniture. In 1939 the value of products manufactured within

Atlanta proper was $165,729,836, and the total sales of Atlanta's retail and wholesale stores amounted to $637,394,000. The city has 47 prominent office buildings with a total square footage of 2,748,619 feet, making it the first city in the Nation in per capita office space.

Labor

THE founders of Atlanta were their own workmen. Though built in the midst of a slave State, the town was fiercely proud of its independence and vitality, and its social aspect was essentially democratic. No newcomer to the city was ashamed to build his own hut or store and personally perform all the daily tasks necessary to a pioneer living. This was largely because most of Atlanta's settlers were migratory workers, accustomed to shift for themselves, while those few early citizens of means were Northerners opposed to slave labor.

In 1847 Atlanta had a population of 2,500 and Dr. William White, a school teacher from New York State, wrote in his diary of that year: "There are not 100 Negroes in the place, and white men black their own shoes and dust their own clothes independently as in the North. All through the upper part of Georgia the labor is done almost entirely by white hands. Carpenters get but ten shillings a day here and labor commands about the same price as at the North."

The few Negroes in Atlanta during the town's early days were freed slaves. Trained on the plantations as wainwrights and black-smiths, they were theoretically free to follow these callings in the hope of accumulating enough money to purchase the freedom of their wives, children, and other relatives still held in bondage. They were rarely successful at making a living, however, and the majority of them returned to the plantations. Some farmers in the vicinity were accustomed to send their slaves into town to peddle produce on the streets. The fact that the city council in 1850 placed a tax of $1 on each Negro sold in the slave market on Alabama Street indicates that the trade was active, but these slaves were rarely purchased for work in the city.

Several years before the War between the States it became fashionable for owners of outlying plantations to build houses and send their families to Atlanta for residence at various seasons of the year. A family was accompanied usually by a young Negro girl who acted as

ladies' maid, a mature Negro woman to cook and do the house clean-
ing, and a grizzled darky who performed the duties of handyman and
carriage driver.

During the War between the States, Atlanta became the chief
military supply base of the Confederacy and business boomed. But,
with most of the young men in the army or engaged in the manufacture of war supplies, there was a serious shortage of labor in the
less important fields of industry. Many an older Atlanta business man
doffed his coat for a clerk's apron and left his executive desk to work
behind the sales counter.

Shortly after the war thousands of "free issue" Negroes crowded
Atlanta awaiting the division of confiscated lands which had been
promised them by the carpetbaggers. Disaster was their lot. With
no means of support, drinking and carousing day and night, running
wild and living in filth, hundreds of them perished from starvation
and disease. The Freedmen's Bureau helped some, building shelters,
feeding and caring for the homeless, and sending many to other sections of the country where there was more opportunity for employment. A few Negroes, trained in various mechanical callings on the
plantations, found their way into industry. Many, however, were
forced to return to their former owners where, facing the contempt
of the older slaves who had remained loyal to their masters, they helped
rebuild the ruined mansions and replant the devastated fields.

So it was that during Reconstruction potential labor went idle
while professional and businessmen carried mortar, bricks, and timber
to repair their residences and shops. Lack of money furthered lack
of employment, and the carpetbagger administration of Governor
Bullock did nothing to improve the labor situation. After his resignation and flight in 1871, business took confidence and there was considerable expansion. A census of that year shows that 75 firms were
employing 846 men, 44 women, and 126 children in Fulton County.
The average weekly wage was $8.42.

The decade of the 1870's brought about a sounder reconstruction
program. As Southerners recouped their fortunes, older business houses
were re-established, while many new ventures, founded with speculative
Yankee money, failed. Reconstruction was physical as well as financial.
Scores of buildings and houses that had been hastily repaired after
the war were torn down, and new structures were erected in their
places. The construction industries boomed, providing employment for
thousands of workers.

A social evil which arose during this decade and had far-reaching
effects upon labor was the system whereby the State leased convicts to
private employers. Originally intended as a humanitarian move to
rehabilitate the criminal, the practice quickly degenerated into one of

abuse and selfish gain. In return for a small per capita annuity paid to the State (ten or twelve dollars per year) the leaser worked the convicts from sunup to sundown with no other expense than the provision of food and shelter. Supervision was often brutal, and many convicts died from neglect or flogging. Since free labor could in no way compete with this enforced service, a general lowering of wage standards followed. In 1873 a survey showed that, although 800 mechanics in the city were out of work, trains were almost daily bringing in additional convict labor.

Some slight progress was made toward organization of workers, however, when a small union of factory workers was formed. In the summer of 1873 members of the Typographical Union struck in protest against the dismissal of a foreman and two printers from the staff of the Atlanta *Herald,* a newspaper edited by Henry W. Grady. When the owners of the paper threatened to suspend publication permanently, the union members returned to work, and the defeat of this abortive strike was considered a triumph for the open shop. But the workers had been impressed by their own audacity in even daring to strike, and they were determined to gain strength for later and more telling efforts.

In 1880 labor conditions had improved considerably in actual employment, but wage scales were still low. In that year Atlanta had 196 manufacturing establishments that employed 3,680 hands, including 538 women and 394 children. But the average wage was only $4.65 a week. Computed on the basis that each of these workers, including children, represented a then typical family of five, estimates show that of Atlanta's 37,409 population in that year almost exactly one half were existing upon substandard incomes.

Under such conditions organization among the workers changed from a mere desire into a compelling necessity. But, although various trades organized local chapters under the leadership of the Knights of Labor, these were but short-lived. Organization among Southern workers was still too new to engender an effective feeling of unity, but unionization was growing. In February 1884, the Woman's Industrial Union was organized to teach working girls how to sew, cook, and perform other duties, paying them while they learned. It was claimed by the union that a girl earning 15 to 20¢ a day in a factory could easily make 75¢ a day after being vocationally trained in the union school. In April of the same year the Women's Industrial Union expanded to establish the Woman's Exchange, a shop which afforded the unemployed women of Atlanta an opportunity to sell homemade articles. Heartened by the success of these ventures, existing unions also introduced training schools.

In 1888 an independent union, the first of its kind in the United

Commerce and Industry

FREIGHT TRUCKS

RAILROAD YARDS, ATLANTA TERMINAL STATION

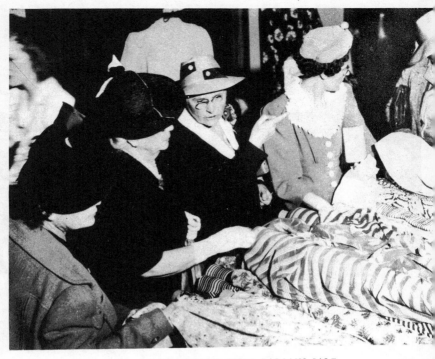

DEPARTMENT STORE BARGAIN SALE

TELEPHONE OPERATORS

MIDMORNING AT THE STOCK BROKER'S

BUS TERMINAL

THREADING AUTOMATIC BANDING MACHINE IN A COTTON TEXTILE MILL

WARPING IN A COTTON TEXTILE MILL

MILL VILLAGE

STORING COCA-COLA SYRUP IN METAL DRUMS FOR SHIPMENT

PACKING CANDY

THE "CONSTITUTION" PRINTING PRESSES

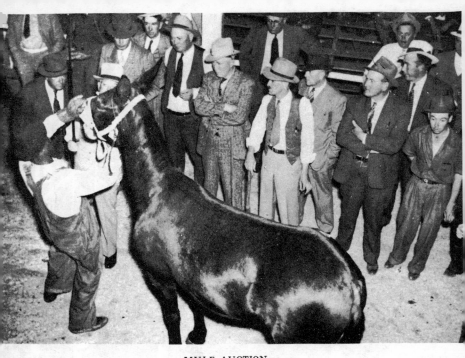

MULE AUCTION

STATE FARMERS' MARKET

States, was formed by 19 machinists of Atlanta. By the following year chapters had been organized throughout the Nation and in Canada, and the name was changed accordingly to the International Association of Machinists. Also in this year the International Brotherhood of Blacksmiths, Drop Forgers, and Helpers was organized in the city.

An investigation by the Atlanta *Constitution* at this time revealed the appalling circumstances of child labor in the city's textile industries. One mill employed 75 to 100 children, half of whom were less than 10 years old. Similar conditions prevailed at another factory, except that the majority of children were even younger, being from 6 to 8 years old. Employed as sweepers, carriers, and doffers, these children worked 12 or more hours every day. As an excuse for the long overtime work, the mill owners claimed that the wet weather affected the machinery, requiring that it be kept running almost constantly. This exposure brought about an agitation for protective legislation that resulted several years later in a child labor law which prohibited the employment of children under 10.

With the expansion of industry in the 1890's, fresh impetus was given to organization among labor. In 1891 workers representing the carpenters, molders, plasterers, tailors, and typographical unions formed a central body known as the Atlanta Federation of Trades. By the turn of the century unionization had been achieved among railway employees, newspaper workers, book and job printers, and many other trades. But, as usual when wage standards and purchasing power are high, interest in organization lagged and many of the unions were short-lived. The depression of 1908, however, brought about a revival of interest, causing the organization of many new locals and a strengthening of the existing ones. By 1910 organized labor had become a power that could not be disregarded.

In 1916 Atlanta experienced its most spectacular strike. In September of that year the motormen and conductors of the Georgia Power Company struck for union recognition, shorter hours, higher wages, freedom from compulsory membership in a company "benevolent association," and "political freedom." Cars were abandoned on the tracks, and when the company hired non-union men to operate them, these relief crews were immediately pulled from the cars. Trolleys were cut, poles were sawed down, rocks were piled on the tracks, and rails were soaped and spiked. Some cars were peppered with gun shot, a few were dynamited. Opposing mobs jammed the downtown streets and hundreds of deputies were sworn in to preserve order. This state of affairs continued for about two months with city transportation completely demoralized. Injuries were inevitable, and, as a result strike leaders and scores of union sympathizers were jailed. On December 23, a compromise was reached in which the most significant clause provided an increase in pay. But union recognition and the rehiring of men laid off for their union activities were not granted.

Resentment growing from these denials brought about a second strike in July of 1918. After a four-day tie-up of trolley service, a satisfactory agreement was reached between the power company and its workers. Since then the local chapter of the Amalgamated Association of Street and Electric Railway Employees of America has become one of the largest, strongest, and best-ordered unions in the city, and the relationship between the power company and its employees has been almost ideal.

Although employment boomed during World War I, labor made no contractual gains because of a shortage of workers and extensive camp-building and munitions developments. Strikes in the war industries were handled in a summary manner, often being suppressed by the Federal Government. Workers in less important industries dared not make any drastic moves, knowing that public opinion would be almost united against them in this critical time. During the boom period of the 1920's the unions did not lapse into the lethargy usually so characteristic of prosperous years. Dues in arrears were paid up and much of the money was spent in a program of organization expansion. Industry, operating at peak production, willingly made many concessions to organized labor, and few strikes marked this period.

The early years of the depression had as disastrous an effect upon organized labor as upon all other phases of national life. The chaos and financial stress caused by thousands of members being thrown out of work was aggravated by the influx of laid-off farm hands who flocked to the city seeking any kind of employment and concerned not at all with unionism. Many groups split over strike issues, feeling that conditions were too precarious to risk jeopardizing their jobs further by radical voluntary action. On the other hand, many union leaders felt that drastic action was necessary to insure the rights of labor. As a result, the first half of the decade of the 1930's was a period of constant strikes, many of which were, for the first time, marked by racial prejudice.

A significant example of this new trend was the formation of The American Fascisti Association and the Order of Black Shirts, an organization founded in Atlanta in 1930 by a group of men who had no legitimate connection with recognized labor movements. Their immediate object was to drive the Negroes out of industry and replace them with white workers. Appealing as it did to the misery and self-pity of the more ignorant unemployed white men who had always regarded the Negro as an economic menace, the Black Shirt association swept the State and, in a few short weeks, claimed a membership of 27,000. Although some employers heeded the demands of the Black

Shirts, the majority did not and, as soon as it became apparent that the organization could not create work for them, members withdrew.

In July 1932, Angelo Herndon, a young Negro Communist, led a demonstration of white and Negro unemployed on the steps of the Fulton County Courthouse. Although the gathering was orderly and city council recognized and granted its demands for continued work relief, Herndon as its leader was arrested and charged with "attempting to incite insurrection." Many groups throughout the country came to his defense, and in time the case assumed international proportions. After five years of alternate imprisonment and freedom on bail, Herndon was acquitted by a ruling of the Supreme Court of the United States.

The middle 1930's was a period of great labor agitation. On September 6, 1934, all textile mills in the Atlanta area, except the Fulton Bag and Cotton Mills, were closed. This was a natural extension of the mill strike conditions which prevailed throughout the State at that time. The workers' demands were the usual ones— shorter hours and higher wages. After two hectic weeks marked by a declaration of martial law, the throwing of tear-gas bombs, and the arrest of hundreds of strikers, the demonstration was called off. But for the next several years hardly a season passed without a strike in some Atlanta textile mill or garment factory.

With the rise of the Committee for Industrial Organization (now the Congress of Industrial Organizations) in 1935, the labor stage in Atlanta became a scene of great activity. Many established unions, feeling that the new industrial organizations offered more strength and security than the old trade unions, wished to affiliate with the C.I.O. The result was a split in the ranks of the Georgia Federation of Labor. In April 1937, William Green, president of the American Federation of Labor, ruled that A. Steve Nance, president of the Georgia Federation of Labor, was ineligible to preside over the annual State convention being held that month because he had become Southeastern director of a C.I.O. body, the Textile Workers Organizing Committee. The various unions immediately chose sides, some supporting Nance and others denying his leadership. For a time there were two groups each claiming to be the real Georgia Federation of Labor. This state of affairs continued until shortly after Nance's death in April 1938. Some of the alienated textile workers returned to the A.F. of L., but many remained in the C.I.O.

In the meantime, many other unions affiliated with the C.I.O. This caused the A.F. of L. to begin its own intensive drives to enlist groups who were for the first time becoming aware of the importance of labor and were seeking leadership. The contest between the two labor movements has been marked by considerable anger and mutual disparagement, but it has been a stimulating conflict, bringing many new workers into the ranks of labor and causing many old-line members of the union to regard their organizations more seriously. Only the campaigning engendered by fierce rivalry could have brought about the organization of the textile workers and other groups which had been long neglected or had remained indifferent to the labor movement.

In November 1936, the United Automobile Workers of America, a C.I.O. body, staged one of the first sit-down strikes in America in the Fisher Body Company, Atlanta. The strike lasted three months and ended when the company granted every demand of the union. These included recognition of the union, 100 per cent raise in wages, establishment of a minimum wage, recognition of seniority rights, restoration of jobs to men dismissed because of union activities, establishment of a grievance procedure, control of the speed-up system, and the granting of vacations with pay.

Encouraged by their success, the automobile workers undertook the task of organizing groups of workers in entirely unrelated industries under the C.I.O. banner. At present 12 separate groups comprising 18 local chapters are so organized. These include workers in the automobile, steel, aluminum, rubber, furniture, textile, quarrying, meat-packing, communications, and garment industries, as well as office and professional and Federal workers. Two of the groups, the aluminum and rubber unions, are composed of Negroes.

The C.I.O. now maintains a council in Atlanta in which all city unions are represented. Its function is to co-ordinate the activities of the various unions, to discuss plans for further organization, and to hold educational programs. The A.F. of L. is represented by 100 local unions with an approximate membership of 20,000. A central body known as the Atlanta Federation of Trades functions in a manner similar to the C.I.O. council.

In recent years the Georgia League of Progressive Democracy, an affiliate of the national Non-Partisan League, has been bringing the unions into closer contact with civic clubs and other groups. This league is composed of representatives from both the C.I.O. and A.F. of L. organizations.

The record of recent strikes in local industries is negligible compared with the national labor agitation. During the period from 1934 through 1938 there were only 24 strikes in the city. These involved 4,845 workers who were laid off for a total of 98,808 man days. Eight of the strikes were called because of wage and hour conditions, 11 were declared for union recognition, and 5 were due to miscellaneous causes.

Labor statistics for 1930 show that there were 50,617 gainfully employed workers in Atlanta proper, of which 24,285 were women. The approximate pay roll total for that year was $200,000,000.

In addition to State-wide labor legislation, various city laws regulate Atlanta workers in certain industries and trades. These apply to plumbers, barber and beauty shop operators, and workers who handle foodstuffs.

Public Welfare

COUNTY funds, church donations, and individual benevolence provided the first relief for the poor of Atlanta. As early as 1853, however, the city was beginning to recognize the need for regular municipal aid, and Mayor J.F. Mims appointed from council a committee on relief of the poor. This body had only advisory powers: after its recommendations had been made, council as a whole voted on each case. Assistance was then rendered not in the form of supplies but as cash, an outlay that was seldom more than a few hundred dollars annually. Once the money was given, little effort was made to learn how it was spent. The minutes of the fifties are full of such entries as "The Committee on Relief report in favor of John Tiller having an order for five dollars on account of helpless daughter" and "The Committee on Relief report that they have employed Mr. Baker to keep and maintain Mr. Gardner who is afflicted with a sore leg, and his two small children, for the sum of one dollar and fifty cents a day, for the present."

Soon after the outbreak of the War between the States, relief costs mounted rapidly—in 1862 the city expended almost $4,000 in caring for the poor, in the following year this amount was increased to $40,000, and in the last year of the war it was more than $80,000. In place of cash relief council set up provision stores for the poor, but with thousands of soldiers and refugees crowding into the city even this arrangement proved too costly. In the midst of this emergency a group of women came to the aid of the city by organizing the Ladies' Soldiers' Relief Society. By charity balls and bazaars this organization raised large amounts for the care of sick and wounded soldiers quartered in the city.

In the period immediately after the war, the problem of existence became still more acute. Refugees returned home, their numbers swollen by hordes of freed slaves, and the young men disbanded from the army often searched in vain for work to support their impoverished families. Fire losses following Federal occupation and the collapse of Confederate finance constituted an appalling drain on the treasury. Hundreds of unemployed were given transportation in order that they might seek employment in other sections of the country. The work of aiding destitute Negroes was largely taken over by the Freedmen's Bureau, the American Missionary Society, and other Northern organizations, while many more were succored by their former masters. In its extremity the city had to appeal to the country at large. Several cities, Northern and Southern, responded generously, and many contributions from individuals were sent in from points as far away as Illinois and New York. The State of Kentucky sent 100,000 bushels of corn to be distributed among the poor throughout Georgia.

In the summer of 1866 a severe smallpox epidemic broke out. Immediate expenditures were necessary, and before the year was out two pest-houses and a makeshift hospital had been constructed. Although the danger from disease soon passed, the condition of the poor still made heavy demands on the treasury. Early in 1867 Atlanta, aided by Fulton County, erected 20 shanties 4 miles west of the city to serve as an almshouse. Minor children of inmates were placed in private homes with their expenses paid by the city. By the early seventies, after a series of court rulings, Fulton County was compelled to take over the entire burden of providing for Atlanta's poor who were committed to the almshouse. While the institution provided for the care of the aged and decrepit, many able-bodied but destitute citizens continued to be without employment as a result of the war and the reconstruction program.

Again the women of Atlanta came to the aid of their city. In rented rooms they established the Atlanta Benevolent Association, the purpose of which was to provide a temporary home "for destitute and helpless women and girls out of employment, in finding suitable work, and, as soon as practicable, to give full instruction in industrial pursuits, thereby enabling such persons to become self-supporting and useful." After giving several entertainments the association succeeded in raising $4,000, with which two buildings on Alabama Street were purchased. In 1881 the property and the entire facilities of the institution were deeded to the city, and soon afterward the name was changed to the Atlanta Hospital and Benevolent Home. By the middle eighties the city was fully maintaining this institution and contributing to several private charitable organizations.

In the same year the Florence Crittenton Home, a branch of the national welfare organization of that name, was opened in Atlanta. Many citizens bitterly opposed the establishment of this maternity home for unmarried girls, but others refuted their arguments by answering that innocent children should not be made to suffer for the sins of the mothers and the unknown fathers. The Florence Crittenton Home was the first national welfare organization to be chartered by Congress, and the Atlanta home was the fourth in the nation.

The Home for the Friendless was established in 1888 by three Atlanta women who solicited church and private donations, rented a cottage on Mangum Street, and opened its doors to the poor of all ages. Applications for entry became so numerous, however, that within a few months admission was restricted to children only. Two years after the home was opened, a large building was erected on Highland Avenue. Here the institution operated for 38 years until it was moved to its present quarters on Courtney Drive, where it is now operated as Hillside Cottages.

Although several attempts had been made to establish a refuge for street waifs, it was not until 1888 that Atlanta Baptist women made definite plans for setting up the Georgia Baptist Orphans' Home. In that year Jonathan Norcross gave a tract of land, and soon afterward the orphanage was opened. At first there were only five children enrolled, but soon there were so many applications that two successive moves to larger quarters had to be made. Before the decade was ended several large gifts made possible the purchase of the 50-acre tract in Hapeville where the home is now operated. The nine buildings provide accommodation for approximately 300 children, and the property now covers 92 acres.

The rapid industrial growth of this period often engendered hard conditions for factory workers. In 1889 an Atlanta woman happened to notice that a woman mill worker, unable to provide home care for her child, was compelled to take it with her to work and tie it to a window sill while she worked at the looms. Deeply moved by what she had seen, the Atlanta matron and six other women pledged the salary of a matron to care for the children of such working mothers. A room was secured in the building of the Barclay Mission, a Sunday school that had been started several years before by John A. Barclay and Miss Sue Holloway, and the Barclay Nursery was opened to the children of working mothers. Soon the institution outgrew its quarters and W.A. Hemphill provided a new building where the additional services of a kindergarten and a cooking school for mothers were added to the nursery. After several changes two permanent places were established, a north-side branch on Baker Street and a south-side branch on Washington Street. Since 1925 all activities besides those of the day nursery have been taken over by other social agencies. Now known as the Sheltering Arms Nursery, this institution cares for an average of 180 children a month.

Until 1889 little or no public assistance had been rendered Negro children, and scores of neglected gamins played perilously about the tracks of the old Union Depot. Carrie Steele Logan, a Negro matron at the depot, became so distressed by these conditions that she quit her job, adopted several of the waifs, and took them into her home on Wheat Street. As she continued to take more orphans, her rooms became overcrowded and her funds gave out, but the kindly woman, respected throughout the city, appealed to both races for aid. Individuals and church groups contributed funds, and to these she added the amount realized from the sale of her home in order to erect a large brick building on Fair Street. The city donates a small amount regularly toward upkeep, and since the new Roy Street building was erected in 1922 the county has assumed part of the maintenance expense. The orphanage, now known as the Carrie Steele-Pitts Home, is one of the most important local charities.

The Hebrew Orphans' Home also was founded in 1889. A large rambling brick structure was erected on Washington Street, and Jewish children from Georgia, North and South Carolina, Florida, and Virginia were given a home. Support was maintained by individuals and organizations in the five States served and as many as 150 children were housed in the institution at one time. In 1911 the directors of the movement broadened their program and began to give aid to half-orphaned children in their own homes. This reduced the number of children actually quartered in the building. In 1930 the program was extended again to provide a foster home for every child. The function of the institution then became that of a child-placing agency; its name was changed to the Children's Service Bureau and an administrative office was opened on Edgewood Avenue. The work of the agency does not cease when the child is sent to board in a private home; general supervision by members of the staff is continued until the child reaches maturity. Regular physical examinations are made and treatment provided, school reports are checked, and vocational training is given.

Prior to the nineties all charity institutions had been instigated and principally maintained by private individuals. Although some of these agencies had been given assistance from municipal funds, the buildings and equipment had become inadequate for the poor of the fast-growing city. Particularly was this true of hospitalization and clinical services, for economy had prompted the city to place its patients as they could be accommodated in various private hospitals. In 1887 a move toward more efficient management was made when all such municipal cases were placed in the King's Daughters' Hospital, but it soon became apparent that this institution was too small to care for all cases. In order to remedy this situation a movement was begun to found a municipally owned infirmary, and the erection of Grady Hospital, named for the Atlanta editor Henry W. Grady, was financed by popular subscription with the provision that the city assume the responsi-

bility for maintenance.   In 1892 the hospital was opened with more
than 100 beds, 4 physicians, and 21 nurses.   At first both private and
charity cases were admitted, but soon services were restricted to the
latter class.   The hospital now consists of 12 buildings with about 700
beds and has a resident staff of 75 physicians supplemented by a visiting staff of 300 physicians and surgeons.   By an arrangement with
Fulton County, rural patients in the Atlanta vicinity are also eligible
for treatment.

By the turn of the century a number of welfare enterprises were
firmly established.   In 1900 the Confederate Soldiers' Home, which
had been erected by the State ten years before but had remained unoc-
cupied for lack of maintenance funds, was opened to a group of 83
veterans.   In the following year the King's Daughters and Sons established the Home for Incurables on the site of the present Athletic Club
on Carnegie Way and, since many of the applicants were patients who
had been dismissed as incurable from Grady, the city appropriated $33
a month toward upkeep.   Through the generosity of A.G. Rhodes,
George W. Stewart, and others, a new building was erected in 1904
on the present site at Woodward Avenue and South Boulevard.

The King's Daughters again came into prominence in 1905 by
establishing the Home for Old Women—an institution that filled a
real need since it was especially planned to care for inmates who,
though indigent, were well educated and refined.   The Associated
Charities, now the Family Welfare Society, was founded in the same
year.   Before this time other charitable organizations of the city had
been concerned solely with clinical work and with the individual
pauper.   The Associated Charities undertook dealing with problems of
personality and family adjustments and lent aid in situations involving
desertion and nonsupport, unmarried mothers, parent-child relation-
ships, and other domestic matters requiring sympathetic counsel.

Two years later further recognition of the need for aid to children
was manifested in the opening of the Atlanta Child's Home by Mrs.
F.M. Robinson.   Here deserted wives and unmarried mothers could
find adequate care for their babies.   In addition to caring for the children, the home also makes provision for a limited number of mothers
during periods when it is necessary that they remain with their babies.

One of the most important of the city's charities is the Atlanta
Tuberculosis Association, which was founded in 1909 under the leadership of Joseph P. Logan.   White people and Negroes of any age who
have been exposed to tuberculosis may be examined and treated at the
clinic.   In 1910 the Battle Hill Sanatorium, also an institution for the
treatment of this malady, was built jointly by Fulton County and
Atlanta.   All residents of this area who have pulmonary tuberculosis
are eligible for entry.

In 1914 Atlanta's first hospital for crippled children was begun when four leading citizens placed a few beds in Wesley Memorial Hospital for the exclusive use of children of impoverished families. The following year the Masonic Order of Ancient and Accepted Scottish Rite, which had become interested in the work, bought two cottages in Decatur and converted them into an infirmary. So great was the demand for treatment of orthopedic afflictions that within a few years a larger building was erected at a cost of $160,000. The institution has become a pattern for similar work by the Shrine throughout the United States.

By the time the World War period had come, the number of Atlanta social agencies was so large that it became necessary to have a co-ordinating body. This led to the creation of the Social Service Index in 1917. An independent governing body, the Index made itself available to all welfare agencies maintained by schools, churches, tax funds, and voluntary subscriptions. As a clearing house for such agencies in both Fulton and DeKalb Counties, this organization seeks to avoid duplication of work and enables each agency to operate more efficiently in its own specialized field.

The Atlanta Community Employment Service, begun in 1919 by Cator Woolford, endeavors to obtain employment for both white people and Negroes without cost to either employer or employee. Although this agency is still in operation, much of its work has been absorbed by the State Re-employment Office. One valuable phase of the work of the Atlanta Community Employment Service is the training offered Negro domestic servants in a school maintained by a grant from the Rosenwald Fund.

For the past two decades scarcely a year has passed without the addition of a new social agency. One of the most active of these is the Atlanta Chapter of the Junior League, which was founded in 1919 by Mrs. J.W. McKenna. The work of the league includes supplying clothing for girls of the Churches' Homes, maintaining a ward at the Egleston Memorial Hospital, supporting the thyroid clinic at Grady Hospital, providing psychiatric workers for the Family Welfare Association, serving as Girl Scout leaders, directing physical training at various day nurseries, maintaining a school of corrective speech, and providing helpers at several clinics.

The prosperous post-war era of the early twenties brought additional charitable enterprises, of both local and national affiliations. The baby clinic of the Central Presbyterian Church, founded in 1922, provides medical care for white babies without restriction on the area from which they are brought for treatment. In 1923 a number of prominent civic leaders organized the Atlanta Community Chest in an effort to centralize contributions to the various social service organizations in the city, more than 30 of which are represented in the annual drive.

National prominence has resulted from the work done by the Good Samaritan Clinic, established in 1923 to provide free treatment for white and Negro residents of Fulton County who suffer from disturbances of the endocrine glands. While the clinic is not the first of its kind in the country, it is the first to be established entirely dissociated from a medical center and to be operated on a charity basis. Research and experimentation here have contributed many innovations in the field of gland correction, and it was one of the physicians connected with the institution who discovered the value of iodine treatments for goiter before research in this field had been published. The clinic is concerned not only with the treatment of abnormal physical developments but more recently with psychotherapy for delinquent and mentally abnormal children. Though originally designed to extend free services to local residents, the Good Samaritan Clinic has attracted from all sections of the State patients who are given diagnostical service on a paying basis.

The Steiner Clinic, erected through funds bequeathed by Albert Steiner and opened in 1924, gives free medical, radiumtherapic, and surgical treatment to Atlanta and Fulton County residents suffering from cancer. This hospital was operated as a ward of Grady Hospital until 1933 when, by ordinance of city council, it was detached and put under a separate board of trustees. Now functioning as a completely separate unit, the clinic is the only cancer institution in the Southeast to be given the full commendation of the American College of Surgeons and the American Medical Society. The personnel includes a resident staff of 6 doctors, a visiting staff of 26, 11 registered nurses, and more than a dozen special technicians. Forty beds are maintained and the total number of observation cases is more than 50,000 a year.

The Atlanta Legal Aid Society, which also began functioning in 1924, extends much needed facilities to the public by providing legal advice and court counsel for those who are unable to pay for these services. Such cases are usually recommended by the various social agencies of the city, but the society sometimes extends aid also to individuals who apply directly.

Long before the national work relief program was initiated, some of the Atlanta charity groups were organizing their programs with an emphasis on self-help for the individual. One of the leading organizations of this type is the Atlanta Goodwill Industries, which was established in 1925 by representatives of almost 50 Methodist congregations of the Atlanta area. This agency maintains a store and workshop in which cast-off garments and house furnishings are made over and sold to provide support for the workers. The program also offers vocational and religious instruction. An organization that is similar in its aims of self-support is the Atlanta Community Shop, which was founded in 1928 by the Community Employment Service. This agency provides employment to the blind workers of Atlanta and its vicinity by teaching them to make brooms and mops which are sold to the public.

Child welfare has been particularly salient in the more recent work of charity organizations. The Henrietta Egleston Hospital for Children was built in 1928 from funds bequeathed by Thomas E. Egleston, its purpose being to provide medical and surgical aid for children who are seriously ill from causes other than contagious diseases. Patients are admitted regardless of sex, creed, nationality, or place of residence. The Central Presbyterian Church Baby Clinic, which is operated on similar lines, is associated with the Henrietta Egleston Hospital in its work.

In 1930 the Child Welfare Association of Fulton and DeKalb Counties was organized. A child-placing agency rather than a child's home, this institution extends its services to children under 18 whose homes are broken by illness, poverty, or family maladjustments. Children brought to the association are housed here only until they can be placed in the proper corrective institution, school, or private home, as the individual case demands. The association works in close co-operation with the county juvenile courts and other agencies.

During the early thirties when the Nation-wide depression was at its height, the scope of social service became so greatly broadened that it was necessary to co-ordinate the work more closely. In 1932 the Social Welfare Society, which had been founded almost 30 years before by Joseph C. Logan, changed its name to the Social Planning Council and enlarged its field of activities. Its objective is to promote efficiency in solving the welfare problems of the city through research and recommendations made by special committees, each expert in its field. Through these activities public opinion is being directed toward a more intelligent appreciation of welfare needs in the city.

As a memorial to Victor H. Kriegshaber, who had worked for many years with the Georgia Association of Workers for the Blind, a Braille library was installed in the old Hebrew Orphans' Home on Washington Street. Though supported by private funds, the library was set up under the supervision of the trustees of the Carnegie Library. Two years later the institution was moved to its present site on Piedmont Avenue. About 500 phonographs for lending throughout the State are furnished by the Federal Government, and the Work Projects Administration supplies two Braille instructors who teach the blind to read raised lettering. Magazines in Braille and about 2,000 "talking books" or records are also available.

The Fulton County Department of Public Welfare, formed by legislative act in 1937, not only administers direct relief but certifies grants for old-age assistance, aid to the blind, and aid to dependent children under the Social Security Act. This department is also a certifying agency for the Work Projects Administration, the Civilian Conservation Corps, and the National Youth Administration, and also for the distribution of Federal surplus commodities.

In 1938 representatives of the Junior Chamber of Commerce, Rotary, Optimists, Lions, and Civitan Clubs founded the Atlanta Boys' Club for underprivileged youths between the ages of 8 and 18. Paid instructors, volunteer helpers, and students from Georgia Tech and the Georgia Evening School provide instruction in woodwork, art, music, and reading.

Religion

"LONG before Atlanta was even known as Marthasville the proverbial Methodist preacher was roving the country round. Wherever the people were, he was to be found in their midst, helping to open up roads, establish communities and to build schools and churches, and settle the pioneers in their log cabins, with a Bible on their tables and the little families kneeling in prayer at the close of day," wrote Dr. Wilbur F. Glenn in his history of the Methodist Church in Atlanta. To these circuit-riders goes credit for the first recorded religious services held in Atlanta. During the winter of 1844-45 the Reverend Osborne Smith, an itinerant Methodist minister, conducted meetings in a frame building which stood just north of the old Union Depot. The following summer Bishop James O. Andrew, whose ownership of slaves had been responsible for the schism in the Methodist Episcopal Church the year before, held a protracted meeting in a cotton warehouse on the southeast corner of what is now Auburn Avenue and Pryor Street. Later the Methodists held regular meetings in the depot itself, and such was their zeal for these sessions that if an itinerant minister was not available, some member of the congregation would arise to "read the Bible and exhort."

Other denominations with as few members were stirred by this Methodist leadership to plan some means for holding their own regular Sunday services. The population of the town, however, was but about 200, and it is probable that barely more than half of these were of adult age. The situation was further complicated by the fact that this number was divided among five different denominations: Methodists, Baptists, Catholics, Episcopalians, and Presbyterians; and although each group desired a separate church the attainment of this aim was numerically impracticable and financially impossible. After considerable discussion the plan was advanced that the five denominations combine their resources and erect a building that could be used by all. Despite dire predictions and grave head-waggings, the plan carried, and a building known as the Union School and Church was erected in 1845 on the triangular site now bounded by Peachtree, Pryor, and Houston Streets. It was a simple clapboard structure with a gable roof and two chimneys, one of brick and stone and the other of clay-daubed sticks, protruding at each side. Short brick pillars supported the building and three wooden steps led up to the one door. Men and women were compelled to sit on opposite sides of the aisle, an arrangement intended to keep attention focused on spiritual matters.

This union of the churches signified no combining of doctrines but merely an economic compromise. It is therefore remarkable, in view of the prevalent dogmatic convictions, that no quarrels marred the gathering of the diverse groups. One reason for this harmony was the sensible manner in which the church was managed. All denominations wished to hold regular Sunday morning services, but, since this was impossible, it was decided that Sunday services should be strictly non-denominational. These nonsectarian meetings were directed by Dr. John S. Wilson, a Presbyterian minister of Decatur, and it is recorded that a "spirit of love and co-operation prevailed." Dr. Wilson, a man of remarkable tact, occasionally relinquished the pulpit to visiting ministers of other creeds who were equally careful to avoid doctrinal issues. If baptism, communion services, or other rites demanded sectarian privacy, the church was always available on week nights for closed sessions.

Even so, the desire for separate buildings was so strong that in 1848 the Methodists, whose numbers were increasing apace with the rapid growth of the town, erected Wesley Chapel on the site just south of the present Candler Building. Funds were exhausted before the structure was little more than four walls and a roof, but the members were determined to hold services in it. Accordingly, rough slabs for benches were obtained from Jonathan Norcross' sawmill, holes were bored in them, and stout pegs were driven in for legs. A crudely built platform, upon which was set a druggist's prescription table, became the pulpit, while a home-made tin chandelier held the candles for night services. Thus equipped, the Methodists became the first congregation in Atlanta to hold meetings in their own house. Before the year was out a Sunday school was organized, and in 1849 a large revival brought several hundred new members into the church.

The Baptists also erected a building in 1848. It was constructed on the site of the old post office and, like Wesley Chapel, was but a small frame shack furnished with rude benches. Yet, to the 6 men and 11 women who formed the first congregation, it was a pleasing reflection of their simple and rugged characters. That they were determined to retain this early simplicity was shown a few years later when new members provided the church with a melodeon and the older members, declaring the instrument a sinful innovation, ordered it removed.

Further evidence of stern discipline was revealed in the serious inquiries into the actions of members, inquiries which sometimes led to excommunication. These included absence from services or business meetings, failure to pay just debts, frivolity in dress, or permitting music and dancing in their homes.

The Roman Catholics were next to withdraw. Less than any other denomination this one had availed itself of the private usage of the Union Church, for visiting priests usually conducted mass and administered sacraments in private homes. In 1848 Atlanta was made part of the Savannah diocese and Father J.F. O'Neill came from that city to fill the office of resident priest. A building was erected the same year on the site of the present Church of the Immaculate Conception.

In 1849 the Episcopalians, though having fewer members than any other denomination, were financially able to withdraw from the Union Church and occupy their own building, St. Philip's. This church was a small frame structure with a modest tower and vestry room, the interior finished in white, with grained seats, pulpit, and chancel rail. For the first year the Reverend John James Hunt, a missionary priest, served as rector, but in 1850 support was pledged for the appointment of the Reverend W.J. Zimmer as regular minister.

The Presbyterians were the last of the denominations to withdraw from the Union Church. In 1852 their building, erected on Marietta Street where the Federal Reserve Bank now stands, was dedicated. It was the finest church in town at the time, being constructed of brick and having a vestibule, a gallery, and a basement. In deference to the wishes of John Silvey, an influential citizen who lived next door, no bell was ever hung in the belfry. Silvey, a firm believer in Benjamin Franklin's "early-to-bed" maxim, retired at seven o'clock every night. In return for a generous contribution to the church, the elders agreed that no bell-ringing would disturb his early evening slumbers. The Reverend Jesse E. DuBose was chosen as regular pastor in 1854.

The First Christian Church, which had been organized by State Evangelist Daniel Hook in 1850, was erected in 1853 on the corner of Pryor and Mitchell Streets. This building was used for only one year, at which time the property was exchanged for a lot on Marietta Street near Ivy and a new building erected.

In 1854 nineteen members of the First Baptist Church withdrew to form a second church. Their withdrawal was caused not only by larger membership that taxed the capacity of the first church, but also by the desire of the separating group, more liberal than the founders, to have musical accompaniment for their services. An appeal to Baptists throughout the State resulted in the erection of a $14,000 building on the corner of Washington and Mitchell Streets. Until the new church was equipped with a tank, the congregation held baptisms at

an open-air pool on the corner of Spring and James Street. This ceremony was always an occasion for the gathering of many townspeople
who were in no way related to the church.

It is recorded that this church had a gallery in which Negro slaves
sat during the services and that they were permitted to share in the
communion after the white people were served. As the restraint of
the services was not satisfying to the more readily emotional Negroes,
however, they were allowed to use the church occasionally for private
services that were given to more abandon. Although no ordained Negro
ministers were available, some kindly white-haired patriarch of the
"Uncle Remus" or "Eneas Africanus" type was always ready to take
the pulpit and exhort the slaves to walk in "de ways ob de Lawd."
Colorful indeed were these sessions with the "amen corner" and the
"hallelejah chorus" responding vociferously to the words of the
"preacher." But the meetings were closely supervised by the white
elders, and the Negro leaders were somewhat restricted in their choice
of scriptural texts lest some of the more socially significant passages of
the Bible lead them into dangerously independent ways of thinking.

Also in 1854 Trinity Methodist Church, an outgrowth of a mission
Sunday school conducted under the auspices of Wesley Chapel, was
erected on Mitchell Street opposite the site of the present State capitol.
For the first year and a half the pulpit was occupied by visiting preachers, but in 1856 it was made a separate charge and a regular pastor
was appointed. Three other Methodist churches were founded between
1854 and 1859, the African Methodist, the Protestant Methodist, and
Payne's Chapel. The African Methodist building was the first Negro
church in the city, and the denomination later played a leading part
in the fight for emancipation and the establishment of educational institutions for Negroes.

The Central Presbyterian Church, founded in 1858, was the last
of Atlanta's pioneer churches established before the outbreak of the
War between the States. Thirty-nine members of the First Presbyterian Church addressed the Flint River Presbytery, of which the
church was a unit, and requested that they be permitted to form a new
congregation and that this body not be designated as the second church.
Both requests were recognized and the Central Presbyterian Church
was erected on Washington Street just north of the First Baptist
Church. This brick building, of Colonial design, with four tall
Corinthian columns supporting the entablature, was the most handsome
church structure in the city when it was dedicated on March 4, 1860,
by Dr. J.C. Stiles.

Thus 1860 found all the principal denominations, with the exception of the Jews, established in their own houses of worship. Churches
had become the center of virtually all public, social, cultural, and edu-

cational activities. Not only were they houses of worship on Sunday, but they were the scenes of spelling bees, box suppers, dramatic readings, and song fests during the week. The growth of the church was definitely keeping pace with that of the city, and spiritual leaders were making plans for even greater expansion.

Then came the war and the bombardment and burning of Atlanta. Strangely enough, even in 1864 while the city was in the path of crossfire from opposing armies, still another Episcopal group found means to build a church, St. Luke's. Dr. Charles T. Quintard, a physician and Episcopal cleric who had been sent to Atlanta from his native Connecticut as chaplain-at-large to the Confederate Army, found that St. Philip's was not large enough to accommodate its congregation. With characteristic zeal he immediately set about organizing a second group of communicants, obtaining a lot and erecting a building. So persuasive was Dr. Quintard that his efforts were quickly successful. A new parish was created; land, lumber, and furnishings were donated; and the building was erected on Walton Street where the Grant Building now stands. Bishop Elliott in his report of the year says: "Friday, April 22, 1864, I consecrated to the service of Almighty God, St. Luke's Church—Atlanta— In the afternoon of the same day a class for confirmation was presented, which I laid hands upon five persons, the first fruits of this enterprise." Seven months later the church was a heap of blackened ashes, destroyed in the fire that devastated Atlanta.

Most of the churches escaped the torch, but many were badly damaged by cannon balls and the use to which they were put during Sherman's occupation. The facades of the Immaculate Conception and the Central Presbyterian Churches were both scarred by exploding shells. Federal troops took over St. Philip's for a stable and bowling alley and tore down the rectory to make room for breastworks, and they converted the basement of the Central Presbyterian Church into a slaughterhouse. By agreement with General Sherman, Trinity Methodist was protected as a storehouse for furniture of the evacuating citizens. Apparently the First Baptist Church was left in a usable condition, for services were conducted there by the pastor on Christmas Day, 1864, for those citizens who had already returned to the devastated city.

The churches still standing among the smoking ruins afforded temporary shelter to many of the returning refugees, who hung makeshift screens of burlap or paper between the pews and along the aisles, thereby fashioning rooms which provided a modicum of privacy. In a short while the more pressing repairs had been made on the churches and, as soon as the more urgent task of rebuilding houses had been accomplished, attention was turned to plans for new church buildings.

Within ten years after the close of the war, every denomination in the city had erected at least one new building. Father O'Reilly, the heroic priest of the Church of the Immaculate Conception, died in 1872 before the new church was completed and he was buried under the altar stone. The year 1875 was significant in church history in that a synagogue was dedicated, the first Jewish house of worship in the city. The Lutherans also erected their first building in this year. During the next decade new buildings were erected by three of Atlanta's most prominent churches: the Central Presbyterian, St. Philip's, and St. Luke's. In 1897 the Sacred Heart Parish was created and the Catholic church of that name was dedicated the following year. The Baptist Tabernacle, an institution which was for years to play a leading part in the growth of that denomination, was established in 1898. In 1899 the Christian Scientists, who had for years been holding classes in various private houses and rented offices, built an imposing church on Baker Street.

Atlanta's population trebled during the first quarter of the new century; this period marked the greatest growth of churches. Most of the older congregations of the city erected buildings that compared favorably with the churches of the newer ones. Even the small foreign elements, the Greeks and the Syrians, had increased to such an extent that they could establish their first churches.

The Baptists attained a definite lead in membership which they have maintained to the present (1942). The church census of 1936 listed 164 Baptist churches in Atlanta with 60,781 members. This denomination entertained in 1939 the World Baptist Alliance, a convention which brought many visitors to the city. The Methodists are second in denominational strength, having 90 churches and 41,655 members. The Presbyterians have a membership of 10,940 and 22 churches. There are 10 Protestant Episcopal churches with 4,420 members, 6 Roman Catholic parishes with 8,430 members, and 6 Jewish congregations with 12,000 members. Smaller denominations include the Disciples of Christ, Lutheran, Church of God, Churches of Christ, Church of Jesus Christ of Latter-day Saints, Congregationalist, Seventh-day Adventist, Church of Christ Scientist, Church of the Nazarene, Universalist, and Unitarian, as well as scores of minor schismatic bodies which have separated from all the foregoing. There are 50 denominations represented in Atlanta, with 354 churches and a combined membership of 152,083.

Education

I N the chaotic year of 1844, before Marthas-
ville had changed its name to Atlanta, Miss Martha Reed courageously
opened a small private school in a shack near what is now the intersection of Decatur and King Streets. Here "for about a year" she
taught the children of "lumbermen, saw-mill workers, teamsters, trainmen, blacksmiths, commissary-keepers, mechanics and laborers" in the
town's first school. Its second school, a one-room shack that also
served as a church on Sunday, was erected by private subscription and
opened in 1845 on the site now bounded by Peachtree, Pryor, and
Houston Streets. No references are available indicating who taught
this school or how long it remained in existence. Apparently both of
these schools were short-lived, for during the following year the town
seems to have been without any educational institution.

Then, in the spring of 1847, Dr. Nedam L. Angier came to Atlanta
from New England and erected a building known as Angier's Academy
on the southwest corner of Forsyth and Garnett Streets. His wife
taught this school for several months during the summer, but the venture failed, for the little town was still too engrossed in its struggle
for survival to find time for cultural enterprises. During the year
almost 200 buildings had been constructed and the population had leapt
from a few hundred to more than 2,000. Children had been pressed
into service helping their parents clear the land and split logs so that
they might have shelter before winter set in. Regular schooling, for
the time being, was out of the question.

By fall, however, with noisy children kept indoors by cold and rain,
parents were more than ready to avail themselves of the services of
Dr. William N. White, an idealistic young man who had but recently
come south from Utica, New York, to regain his health while earning
his living as a teacher, ". . . which, with God's blessing, I trust I
shall be able to do." On October 21, 1847, he made this entry in his
diary: "There are lots of children who I am assured would go to a
school worth patronizing, and from what I can see I am sure, with a

good building, in a very short time I could make a thousand dollars a year. But there is a difficulty; the only building I can get is a miserable shell of a thing without ceiling, and it cannot be finished this winter. I have been to all prominent men of the place, who promise their influence, and those who have children, their patronage. For two years there will be great difficulties on account of the unfixed character of the inhabitants, the poverty of most of the present settlers and, this year, the discomforts of the old building."

On November 8, White took over Dr. Angier's academy, "which has a bell, but is quite unfinished and is merely covered and enclosed," and opened his first class with an enrollment of 25 pupils. On November 18, he writes: "School goes off very pleasantly; have several new scholars." A few days later, however, he declares mournfully, "Surely there is no work in the world as onerous as the employment of the teacher. It needs all the wisdom in the world. . . ." This entry offers some clue as to why White, never the stern disciplinarian, closed school within three months and departed for Athens to enter the book business. Yet he was not embittered; he left believing "my scholars love me, and I am sure I love them." Other teachers of the period were not so sensitive, for various writers with first-hand information stress the fact that a bundle of "wyths" or hickory sticks was always kept in sight of the whole school. Thrashings were administered not only for misconduct but for "missing lessons," and the mildest punishment the derelict student could hope for was the wearing of a red dunce cap.

Records indicate that the academy was taken over by a teacher named Adair, who was followed by W.W. Janes. Janes' charges for instruction are interesting: "For orthography, reading and writing, $4 per term; arithmetic, grammar and geography, $6; Latin, Greek and Mathematics, $8." Mrs. T.S. Ogilbie, who opened a school early in 1851 on the corner of Hunter and Pryor Streets, offered instruction in these same subjects at the same price, but added ". . . philosophy, botany, rhetoric, astronomy, geography of the heavens, ancient and modern history, moral and intellectual philosophy, $6; waxwork, fruit and flowers, $10; music and use of the piano, $12.50; painting and embroidery, $5."

Several other institutions also opened in 1851, among them Miss Nevers' "school for the instruction of children of both sexes" on Marietta Street, Miss C.W. Dews' "School for females," T.O. Adair's "literary school on the Humphries lot," the Misses Bettison's and Daniel's school "near Walton and Spring" on the site of the present old post office building, and two schools by the name of Atlanta Male Academy, one directed by J.T. McGinty and the other by G.A. Austin. It was not until 1853, when Atlanta's population had increased to

4,000, that the first free school was opened. This was the Holland Free School, named for Edmund Weyman Holland, a banker who leased the old Angier Academy property free of rent to the city for five years. A South Carolinian who had been a schoolmaster in Alabama, Holland decided upon a free school as a fitting philanthropic gesture toward his adopted city where he had made his fortune. Although the students' tuitions were financed by the State poor school fund, an aid usually resented and spurned by the citizens, the school continued in successful operation for six years after Holland's extension of the lease. But, as Atlanta continued to grow, some of its people began to show certain genteel snobberies of attitude frequently found in a new society, and it was this element that revived the old feeling toward the poor school fund.

In 1858 a group of citizens, unwilling to utilize this educational system and unable to afford private tuition, began agitating for the establishment of public schools. Foremost in this progressive group was the Scotch-Irish schoolmaster and unionist Alexander N. Wilson, who at that time was teaching his "classical and English school" in the building first occupied by Martha Reed. Wilson made a special trip to Providence, Rhode Island, to study its public school system and returned enthusiastic for the establishment of a similar one in Atlanta.

Mass meetings were called and success seemed at hand, but an opposing group, which regarded a public school system as merely a substitute for the old poor school fund, came forward and began soliciting for the founding of a "female institute." It is difficult to understand why such an institute was deemed an acceptable alternative for a public school system providing for both sexes and for a greater range in ages. Nevertheless, the majority of the people supported this proposal and, when council refused to appropriate funds for its establishment, raised $15,000 by private subscription. The Female Institute was opened in 1860 on the corner of Ellis and Courtland Streets. The defeated proponents of a public school system, seeing that victory must be deferred, adopted a conciliatory attitude and expressed approval of the new school for young ladies "first because they believed education from that source was better than none, and second because they believed that educated women would be the strongest advocates in the future of a system of public schools."

By 1860 more than a score of private schools had been established, but during the years of the war all were closed and those that were spared destruction in the burning of the city were converted into hospitals. Yet, as soon as the more urgent needs of the reconstructed town were met, attention was given to the re-establishment of schools, and by 1866 there were 19 private institutions operating. But Atlanta's population had now grown to 10,000, and, while these private institutions were more than sufficient to accommodate the children of the few families of means, many less fortunate were growing up in a state of illiteracy. Some momentum for the public school movement was left from the pre-war period, but this alone was not sufficient for an advance. Also at this time the carpetbaggers began to agitate for racial equality in the schools throughout the State. The result was that a public school system, which would have been subject to this racial inter-mingling, was further delayed and the position of the private schools strengthened.

In 1866 four schools were established for Negro children. The American Missionary Society sent the Reverend E.M. Gravath to Atlanta early in the year and he immediately organized a class in the African Methodist Church on Gilmer Street. Within a few months a second school was opened in a building brought from Chattanooga and re-erected on Walton Street. These two schools housed about 1,000 children. During the summer this overcrowding was relieved somewhat by the Freedmen's Bureau which made available a small structure on the site of the present Candler Building. Later in the year the Missionary Society and the Freedmen's Bureau co-operated in collecting funds for a larger building. Dr. Storr's church, of Cincin-nati, gave the largest sum, $1,000, and, accordingly, the new building completed in December 1866 was called Storr's School. This building stood on the corner of Piedmont Avenue and Houston Street and was for years the principal grammar school for Negroes.

By 1870 it had become apparent that the Negro children of the city were provided with better educational facilities than the white children. But, with the removal of the threat of racial intermingling in the withdrawal of the military government in the latter part of that year, the position of the earlier advocates of a public school system was now fortified by economic conditions, and citizens who had formerly been in opposition began to clamor for it.

The council hastily amended the city charter to permit the estab-lishment of public schools and imposed taxes and issued bonds to assure their maintenance. A board of education, consisting of 12 members, was appointed, and in November 1871, M.B. Mallon was elected super-intendent. In January 1872, the first three buildings were opened with an enrollment of 1,839 pupils and with a faculty of "24 females and 6 males." By the end of the scholastic year, the number of chil-dren in attendance was almost 4,000, the faculty had increased to 56, and the buildings, either rented or erected for the purpose, included seven grammar and two high schools for white children and three schools for Negroes. Most of the "private and select" schools were forced to close their doors and many of the teachers were absorbed into the public system.

An unanticipated problem arose in 1873 when the Roman Catholics of the city petitioned the board of education for separate schools to be provided for their children. The petition was refused, but the Catholics returned the following year with the request that their children at least be taught by teachers of the same faith. This petition also was denied. Not until the turn of the century were the Catholics able to erect their own parish school.

Running parallel to the expansion of the public schools was the growth of institutions of higher learning. In this direction Negroes received more outside philanthropic aid than the white citizens, and from 1865 through 1885 six Negro colleges and universities were founded in Atlanta. These institutions are now known as Clark College, Gammon Theological Seminary, Morris Brown College, Spelman College, Morehouse College, and Atlanta University. The last three, and the Atlanta School of Social Work, are affiliated under the Atlanta University System, and Atlanta University is the only Negro institution in the city offering a degree for graduate work.

In 1870 Oglethorpe University, formerly located in Milledgeville and closed during the war, reopened in Atlanta. Financial difficulties forced it to close two years later. The Southern Medical College was founded in 1879 and was later combined with the old Atlanta Medical College, which had been established in 1855. In 1882 the general assembly, recognizing the need for skilled technicians to develop the natural resources and build up the industries of the State, passed a resolution calling for the establishment of a technical school. As a result, the Georgia School of Technology was opened in Atlanta six years later. Decatur Female Seminary, which was opened in 1889, is now Agnes Scott College, an outstanding institution for the higher education of women.

Educational progress was not made, however, without much opposition from reactionaries. An editorial in the Atlanta *Journal* of 1883 expresses the passing mood of an era. "Some of our best men appear to rest under the impression that education is a sort of panacea for every evil which affects the body politic. This is a mistaken notion. What is education doing for the Negro? A Southern editor who has been a close observer of affairs since the war answers this interrogatory with the statement that every educated Negro goes into politics or into the penitentiary. The truth is, education in the customary sense of the word makes better citizens of those only whose natural bent inclines them to a moral and law-abiding mode of life; with the naturally vicious the education of the schools goes for nothing, except that it increases their power for evil. Perhaps it would be well to make haste slowly in the matter of public education. A too rapid growth would inevitably make us a nation without a conscience, and give us over to infidelity and dangerous political heresy."

Despite these views, the establishment of schools went forward and by 1892 Atlanta had 16 grammar and 2 high schools. There were also many private preparatory schools and several special schools. Washington Seminary, which had been established in 1878 as an elementary school, was continually adding more advanced subjects to its curriculum. In 1895 the Peacock School for Boys was opened to teach college preparatory work, and the Southern Female Seminary moved to College Park from LaGrange and reopened as Cox College. In 1900 the Georgia Military Academy was established in the same Atlanta suburb. These were followed by Marist College, a Roman Catholic preparatory school for boys, in 1901 and by the Southern College of Pharmacy in 1903. In 1909 the Sacred Heart Church, under the ministration of Father John E. Gunn, established a parish school, thereby fulfilling the desire which the Catholics had harbored since the seventies. In the same year members of the North Avenue Presbyterian Church opened an elementary school for girls and boys in the Sunday school room of the church; high school work for girls was added in 1912.

In 1914 the old Emory College at Oxford was moved to Atlanta and established as a university, and it later took over the combined Atlanta School of Medicine and the Southern College of Physicians and Surgeons. Oglethorpe University reopened in 1916, aided in its re-establishment by a gift from Atlanta citizens of $250,000 and 137 acres of land.

The Negroes again assumed a prominent position in the educational field with the founding of the Atlanta School of Social Work in 1925. Set up through the efforts of leading educators of both white and colored races, the institution achieved such excellent standing that within three years it was admitted to the American Association of Schools of Social Work, holding the only Negro membership in that organization.

In 1933 the University System of Georgia took over the Georgia Tech Evening School of Commerce, which had been established downtown in 1914, and developed a university extension center. The evening college grants only the degree of Bachelor of Commercial Science, but credit for three years' work toward a Bachelor of Arts degree can be earned here and transferred to a senior college in the university system. A junior college was added in 1934, with day classes.

During all these years the city had been hard pressed to build enough public schools for its rapidly growing population, but, with growth slowing after the boom years of the 1920's, Atlanta had time to adapt itself to the building needs of the system and to consider the quality of its educational facilities. The progressive methods of

Atlanta's public schools now compare favorably with systems found in cities of much larger size. Textbooks and curriculum constantly undergo modernizing processes designed to keep them attuned to the trends of public opinion. In addition to the basic studies found in every modern system, the Atlanta schools give instruction in creative art, music, and physical training. Free textbooks are supplied to all grades, free lunches to undernourished children, and free clinical service to the entire student body.

The system is administered by a board of 6 members, one from each city ward elected for a 4-year term, who appoint and have control over the general superintendent and his 3 assistant superintendents. There are 73 school buildings, housing 44 elementary schools for white children and 12 for Negroes, 6 junior and 4 senior high schools for white children, and 2 senior high schools for Negroes. The remaining buildings are allotted to special classes, such as those for the blind, the mentally defective, and the hard-of-hearing.

The enrollment numbered 64,950 for the 1939-40 term. Maintenance cost approximates $3,500,000 yearly, a sum amounting to 30 per cent of the city's annual revenue. As funds become available, a further expenditure of $6,000,000 is planned to modernize and increase the number of buildings and facilities.

Because of the city's metropolitan spread, three other school systems are operated within the vicinity: the Fulton County Schools, the De-Kalb County Schools, and the Decatur Schools. Fulton County maintains 94 schools, of which 39 are for Negroes, and has an enrollment of 21,733. DeKalb County, with Decatur as its seat, has 51 schools with 10,122 pupils. Decatur organized its public school system in 1902 and now has 9 schools with an enrollment of 3,066 children.

Atlanta children can obtain complete schooling from kindergarten to college without going out of the city. Further co-operative plans among the city's institutions are contemplated for Emory University, Agnes Scott, and Georgia Tech. Actual realization of this plan will definitely establish Atlanta as the leading educational center of the South.

Newspapers

THE history of Atlanta's early newspapers is a series of enthusiastic beginnings followed almost immediately by failures. Newspaper publishing too often was regarded as a mere avocation for the entrepreneur with a little idle money, with the result that many papers served no other purpose than to express the personality of the owner or to report news limited in interest to one particular group in a town too small to support even a paper of general appeal.

Many of these early papers were largely one-man affairs, owned, edited, and published by a single individual. It mattered little that these men had no previous journalistic experience; word had but to be passed around that a Washington hand press and an ink roller were available at the sheriff's sale and some self-appointed molder of public opinion would be there with his bid. Within a few days dog-eared manuscripts of long-cherished editorials would be set up in type and another paper was launched. These ventures, however poorly conceived and directed, nevertheless served to accustom the people to the regular appearance of a newspaper and to create a demand for printed news.

Historians disagree as to which of the early Atlanta newspapers began publication first. C.R. Hanleiter, an early newspaperman, said in 1861 that he was in doubt as to the order in which the first three newspapers were established but that he thought the *Enterprise* was the first; years later he stated without qualification that the *Democrat* was the first. Most historians, however, credit the *Luminary* with being the earliest, saying that it appeared in 1845 about the time the Georgia Railroad reached the city. But doubt is cast on this date by a news item in the Athens *Banner* of July 21, 1846, commenting on the first number of the *Luminary*, ". . . a capacious and handsome newspaper . . . published at the new town of Atlanta, by Messrs. Baker & Wilson. . . ."

The Reverend Joseph Baker used a Washington hand press for printing the *Luminary*, and indications are that it was really a small, crudely printed sheet consisting chiefly of religious items—Bible lessons, moralizing editorials, and the like. Because of its limited appeal subscribers were few, and within a short time Baker was forced to sell his paper. The new owners, J.B. Clapp and L.W. Bartlett, made drastic changes in the format, and a commentator of 1847 writes that the December 9 edition "came out in a blaze of glory with four columns of original matter, a poem, and odds and ends." Early in the following year Clapp's interest in the paper was bought by Charles L. Wheeler and the name was changed to the *Tribune.* The venture failed, however, and publication was suspended before the year was out.

The *Democrat,* it is said by most of the local writers, was the city's second paper. Dr. William Henry Fonerden set up a little hand press in 1846 in the upper half-story of a building at the junction of the Peachtree and Marietta roads and began printing the paper as a weekly. But after a few months he moved his family to Spring Place near Dalton, Georgia, and, changing the paper into an educational journal, continued publication there.

The *Enterprise,* another weekly, was published in the fall of 1846 by W.H. Royal and C.H. Yarbrough in an office just a few doors south of Alabama Street on Whitehall Street. In the same year, however, the paper was discontinued and the material and equipment sold to C.R. Hanleiter, who in 1847 moved to Atlanta with his *Southern Miscellany,* which he had been publishing for six years in Madison, Georgia. The paper asserted itself to be "A Weekly Family Newspaper Devoted to Literature, Education, Agriculture, Mechanical Arts, News, Humor, and Politics." Of the nine subscribers, three paid in money, one in candles, and five nothing at all. A copy of this paper, dated December 4, 1847, gave four and a half of the six columns on the first page to "A Selected Tale, from the Columbian Magazine" entitled "Charity Begins at Home." A speech by Henry Clay filled the remaining column and a half of the first page, the entire second page, and a half of the third page. The remainder of the third page was devoted to national political news. Henry Clay was endorsed for President and John McLean for Vice President.

In keeping with the custom of the day, no local news was published. Aside from the town's small size, which rendered this unnecessary, it was considered a confession of failure for an editor to be forced to fill his pages with local happenings. If civic undertakings demanded newspaper comment or support, the custom was to publish separate handbills for distribution in order that they might be in no way associated with the regular issues. If regular issues failed to appear after one of these handbills exhausted the week's supply of paper and ink, it was politely overlooked by subscribers who were also the editor's friends. Another taboo of the day was the mention by name of any citizen except by way of a business advertisement. Not for several decades yet was such mention to be regarded as anything but a serious breach of good taste.

True to form, the *Miscellany's* only indication (aside from the masthead) that it was published in any specific place was found in the advertisements on the fourth and last page. Here it was announced that the Washington Hotel was under new management; that Major Wyllys Buell, the portrait painter, was recommended by the editor; and that Jonathan Norcross had a new supply of "fine hardware and dry goods selected in New York" and was quoting attractive prices on "meats and feathers."

Hanleiter continued publication of the *Southern Miscellany* until the fall of 1849, when he was forced to discontinue the paper because of a raging smallpox epidemic that made it impossible to secure workers. The type and press were purchased by four men, one of whom was Jonathan Norcross, the town's foremost merchant and later its mayor. The name of the paper was changed to the *Intelligencer* and, after several other changes in ownership, came into the possession of John Duncan and Colonel Thomas C. Howard in 1855.

Two years previously the *Daily Examiner,* Atlanta's first daily, had appeared under the editorship of J.H. Steele and J.W. Dowsing. It consisted of one sheet "devoted to the advocacy of democratic principles." After four successful years it was purchased by John Duncan, who had become sole owner of the *Intelligencer.* He merged the two papers and continued publication under the name of the *Atlanta Daily Intelligencer and Examiner.*

During the decade of the fifties no less than 28 papers appeared in Atlanta. These included the *Herald,* the *Weekly Republican and Democrat,* the *Christian Advocate,* the *Olive Tree,* the *Knight of Jericho,* the *Georgia Blister and Critic,* the *Southern Blade,* the *Discipline,* the *Literary and Temperance Crusader,* the *National American,* and the *Medical and Literary Weekly.* The circulation of these journals was limited because of restricted appeal or hidebound dogma, or their columns were devoted too exclusively to political propaganda, with the result that they survived but a few months.

Although the dawning sixties brought the threat of war nearer, there was no abatement in the appearance of new sheets on the streets of Atlanta. During the first year of the decade five papers were established, the *Educational Journal & Family Magazine,* the *Georgia Weekly,* the *Temperance Champion,* the *Daily Locomotive,* and the *Gate City Guardian.* During the four-year period of the conflict 15 newspapers were published at various times. Three of these were papers which were moved to Atlanta from other besieged towns, the Memphis *Appeal,* the Knoxville *Register,* and the Chattanooga *Rebel.*

Education and Welfare

CANDLER SCHOOL OF THEOLOGY, EMORY UNIVERSITY

MEDICAL STUDENTS, EMORY UNIVERSITY

MACHINE SHOPS, GEORGIA SCHOOL OF TECHNOLOGY

TOWER OF ACADEMIC BUILDING, GEORGIA SCHOOL OF TECHNOLOGY

STUDENT PRINTERS, OGLETHORPE UNIVERSITY PRESS

AGNES SCOTT COLLEGE

ART STUDENT, ATLANTA UNIVERSITY

LABORATORY AT THE MUNICIPAL GRADY HOSPITAL

RECREATIONAL CENTER FOR ENLISTED MEN

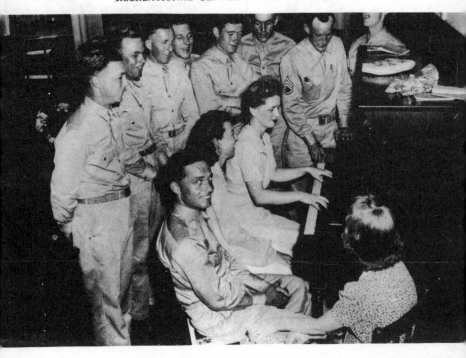

HENRIETTA EGLESTON HOSPITAL FOR CHILDREN

HILLSIDE COTTAGES

MARIST COLLEGE CADETS

MODELING AIRPLANES IN TECH HIGH SCHOOL SHOPS

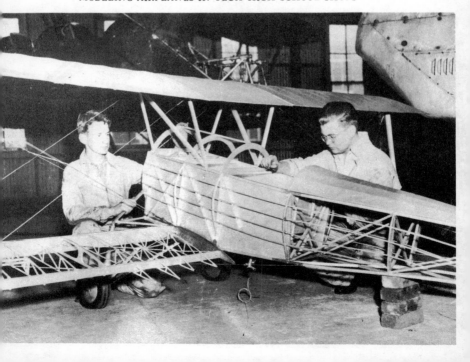

The *Gate City Guardian* changed its name to the *Southern Confederacy* as "a more appropriate title" in 1861 and claimed a circulation of 5,000. This was undoubtedly surpassed by the old *Intelligencer,* which was still carrying on under a constant change of management. The amazing number of less important papers may be partly explained by the law that exempted newspaper editors and workers from military service.

Wire service was supplemented by letters from correspondents and soldiers at the battle fronts, and contact was maintained with the telegraphic offices of the railroads for any additional news concerning activities of the fighting forces. Some of the most dramatic scenes of the war period occurred in the streets before the newspaper offices, as reports of another battle brought distraught crowds for news of relatives and friends. Office boys and printers' devils were kept busy running up and down stairs delivering hurriedly printed lists, still wet with ink, as fast as they were taken from the presses. Grief-stricken hysteria often hung upon the spelling of a name and, because of the probability of errors in the hastily compiled lists, tension was heightened by people pushing into the offices to check the original spelling.

With the beginning of the siege of Atlanta, the presses of the *Intelligencer* were moved aboard a freight car, where publication continued. Since supplies were cut off from the besieged city, papers were printed on any acceptable material that came to hand. Issues appeared on wrapping paper, wallpaper, and even cardboard. When it became evident that the Confederate forces could no longer hold the city and that Federal occupation was imminent, the car containing the press of the *Intelligencer* was pulled out of town and for the duration of the war was shifted about the State, papers being irregularly published wherever circumstances permitted. This was the only Atlanta paper to survive the war.

During the period of Reconstruction many new papers appeared. Most important among these were the *Daily Commercial Bulletin* and the *Ladies Home* in 1866; the *Daily Opinion* and *Adair's Georgia Land Register* in 1867; the *Constitution* in 1868; the *Weekly Republican,* the *Sunny South,* and the *Southern Advance* in 1874; and the *Daily Tribune* in 1875. Many others, like the *Acanthus* ("Devoted to the True, the Beautiful and the Good") had an ephemeral existence.

Only two papers inclined toward Northern sympathies during the Reconstruction Period. The first of these was the *Daily New Era,* which was acquired by Dr. Samuel Bard in 1866. In retrospect Bard's allegiance seems to have been more to supporting the Constitution than the Federal regime, but even this was unpopular among a defeated people living under military rule. In the first issue of the paper Bard outlined his policy of accepting the reconstruction methods of President Johnson and advised a conservative political course that he believed would result in an ultimate union with full restoration of the South's rights under the Constitution. Adhering to his conservative principles, he refused to comment on the Sherman Reconstruction Bill. This caused much bitter censure, and finally the paper was forced to declare that it was accepting the Reconstruction Bill unconditionally and was determined to co-operate with the United States authorities. Subscriptions were immediately canceled and the *Daily New Era* was scathingly denounced by other papers as a Republican sheet. Nevertheless, the *New Era* survived and began an attack on the irregularities of the carpetbag administration of Governor Bullock in Georgia, which Bard so effectively exposed that Bullock was forced to silence the paper by purchasing it for $25,000 in 1870. He neglected, however, to insert a clause in the deed of transfer prohibiting Bard from beginning another paper. The result was that Bard, now armed with the additional weapon of the facts of the sale, opened an office across the street from the *New Era* and began publishing the *Daily True Georgian*. More than any other individual, this resourceful editor was responsible for the defeat of Governor Bullock and his ultimate resignation from office.

On November 17, 1870, the *Daily True Georgian* announced that in acting with the Republican Party in support of measures for the restoration of the Southern States it had discharged a duty to the people; it declared sympathy with the National Democratic Party, believing the principles of that party guaranteed the best interests of the people. Thus, having defeated the Bullock administration and returned to the Democratic fold, Bard discontinued the publication of the *Daily True Georgian* early in 1871.

The *Intelligencer,* which had admirably spurred Atlanta's citizens in the work of reconstruction, likewise passed out of existence in 1871, but the work was carried on by the new sheets. Most prominent of these was the *Atlanta Constitution,* a morning daily founded by Colonel Carey W. Styles in 1868. The *Constitution* led the fight for the re-establishment of State government under the rule of its own people while it was still under the military control of the Federal regime. Because of this courageous stand the paper became instantly popular, a regard which was justified when it proved itself the most conspicuous newspaper factor in the complete triumph of 1871 when the native white people succeeded in recapturing the State and routing the scalawags and carpetbaggers.

Styles maintained his connection with the paper for only a year and was succeeded by G.H. Anderson, who took into partnership his son-in-law, William A. Hemphill, a young Confederate veteran then teaching school in Atlanta. Following Anderson's retirement in 1871, Colonel E.Y. Clarke became associated with Hemphill, and the two were chief owners of the paper until 1876. Clarke then sold his interest to Captain Evan P. Howell. A few years later Henry W. Grady, a young man who later became the South's most outstanding orator, bought one-fourth interest in the paper and was made managing editor.

Some knowledge of the type of reading matter contained in the papers of this period may be learned by a review of an 1882 issue of the *Constitution*. It consisted of eight pages of six columns each. The first column of the front page was allotted to advertisements. The second column contained two ghost stories and an article on the "Treacherous Thirteen," dealing with the superstitious regard of this number. The third and fourth columns were given over respectively to Ben Hill's and ex-Governor Colquitt's speeches. The fifth column was a travelogue in the Burton Holmes manner entitled "Life and Nature in the Far Northwest." But the most striking notice on the first page was the last column headed "Women's Feet," in which the avid reader learned that "Mme. Patti has the plumpest of legs that hang over her trim little boots," while "the spindle limbs of Bernhardt borrow rotundity from bull red, block blue and dull pink stockings." The inner pages contained news items with such captions as "Cruelly Deceived—A Young Woman Made Crazy by the Neglect of a Faithless Lover" and "The Evils of Drink—Drunken Young Man Arrested for Loitering Confesses He Has Led Many Young Girls Along the Road to Ruin." The "Personal Intelligence" column contained such confidences as "the season in the deer forests of Scotland is now pretty well over" and "The elevated railroads in New York are being repainted."

The reporter of the day pictured himself not as Mercury but as Aesop. In any news story concerning unfortunate persons every possible opportunity was taken to squeeze out the utmost of sentiment and to point out the most telling moral. Story captions were standardized, and "The Wages of Sin" led the lot. The line drawn between conceivable news and actual fiction was hardly discernible.

Although the *Constitution* excelled in the approved reportorial lushness of the day, it also plunged candidly and dynamically into critical controversial problems. Because of its courageous policies, it soon became the most important paper in the South, and its editorial offices were a training school for a number of men who later became impressive figures in the world of journalism and literature. Among these were Joel Chandler Harris, whose first "Uncle Remus" stories appeared in the columns of the paper; Major Charles Smith, whose homely philosophies and dry witticisms were published under the pseudonym of "Bill Arp"; and Frank L. Stanton, whose poems expressed in distinctive style the "soil and soul of America" in a column known for years as "Just From Georgia." Wallace P. Reed and Lucian Lamar Knight, two other reporters on the early staff of the *Constitution,* became noted historians of Atlanta and Georgia.

For many years the *Constitution* was undisputed leader of the city's daily newspapers. Then, in 1883, its predominance was challenged by the appearance of the Atlanta *Journal.* In its first issue the *Journal* proclaimed, "Our editorial department will be under the exclusive control of those who are 'to the manor born,' and, therefore, our patrons need not fear that any offence will be given through ignorance of Southern sentiment or lack of sympathy with it. In politics the *Journal* will be Democratic, though not so loosely buckled in the harness that it will unthinkingly yield to the party lash in the hands of those who may assume the right to rule."

The four-page paper was founded by Colonel E.F. Hoge, a lawyer and legislator. While it caught the public interest immediately, the *Journal's* future was assured by a chance occurrence which made it the talk of the town and the State and proved more effective than any planned publicity stunt. This was the issuance of an extra covering the burning of the Kimball House, at that time the largest hostelry in the South, a favorite haunt of legislators, the center of many territorial conventions, and the symbol of Atlanta to thousands of travelers. The fire broke out at 4:30 on the morning of August 12, 1883, after the day's issue of the *Constitution* was off the press. The *Journal* called in its workers and hastily composed the extra, which was quickly rushed onto the streets. Other copies were sped to trains for distribution in cities throughout the State.

The extra, an almost unheard of innovation, caused more excitement than the fire. Commenting on its *tour de force* the next day, the *Journal* stated, "The extra edition of the *Journal* yesterday was a phenomenal success. Long before the paper went to press the sidewalk in front of the office was crowded with people eager to secure an early copy. The regular carrier force of the *Journal* numbers twenty-one boys, and as it was impracticable under the circumstances to notify them of the extra edition, it was, of course, out of the question to attempt a delivery to the regular subscribers. The demand for the papers continued until dusk, and fully five hundred enterprising boys were kept busy selling papers all over the city and in the suburbs. In the neighboring towns the afternoon trains were besieged by people clamoring for the *Journal* and thousands of copies were disposed of in this way."

But as though to demonstrate that it could take such success in its stride without undue excitement, the very next item in the column showed a return to the great tradition: "Among the society women of London is an old lady eighty-three years of age, who is quite a wonder. She has a very youthful figure, and across the room would be taken for a woman of thirty."

Until 1906, the *Journal* and the *Constitution* had the newspaper field in Atlanta virtually to themselves. Only seven other papers appeared during the quarter century after the establishment of the *Journal* and four of these were for Negroes. Of the remaining three, two, the *Peoples' Party Paper* and the *Daily Press*, were published by the fiery Tom Watson, State representative and United States Senator. The *Peoples' Party Paper* was established in 1891 and achieved a moderate circulation among Watson's political followers. Encouraged by the success of this weekly, Watson brought forth the *Daily Press* in 1894 which was intended to have a more general appeal. The new sheet, however, soon began to show the old Watson trait of biased news, and although Watson's followers were numerous enough to support a political weekly, the general public refused to subscribe to a daily paper largely given over to the self-glorification of its publisher. *The Daily Press*, therefore, was discontinued within the year, but the *Peoples' Party Paper* continued in publication until 1898.

The *Daily News*, which had been published since 1902, was bought in 1906 by F.L. Seely who merged it in the establishment of a new paper, the Atlanta *Georgian*. Six years later the *Georgian* was taken over by the powerful Hearst interests, and for almost 30 years it constituted a serious rival to the *Journal* in circulation. The *Constitution*, being a morning paper, was not directly involved in this struggle.

John Temple Graves, a South Carolinian who began his newspaper career on the Rome *Daily Tribune* and was later editor of the Atlanta *Journal* and the New York *American*, was the first editor of the *Georgian*. His oratorical brilliance equalled that of Henry W. Grady, and his eloquence in political debate led to his first appointment in newspaper work. Under his direction the *Georgian* conducted successful drives against open saloons and the convict lease system and championed the passage of child labor laws. But the odds were against the *Georgian*, and it never quite attained the circulation of the *Journal*.

In 1900 the controlling interests of the *Journal* had passed into the hands of James A. Gray, under whose astute guidance the *Journal* introduced many features. It was the first Southern paper to feature business, agricultural, and educational news; the first to give sports the prominence of major news; and the first to issue a magazine section (1912). In 1917 Gray died, but, although Major John S. Cohen succeeded to the presidency, the Gray family retained their stock ownership and their personal interests in the paper. Major Cohen continued to establish precedents. In 1919 the *Journal* became the first Southern paper to publish its own rotogravure section; in 1922 the first to construct a radio station, WSB; in 1929 the first to employ teletype mechanism in sending news direct from the source to the editorial room; and in 1935 the first to introduce wire-photo service. In 1937 the *Journal* opened its second radio station, WAGA.

On December 15, 1939, James Cox, thrice governor of Ohio, made a flying visit to Atlanta and announced that he had bought both the *Journal* and the *Georgian*. The deal included full possession of the *Journal's* 50,000-watt radio station WSB and a 40 per cent interest in the less powerful WAGA. The total cash payment was approximately $3,500,000. Within a week the *Georgian* suspended publication and many of the workers and features of the paper were added to the *Journal*. The addition of the *Georgian's* subscribers now probably gives the *Journal* the largest circulation of all papers in the South, 150,000 copies daily and 200,000 on Sunday.

Atlanta has had several Negro papers, both weekly and daily. The earliest, the *Weekly Defiance,* was published in 1881 but quickly failed. It was followed by the *Atlanta Age,* established in 1893 and discontinued in 1908. More successful was the *Atlanta Independent,* a weekly founded in 1903 by Benjamin Jefferson Davis who was a prominent Republican and officer in the Order of Odd Fellows. The paper was published until 1932 when Davis discontinued it in order to devote more time to his political and fraternal activities.

The Atlanta *World,* a weekly, was founded in 1928 by William Alexander Scott, a young, well-educated Negro. The paper was an immediate success and in 1930 was made a semiweekly. In 1931 it became a triweekly and in 1932 a daily, the name being changed in this year to the *Daily World*. The paper maintains its own wire service and features a full page of comics drawn by Negro artists and a Sunday rotogravure section. It is the only Negro daily published in the country. A newspaper syndicate founded by Scott owns or controls 34 newspapers appearing in various Eastern cities.

Radio

I<small>T</small> is estimated that early in 1922 there were about 1,000 homemade radio receivers in Atlanta and its vicinity. At that time, however, there were no broadcasting stations in the South, and radio fans of the region had to content themselves with the reception of alternate whisperings and squawks which indicated that the broadcasts of some of the up-East seaboard stations had wandered within range of their makeshift tube and crystal sets.

Then, on the evening of March 15, 1922, these hopeful listeners were thrilled to hear the by no means overpowering strains of a jazz band rendition of the "Light Cavalry Overture" coming through their earphones and loud-speakers. This surprise broadcast was the initial program of the Atlanta *Journal's* radio station, a station just authorized by a telegram received that same afternoon from the acting Secretary of Commerce and operating under the call letters formerly assigned to a ship's wireless in the Pacific Ocean—WSB.

With this broadcast WSB set the first of many precedents which were to establish it as one of the leading stations in the country. Even before entering the field of broadcasting the *Journal* had published many articles instructing amateurs how to build receiving sets. A sound truck equipped with receiving apparatus cruised the city, and loud-speakers were set up in Piedmont and Grant Parks.

With the inauguration of its own station, the *Journal* immediately began a series of important innovations. WSB was the first station in America to adopt a slogan, "The Voice of the South," and early in its career it originated a mechanical effect for station identification, the famed chimes intoning the first three notes of "Over There." A musical signature was later adopted by the National Broadcasting Company. Night programs were not given in those early days, but WSB took the initiative here by introducing a 10:45 P.M. transcontinental broadcast. The *Journal's* station also led the field in employing radio as an educational medium by effecting a city-wide installation of radio receivers in the public schools and transmitting daily programs as an integral part of school work and also by establishing "WSB's University of the Air," a daily schedule of broadcasts conducted by the faculties of Georgia Tech, Emory University, Agnes Scott College, and Cox College. Radio broadcasters and listeners were on more informal terms in 1922 than is the case today, and WSB, always alert to please its fans, organized radio's first fraternity of listeners, the "WSB Radiowls."

The fact that all of these "firsts" were originated before its initial year of broadcasting was completed is indicative of the progressive spirit of the station's general manager, Lambdin Kay, known as "The Little Colonel" throughout the world of radio. Kay persuaded many celebrities to make their first radio broadcasts over WSB microphones. Among these were Otis Skinner, Efrem Zimbalist, Alma Gluck, Rudolph Valentino, and Rosa Ponselle. Miss Ponselle, after singing two numbers during an informal broadcast, was so awed and excited by the new medium that she heartily joined the studio audience's applause, explaining that it was "the first time I have ever had the chance to applaud myself and not seem immodest." Henry Ford, Octavus Roy Cohen, and Roger W. Babson are a few of the other noted personages who made their acquaintance with radio at WSB in the early years of broadcasting.

WSB entered the field of commercial broadcasting when it became affiliated with the National Broadcasting Company in 1927. This was a definite recognition of the station's accomplishments in the radio world, and WSB is now regarded as one of the most important links in this national chain of stations.

The amazing growth of WSB since its opening in 1922 in hastily constructed and cramped quarters on the roof of the *Journal* building to its present status in capacious studios in the Biltmore Hotel is marked by its increasing wattage. On March 15, 1922, its broadcasting power was a mere 100 watts; on June 13, 1922, this was raised to 500 watts; on July 13, 1925, to 1,000 watts; on February 8, 1930, to 5,000 watts; and on September 9, 1933, to 50,000 watts.

The station operates 18 hours a day on a regional frequency of 750 kilocycles and transmits its broadcasts via a 650-foot vertical antenna, the tallest man-made structure in the State, which is located near Atlanta at Tucker. Although known as "The Voice of the South," WSB's reception range extends far beyond the territory which gives it its slogan. Not only has WSB been heard in every part of the United States, but, because of occasional "freak" conditions of the atmosphere, it has been reported from South Africa, Australia, New Zealand, and numerous Central and South American countries.

WGST, Atlanta's and the South's second radio station, opened March 17, 1922, just two days after WSB's initial broadcast. At that time the station's charter was owned by the Atlanta *Constitution*, and its first program, a news broadcast, was transmitted through the radio plant of the Georgia Railway & Power Company under the signature of 4-F.T. When the *Constitution* built its own station within the year, it began broadcasting as WGM with a power of 250 watts.

In 1929 Clark Howell, owner of the *Constitution*, gave the station to the Georgia School of Technology so that the students might have the opportunity to study radio engineering. At that time the station acquired its present designation of WGST. The following year the station was leased by the school to the Southern Broadcasting Stations, Inc., and became a member of the Columbia Broadcasting System.

WGST has the distinction of being one of the few stations in the United States which was heard by Rear Admiral Richard E. Byrd at the South Pole on his first expedition in 1929. The studios are on the ninth floor of the Forsyth Building and the station operates 18 hours a day on an assigned frequency of 920 kilocycles, with a power of 5,000 watts during the day and 1,000 watts at night.

WATL was established in 1931 as WJTL by Oglethorpe University, and for years its broadcasts consisted solely of educational programs designed to offer the public complete extra-mural instruction on university subjects. In 1935 the station was purchased by a private organization; the call letters were changed and studios were opened in the Shrine Mosque. These were later moved to the Henry Grady Hotel.

The majority of the station's programs in the past have been electrical transcriptions, although a unique arrangement existed whereby the station broadcast programs originating in the studios of WLW in Cincinnati, WLS in Chicago, and WSM in Nashville. In January of 1940, however, this arrangement with added features was given permanency when the station became a member of the Mutual Broadcasting System.

Although a station of small power (100 watts day and night), WATL is especially popular with Atlanta's younger set because of its recorded programs of dance music on Saturdays. A notable feature of the station is its broadcasts of "news on the hour every hour" during the 18 hours of daily operation. WATL's frequency is 1400 kilocycles.

WAGA, like WSB, is operated by the Atlanta *Journal*, but it is owned by the Liberty Broadcasting Company. The need for its establishment arose from the difficulty with which WSB was faced in attempting to choose between programs emanating from both the Red and Blue networks of the National Broadcasting Company. For eight years WSB had to broadcast an alternation of Red and Blue programs, with the result that many of the better offerings of both schedules were blocked. To overcome this difficulty, station WAGA was opened on August 1, 1937, to carry the Blue network programs, leaving WSB free to transmit the broadcasts scheduled on the Red network.

Known as "Atlanta's Wave of Welcome," WAGA operates on a frequency of 1480 kilocycles with a power of 1,000 watts during the day and 500 watts at night. Its studios are located in the Western Union Building and its transmitter is at Sugar Creek, three miles from the heart of Atlanta.

Atlanta's police department maintains a two-way contact with all of its cruising cars, an installation that has proved indispensable for efficient police service. All messages are broadcast in code which is changed monthly in order to prevent the public from crowding around scenes of fires, accidents, and similar spectacular happenings when private radios pick up the police wave length.

In addition to the city's commercial and police radio stations are the scores of sending and receiving sets operated by wireless fans who maintain nightly contacts with others of their kind throughout the western hemisphere.

Certainly no medium has contributed more in recent years to the education and entertainment of the public, not only in Atlanta but in the entire Southeast, than this city's radio stations. Complete coverage of all local and national events in the fields of news and amusement are assured by the four commercial stations. On occasion, programs of national importance originate in the various Atlanta studios and are broadcast via the networks throughout the country, while the music of various noted orchestras playing engagements in Atlanta hotels is almost a nightly feature of the Eastern radio chains.

Sports and Recreation

O N THE land where Atlanta's tallest buildings now stand, Cherokee tribes once fished, hunted, and played a kind of lacrosse with a flattened wooden bat and a ball made of stuffed deerskin. The first white men's sports on record were introduced early in the 1830's by the militia on muster day at Whitehall Tavern. After the brief drills had been finished, the air crackled with rifle fire as the men carried on their keen trials of marksmanship, contests that sometimes ended with fist fights and bloody noses. More often, however, the occasion ended in a hilarious feast. The winner's prize, a yearling heifer, was roasted and eaten on the spot, washed down with mighty drams from the tavern's whisky barrel.

During these pioneer days, the railroad men and sawmill workers brought not only gambling and card games but some lusty athletic sports. Among the most popular were wrestling, cock-fighting, and turkey or gander pulling in which the prize, a live fowl, was hung by its feet while the mounted contestants galloped very fast beneath it and tried to snatch off the head.

The wives who soon came to the settlement could not immediately abolish these elementary and often brutal games, but they gradually broke down their popularity by substituting more genteel forms of entertainment. An amusing account of a dance in 1844 is given by "Cousin John" Thrasher, contractor for the Monroe Railroad. According to the story, Mrs. Mulligan, the wife of Thrasher's Irish foreman, refused to move into her cabin until a puncheon floor had been installed. When she moved in, this dynamic lady was so delighted by the elegance of her new abode that she immediately invited the workmen and their wives to a ball and insisted that Thrasher lead the first dance with her. Although he stumbled and had the heel of his boot wrenched off by the rough boards, he contrived to hop through the figure, and the ball was a great success—the forerunner of the innumerable brilliant social affairs for which Atlanta has since become famous.

Despite strong opposition from some strict church-goers, dancing quickly became popular. The Atlanta *Intelligencer* of November 18, 1857, notes that "Mr. and Mrs. J.S. Leonard, together with Prof. Duesberry, will open their Dancing Academy today at Hayden's Hall . . . being in every way qualified to teach the most fashionable, plain and fancy dances of the day." As the town grew, the people also began to find entertainment in devices of the kind later offered by amusement parks. A ten-pin bowling alley did a lively business in the 1850's and at about the same time Antonio Maquino advertised his confectionery shop by a large wooden Ferris wheel upon which his customers were given free rides. Housewives brought their cakes and preserved fruits to the fair sponsored by the Southern Central Agricultural Society.

During the early 1860's, Confederate soldiers were put into barracks in the city, and these men, many of them from the farms, often worked off their energy in wrestling and fist fights. They were not left very much to their own devices, however, for the ladies of Atlanta kept them busy with bazaars, *tableaux vivants,* balls, picnics, and barbecues. Despite the bitterness of the Reconstruction Era that lasted into the following decade, Atlanta continued to regale itself with the theater and with many evening parties graced by music and amateur theatricals. The church, from the first an important social factor, now strengthened its hold on the impoverished but undaunted people, and on Sunday afternoons the dusty thoroughfares were gay with young couples carrying on their courtships on the way from Sunday school. Although this period had so many dark aspects, there are records of many gayeties—of the entertainments of the volunteer fire companies, of people visiting the summer resort at Stone Mountain and climbing the great granite mass, of roller skating on an upper floor on Forsyth Street, and of merry parties pedalling their way around the hall of the velocipede rink at Marietta and Forsyth Streets.

The rapid growth of the city brought many newcomers—merchants, insurance salesmen, real estate promoters, soldiers in the Federal army of occupation—who introduced new forms of entertainment. A German society, the Turn Verein, organized an Atlanta unit in 1873. Its members were required to participate in gymnastic exercises twice a week; and on Sundays, with music and beer, they entertained their families with exhibitions of skill at their hall on Broad Street.

By a trade with the Macon & Western Railroad, the city acquired a land plat bounded by Whitehall, Pryor, and Alabama Streets and the Western & Atlantic Railroad, and for about 15 years these grounds were rented out to circuses, medicine shows, auctioneers, and fortune tellers. These fakirs, shouting up their evening trade in the flare of kerosene torches, caused the block to be locally christened Humbug

Square. Here in 1868 there was erected the bush arbor at which crowds were stirred by the oratory of Robert Toombs, Howell Cobb, Benjamin H. Hill, and Raphael J. Moses.

During the 1870's when baseball became popular, the young men of Atlanta made up their own nines with the exception of pitchers and catchers, who usually were engaged from professional ranks. Matches were arranged not according to a regular schedule but simply by challenging the teams of neighboring towns, and no admission charge was made until July 25, 1884, when Atlanta defeated Augusta in the year's first professional game. This was played in what is now Peters Park, where a new diamond had recently been laid out with grandstand and bleachers and enclosed by a high wire fence. It is worthy of note that only about half the spectators were men, for women were beginning to interest themselves more fully in public sports, though still as onlookers rather than participants. In the following year Atlanta won the pennant for the first year of the Southern League, which was composed of cities of Georgia, Alabama, and Tennessee. It was not until some years later that the Atlanta team took its present name of the Atlanta Crackers.

With recovery definitely assured, Atlanta soon developed a graciously worldly society that learned to enjoy more varied recreations. Croquet was a favorite game with the young ladies and gentlemen, and lawn tennis also came in—soon to be developed for clay rather than grass courts because of the abundance of red clay soil in this region. More dancing academies opened and flourished. A few of the city's older citizens remember one of the earlier ones held in Jones Hall on Whitehall Street, where Professor Nichols of Marietta, a tall, gaunt man wearing cloth gaiters with patent leather tips that gleamed as he danced, instructed Atlanta children in the waltz, schottische, mazurka, polka, and Virginia reel. Young people of slightly more advanced years enjoyed the dancing and roller skating at Ponce de Leon Springs. A great pleasure of summer evenings was to board the electric car for a ride past the dark woods and fragrant meadows of the nine-mile belt.

Atlanta society was still of a size to gather comfortably in its own homes, where the entertaining often was sumptuous. The city's most prominent men and women would assemble to honor some debutante who stood to receive them with an armful of red roses held against her white silk and lace. The guests would waltz for a time and then be seated on gilt chairs to eat a buffet supper of cold turkey, chicken salad, beaten biscuit, oysters in molds of ice, and ice cream with cake. A young belle and her escort could drive to a dance unchaperoned in a hired landau if another couple accompanied them. They attended the balls at the Kimball House, the Girls' German Club monthly dances at Concordia Hall, or the Germans of the newly organized Nine O'Clock Club, where they received favors of papier-maché figures, feather fans, and little barrels of candy. New Year's visiting was popular; groups of young men would start walking at opposite ends of the city, stopping for visits as they went and finally meeting at some central home to enjoy eggnog and fruit cake.

The first football game in the State was played at Piedmont Park, February 10, 1892, between the state university and Auburn (Alabama Polytechnic), which won 11-0. Georgia Tech's first football team was organized in the following year by Leonard Wood, who at that time was assigned to duty at Fort McPherson as a lieutenant. Wishing to play the game but having no players, Wood enrolled for two courses at Tech and organized a team there. Tactics consisted principally of line bucking and the famous flying wedge. One of Tech's first football games was in 1893 with St. Albans of Virginia. On this occasion the student body met on the campus and followed the team to Piedmont Park, where the game was to be played. It was on this march that the well-known "wreck Tech" yell was composed.

Beginning about 1895, Atlanta people flocked to Lakewood Park for the harness races, in which horses pulling sulkies were driven very fast around the one-mile track. More than one record was established here during the Grand Circuit races. The horse Single G paced the three fastest beats on record in a regular race. Scott Hudson, a prominent sportsman of Atlanta, is said to hold a world's record, that of being the only man to drive all six winners on the same card in one afternoon.

Golf in Atlanta first appeared very inconspicuously in 1896, when the city's first course, with seven holes, was laid out by the Piedmont Driving Club. No lessons were given by the first professional, Jamie Litsner, whose principal duties were the supervision of caddies and the repairing of golf sticks. The game soon attracted more attention, however, and by 1906 the Atlanta Athletic Club had provided a better course. The first professional was Alec Smith, the second was Jimmy Maiden, and the third was his brother Stewart Maiden, who became internationally famous as Bobby Jones' first coach. Soon other clubs were providing facilities, but the game had not attained even a small part of its present popularity. In 1911, when Bobby Jones at the age of nine won the city Junior Championship Cup, only a comparatively small proportion of the population was interested.

Atlanta citizens of the early twentieth century found their recreation in tennis and baseball, in hunting and fishing in the nearby woods, in swimming at the indoor natatorium on Capitol Square, and in watching the dazzling feats of Bobby Walthour, Atlanta's famous bicycle

racer. Widespread public interest in automobiles was first aroused by
a show in 1909, and soon large crowds were watching races on the
old Hapeville oval, a two-mile dirt track. The gayer social set gave
more sophisticated entertainments—dances, whist and bridge parties,
Saturday night poker games, and opulent Sunday morning breakfasts
with champagne cocktails and Potomac herring roe.

A system of integrated parks and playgrounds was inaugurated
in 1905. Little supervision of recreation was given at first, but in
1907 four supervised playgrounds for children were set up by the
Associated Charities of Atlanta under the direction of Joseph Logan.
Funds for this service were included in the budget of the charities for
several years until this function was absorbed in the general jurisdiction of the city park authorities. With the growth of the park system,
recreation facilities also expanded to include more attractions for both
children and adults. For a number of years golf links, tennis courts,
baseball diamonds, and swimming pools have been provided under
municipal auspices.

During the war period of 1917-18, Atlanta streets once again were
thronged with soldiers, this time the men in khaki who were in training at Camp Gordon and Fort McPherson. Like the Confederates
in the 1860's these men were given the best hospitality the citizens
could afford, and during their hours of leave they went to many dances
and theatrical entertainments. Motion pictures were shown at the
municipal auditorium on Sunday afternoons; after the show the soldiers
uproariously sang such favorites as "Over There" and "K-k-k-katy."
At the cantonment the YMCA took charge of sports, which included
boxing, wrestling, football, baseball, and various relay contests and
races. Often the young soldiers were brought to town to swim in the
indoor YMCA pool.

The war over, Atlanta people flung themselves wholeheartedly into
recreations of every sort, particularly the lavish and showy spectator
sports. Football games became great events, especially after Georgia
Tech and the University of Georgia had resumed their severed athletic
relations in 1925. Atlanta became the scene of the regularly scheduled
automobile races approved by the American Automobile Association.
These contests were held on the Pace's Ferry Track, laid out in 1929,
which was regarded as the fastest half-mile oval in the country.

The post-war years brought prominence to many Atlanta golfers.
Alexa Stirling won the women's national championship in 1916, 1919,
and 1920. Bobby Jones, after years of taking lesser awards, in 1930
made his "grand slam" capture of the four highest golf trophies—
the American Amateur, American Open, British Amateur, and British
Open—regarded as one of the greatest feats in sports history. Charlie
Yates was a member of the Walker Cup Team in 1936 and again in

1938, the year in which he won the British Amateur Tournament. Also in 1938 Howard Wheeler was winner of the Negro national golf championship. Frequently Atlanta golfers have held the State championship and been contenders in national meets.

Atlanta athletes have also won honors in the swimming pool, on the tennis court, and in the boxing ring. In 1932 Louisa Robert was national junior backstroke swimming champion. Bryan ("Bitsy") Grant, whose small stature caused him to be known as "the mighty atom of tennis," has carried off the championship in an imposing list of tournaments, including the United States Clay Court Championship in 1930, 1934, and 1935. Third place was accorded him in the national ratings in 1936, and the following year he was a member of the Davis Cup Team. Among the Negroes famous in sports are "Tiger" Flowers, who won the world's middle-weight championship in 1926, and Ralph Harold Metcalf, who established new track records in the Olympic Games of 1932, 1933, and 1936.

The depression of the 1930's did not permanently curtail attendance at large athletic tournaments; indeed, in many instances, greater crowds than ever were attracted. By putting on more spectacular shows with bands in gay uniforms and high-stepping drum majors, the high schools have greatly increased attendance at their football games. The popularity of baseball also has increased enormously since floodlights have been installed on the field of Ponce de Leon Park so that the Atlanta Crackers and their opponents are now enabled to play night games. Leisure for greatly increased numbers of people has created a new spectator public which is interested in a much broader variety of sports than were the crowds of the post-war boom era.

But a still more significant trend has been shown in the greater numbers who take part in recreation not as onlookers but as participants. Various industrial organizations support baseball and basketball teams for their workers. A more widespread general interest in such activities has been furthered by the co-operation of municipal agencies and the Work Projects Administration. For supervised recreation and playground equipment, the city contributes an average of $330 a month and the Work Projects Administration an average of $6,000 a month, of which approximately half covers Fulton County activity. In 1939 the city created a distinct branch of the Parks Department known as the Recreation Division, with funds allotted under the annual municipal budget to administer Atlanta's supervised playgrounds for children and a system of athletic leagues with regularly scheduled games. Of these 33 playgrounds, 8 are exclusively for the use of Negroes. During 1939 public basketball facilities were used by about 700 players, while 1,200 men and women team members played softball on public diamonds in leagues supervised by the Greater Atlanta Softball Association. More than 1,000 boys under 16 years old played baseball on the supervised sandlot diamonds of the city. The Recreation Division, during this year, presented numerous dramatic and musical performances including an amateur production of the Gilbert and Sullivan operetta *Pinafore* with a cast of 40 children and 20 adult singers.

Large crowds watch football at Grant Field of Georgia Tech and at Hermance Stadium of Oglethorpe University; boxing, wrestling, and basketball at Ponce de Leon Park; and Sunday afternoon polo matches at Fort McPherson. The Golden Gloves Boxing Tournament, conducted by the Atlanta *Journal,* also draws a large attendance. The city has 88 municipal tennis courts and many private ones, 10 private golf courses and 5 municipal links (4 nine-hole and 1 eighteen-hole), six municipal swimming pools (5 for white and 1 for Negroes), 12 or more private or club pools, and many gymnasiums and basketball courts. There are 83 parks comprising almost 1,600 acres. Of these Lakewood (leased to the Southeastern Fair Association) is the largest with 370.9 acres, Piedmont Park second with 185 acres, and Grant Park third with 144 acres. There is good provision for bowling, ping-pong, roller skating, badminton, riding, and numerous other sports.

Atlanta, a busy and crowded commercial city, is only beginning to utilize its many natural advantages for recreation. These advantages include well-wooded rolling lands, abundant water resources, and a mild yet invigorating climate that permits outdoor sports the year around. With such natural facilities combined with many prosperous and energetic citizens, the community is well able not only to maintain but to enlarge the scope of such activities. Atlanta has no pretensions to being a resort town, but in the natural course of its development it is learning to concentrate on the recreational phases that both attract tourists and add to the well-being of permanent residents.

Architecture

ATLANTA is renowned for the taste and sumptuousness of its residences in their green setting of trees, shrubbery, and sweeping hills. The audacious variety of its architecture sets it apart from older cities of the South. Here are no quiet streets of columns and magnolias—although both of these are seen sometimes—but humming thoroughfares where Gothic, Renaissance, Tudor, Romanesque, Southern Colonial, and modern dwellings are blended with harmony and vivacity.

Yet this notable architecture has developed from an origin of pioneer crudeness within only a century. Before the city was founded, the only substantial building in the vicinity was Whitehall Tavern, erected early in the 1830's. When John Thrasher, contractor for the Monroe Railroad, came in 1839 to the site of the terminus, the only dwelling he found was a rude structure of logs. Similar dwellings were quickly erected for the railroad workmen, huts of two rooms with sometimes a lean-to added. These huts were made of puncheons, logs roughly sawed in half, with the smooth side turned in and the cracks daubed with mud. At first the floors were only of earth, but, as soon as the railroad workmen began to bring their families, puncheon floors were installed.

The first builders, uncertain of the future for their little community, erected no substantial buildings until the City of Atlanta had been incorporated on December 29, 1847. Two months before that date Dr. William N. White, who had come from New York to teach school, noted: ". . . the woods around are full of shanties, and the merchants live in them until they can find time to build." He further added: "Atlanta so far has not a good house in the place—except the hotel."

After the city was incorporated, however, conveniences and even decorative details were not long in appearing. The Greek Revival had passed from its pure beginnings into an era of departure from the classic perfection of its friezes, cornices, and columns. Some such details there were in early Atlanta houses, but they were seldom of the finest. In near-by Roswell, Barrington Hall, Bulloch Hall, and Mimosa Hall showed the fine simplicity of this classical influence; Atlanta was built too late to receive it. By the beginning of the 1850's the first unpainted two-room huts were being replaced by geometrically trim white plank dwellings with two rooms on each side of a hallway, sometimes with a stairway leading to a second story. Fireplaces were usually set flush with the inner walls, and the brick chimneys towered above each end of the peaked shingled roofs. The Huff House, built 1854-5, is one of the few surviving buildings of this period.

Builders began to use brick also in the main body, frequently mortising the outer walls with lime and the inner ones with mud. In 1852 Patrick Lynch, an Irish stone mason, erected on Gilmer Street Atlanta's first brick house. A fine example of brick construction during this period was the compact two-story city hall and courthouse erected in 1855. Dignity and strength were implicit in the unpretentious lines of this edifice, with its central cupola, balconied Doric entrances, and high windows with plain lintels and louvered green shutters. The red brick of the courthouse was matched in the posts of the encircling fence of white wooden palings. Also erected during this period were the Central Presbyterian and First Baptist churches, substantial brick structures with wooden spires that stood west of the courthouse. A still more striking achievement of the fifties was the red-brick depot, one of the first in which the train could be taken under the shed.

Other buildings of the late ante-bellum period were constructed of rock from the near-by granite quarries, a novel example being the Calico House built by Marcus Bell in 1860 and later used by General Sherman as his first headquarters during his occupation of the city. The rock surface was covered with plaster, which was painted gayly in blue, red, and yellow in imitation of the marbling process used inside book covers. Most of the domestic architecture, however, whether the material was wood, brick, or stone, followed more academic designs. The variety among Atlanta residences a year or so before Sherman destroyed them is shown in Margaret Mitchell's *Gone With The Wind*: "Scarlett picked them out as old friends, the Leyden House, dignified and stately; the Bonnells', with little white columns and green blinds; the close-lipped red brick Georgian home of the McLure family, behind its low boxwood hedges."

During the fighting around Atlanta most of the houses were shattered by exploding shells or burned by Federal soldiers. After peace was declared the citizens, their cash rendered worthless, had to rebuild and repair largely by their own labor. Sometimes, when only the four walls of a dwelling were standing, shelter would be provided by merely laying on a roof. Some formerly fine residences presented a tragic appearance with their clapboards patched with roughly dressed lumber, and it was some years before the survivors of the siege had sufficient money to improve their habitations.

But at this time history changed the course of Atlanta's architectural development. After the war the bustling railroad city was crowded with Northern soldiers, merchants, and speculators, many with ample cash to build for themselves. The services of architects were demanded, and William H. Parkins, probably Atlanta's first practicing architect, came to the city early in 1868, soon followed by Calvin Fay, who had lived here before the war but had not practiced. Both these men and others now opened offices. In 1869 Parkins designed the brick Gothic Church of the Immaculate Conception, which still serves an active Roman Catholic congregation.

Building operations, vitalized by capital from outside, began to push out in all directions and to develop new sections out of the surrounding forest and pasture lands. The features of the rebuilt city were being changed by a type of architecture that was the antithesis of the old. Even as early as 1868, the new four-story building that was begun as Kimball's Opera House and later used as the capitol, despite the classical work on its ground floor exterior, presaged the coming romantic trend in its cupola and mansard roof. Sometimes the two styles were combined incongruously, and Corinthian columns stood in grotesque juxtaposition to scrollwork and towers. In Atlanta as elsewhere the seventies and eighties constituted a period of reaction against the simplicity of the Greek Revival, so that both commercial and domestic architecture took on the characteristics of what has since been christened the "gingerbread era"—balustrades, scrollsaw banisters, snuffbox turrets, broken roof lines, leaded glass windows. During the last two decades of the century the Romanesque Revival brought circular windows, clustered pillars, sweeping arches, and heavy asymmetrical masses.

Northward out Peachtree Street spread miles of this fanciful decoration executed in wood or brick or stone, but the houses it adorned, despite some overcrowding of details, often presented a handsome appearance with their ivy and softening shrubbery. The stern colors of stone and iron made a fine background for the vital green of the grass lawns that were supplanting the bare yards and tangled gardens of the sixties. Some of the older Peachtree residences still standing are excellent examples of this period, such as the brick and brownstone Silvey-Speer House and the stone houses of Mrs. Samuel M. Inman, Sr., and A.G. Rhodes (now Rhodes Memorial Hall). The public edifices of the time include the Kimball House, the Atlanta *Constitution* Building, and Sacred Heart Church.

From the turn of the century to the World War, Atlanta architecture was greatly affected by the rise of speculative builders, who bought entire blocks, divided them into lots, and erected small dwellings. The architecture of these houses was often a conglomerate, for the builders sought to combine on a small scale the characteristics they deemed most arresting in more expensive dwellings. Sometimes utility was lost in adaptation to a new material. The broad Romanesque arch, for example, had been a structural unit of masonry, but in wood it became a mere decorative detail. The new bungalows, long and low, were admirably suited to their narrow city lots; but later examples were despoiled of the early attractive simplicity by the crowded impression of turrets and other "gingerbread" features. A little dignity was gained when these features were applied to two-story dwellings, but the effect generally was not pleasing. Innumerable houses of this time may still be seen along Juniper Street, Piedmont Avenue, and many other sections that developed near the beginning of the twentieth century. The most attractive section that developed during this time was Ansley Park, with its streets running in intricate circles. Although few of the Ansley Park dwellings are of distinguished style, their builders avoided the worst decorative offenses, and the impression as a whole is agreeable.

Some of the churches were well executed, especially the simpler modernized Gothic ones such as All Saints' and St. Luke's. Likewise there was good ornamentation in some early skyscrapers. The Candler Building, the first of these in Atlanta, is somewhat overburdened with classical decorations, but later office buildings showed a more discriminating simplicity. The Healey Building is a good example of "business Gothic" architecture, and the old post office shows the good taste of the architect in adapting the Italian Renaissance style to commercial purposes. From the first days of its tall buildings, the Atlanta downtown section has presented difficulties to architects because of the irregular shape of its lots; but these lots have been utilized with increasing ingenuity.

In 1915, when the first buildings of the new Emory University were erected, the material and style were considered daringly experimental. In contrast to the nondescript buildings characteristic of older colleges in this region, the Emory structures are of pink Georgia marble in Italian Renaissance style modernized to plane surfaces and simple lines. In their setting of pines and shrubbery these buildings now stand as an appropriate as well as a striking example of school architecture.

After the first World War the real estate boom developed new residential areas, where the more expensive homes began to show the harmony of building and landscaping for which Atlanta is known.

Crowning the boldly curved lawns of the Druid Hills and Pace's Ferry sections arose houses as dissimilar as they were handsome; but, although Gothic, Cotswold, Tudor, neoclassic, and all phases of the Renaissance and Colonial styles followed one another indiscriminately, they usually were set far enough apart to avoid architectural disharmony. No single type was noticeably predominant. The Spanish influence that became nationally popular with the Florida boom was generally thought too austere for Atlanta's irregular landscape and softly massed shrubbery; but a few good examples, such as the Whitehead-Riley House and the Rogers-Haverty House, remain to show this trend. Types still rare in Atlanta are exemplified in such structures as the J.B. Horne House, which is Tudor executed in white brick with Cotswold cottage inspiration showing in the sharp roof lines and casement windows; and the Norman farmhouse Roper-Riley House, with its red-tile roof .and half-timbered white brick facade. A type much more popular during the 1920's was the green-shuttered white frame house of balanced masses, with Colonial influence showing in its slanting roof and fan-lighted doorway. This style was somewhat standardized for less expensive dwellings, but most of them present an attractive if not striking appearance.

One of the strongest influences of the war and post-war eras was brought by the architect Neel Reid, whose previous studies abroad found expression in numerous houses of fine fidelity to European classical patterns. Reid's execution was not limited to any particular style, but his talent was shown most frequently in houses of Renaissance or Georgian inspiration. Among the distinguished examples of his work are the Case-Martin House, a limestone edifice of eighteenth-century classical style with Renaissance details, the front facing on a cobbled courtyard and a limestone wall; the Andrew Calhoun House, of Italian baroque in sunburned stucco with pale green shutters; the Georgian white stucco Edward Inman House, flanked by tall Egyptian obelisks; and the gray stucco Cooper-Brooks House of Italian Renaissance style. Reid was only in his prime at the time of his death in 1926, but he had lived long enough to inspire other talented architects who have insisted on purity of detail in their work.

The most important trend of the 1930's has been the stronger affirmation of good taste in smaller houses, several of which have received national notice. A good example is the Harold Bunger House in Decatur, of French Provincial design executed in red brick with a mansard roof and long green shutters. The great improvement in the smaller dwellings is due in part to the rise of functionalism with its greater simplicity and utility and in part to the long-term loans of the Federal Housing Administration and the strict architectural requirements attendant on such loans. Atlanta has only recently become acquainted with what is known as "modernistic" architecture in its dwelling houses, and this influence is still negligible.

One of Atlanta's many paradoxes is that its Southern Colonial, or Greek Revival, architecture did not come in the mid-nineteenth century, as it came to other Southern cities, but in the 1930's as a new and modified second revival. The old form of interior planning has been altered to suit modern conditions, but many classical decorations are being employed with grace and distinction. There are no examples of the pure Greek temple type, but many of the finer new houses show columns, chaste friezes, and well-proportioned porticoes. Among the best examples of new houses showing the later classical influence are the Hal Hentz, Robert Alston, and Hugh Nunnally houses.

Atlanta contains both good and bad examples of modern design in stores, office buildings, and industrial plants. The two leading department stores are admirably arranged for commercial purposes, and their unadorned surfaces—Rich's of brick and limestone and Davison's of red brick—are agreeable and restful to the eye. The newest skyscrapers also have been modeled on the plan of a shaft with unbroken lines; and the William-Oliver Building and Rhodes-Haverty Building, with their long lines and simple fenestration, exemplify the modern trend away from cornices, consoles, and virtually all exterior decorations not strictly necessary to functional purposes. The new Coca-Cola bottling plant, a broad low building of brick and limestone with clear glass windows, also combines functionalism with attractive, unpretentious decorative features. Several large slum areas in various parts of the city have been replaced by the long low brick or stucco buildings of Federal Housing projects.

An article by Marguerite Steedman in the Atlanta *Journal,* December 15, 1935, presents an acute observation on modern downtown Atlanta: "The ground floors of many buildings . . . have been altered repeatedly for the benefit of progress or a new tenant. But the upper stories often remain as our mothers and grandmothers knew them . . . one glances up, past modern plate glass and chromium, to discover overhead windows still shadowed by sculptured arches or old signs and dates which form integral parts of the walls themselves and so have escaped removal. Dates running from 1875 to 1890 are often found, half hidden in the shadow of a chimney or a steep, fancifully plastered gable . . . many Atlanta buildings still boast their chimneys, relics of the day when every office had its small coal grate or air-tight stove. . . . One structure, at the corner of Alabama and Broad Streets, has second story windows which are shadowed by thick overhanging 'eyebrows' of molded terra cotta, wrought into wreaths of fruit and flowers."

Atlanta's irregular downtown pattern, with its slanting, narrow

streets, makes congestion inevitable in this area. Its best office buildings are not seen to best advantage, for they frequently are obstructed
by other edifices. The residential sections, however, are justly noted
for their beauty. The antiquarian in his journey over the South may
miss the flavor of time in Atlanta architecture, but he will find contrast, beauty, and vitality.

IN 1847, the year in which Atlanta was incorporated, there appeared in the columns of the *Southern Miscellany and Upper Georgia Whig* an advertisement of Major Wyllys Buell, portrait painter. The editor recommends him and urges readers to have likenesses made of wives, sweethearts, and children. This notice, which is among the earliest records concerning art in Atlanta, indicates that there was at least a small measure of artistic appreciation in the community even when it was little more than a frontier settlement. It seems that Buell did not let art interfere with political affairs, however, for he became mayor of the city in 1850, and nothing further is found about him as a portrait painter.

Indeed, the bustling, practical citizens of Atlanta were working too hard for a living to support an artist group. Probably they shared the conviction of most of the United States that a little elegant painting and embroidery were desirable for young ladies but that painting pictures was no job for a virile young man. Boys were seldom urged to scribble or strum or paint. Yet there are numerous indications that the arts had their admirers, as is shown not only in the advertisements of "photographs, ambrotypes, and oil paintings" that continued to appear in the newspapers but in the practical measures that occasionally were taken to stir appreciation and encourage talent. In 1850, at the fifth annual fair presented by the Southern Central Agricultural Society, there were "five beautiful oil paintings by Orgali, an Italian," lent by an Atlanta citizen, while two Atlanta ladies were commended for their own paintings as follows: "By Mrs. V. Foster . . . landscape, horses, domestic animals, & c.—executed in India ink. An elaborate and beautiful picture. Premium $3. Also two pieces of Flowers and Fruits. . . . By Miss Guthrie . . . two Monochromatic Drawings. Landscape, Domestic animals, & c—well executed. Honor."

The *Intelligencer* even ran an article in 1858 minutely describing the paintings on the splendid new fire engine of Atlanta Fire Company No. 1. One of these pictures showed the classic race of the redoubtable huntress Atalanta and her suitor Meilanion, who won both the race and the huntress by casting golden apples before her, and "the paintings are all very spirited, and finished most exquisitely, doing credit to the genius of the artist, M.J. Shreeves, of Philadelphia."

During the 1860's the creative impulse sometimes seemed almost extinguished as the civilians of Atlanta, with the rest of the Confederacy, strained every effort to the breaking point. With the blockade runners loading their cargoes with food, medicines, and—most strangely —fashionable ball gowns, artists' materials were scarce. Nevertheless, the women's defiant gayety was shown in the silk flags they made to float, proud in their fringed gold and scarlet, above the lines of fighting regiments. Atlanta women also directed their instinct for design into the making of screens, fans, feather-and-beeswax flowers, and all sorts of embroidered articles that were sold at bazaars to aid the Confederate cause. When the supply of thread failed, human hair was used to execute the skillful embroidery stitches.

The harsh days of Reconstruction did nothing to awaken the impulse. In January 1869, an *Intelligencer* reporter "visited two art galleries in the city . . . and saw some nice pictures and excellent likenesses. We regret that it is true . . . that in a great measure the arts are looked upon as useless or supernumerary." The people had little money to buy pictures, although it is remembered that one Atlanta citizen, who later amassed great wealth, earned a little cash by peddling the popular Currier and Ives prints of the American scene. From the early 1870's on, the number of professional artists in Atlanta increased steadily. C.W. Motes set up a studio, where he took photographs, instructed in miniature painting, and entertained his friends by exhibiting his life sketches and paintings done while he was on the march with Confederate forces. Among his visitors was Horace Bradley, later to attain some celebrity as a painter and still remembered by a few old citizens as having demonstrated his youthful talents by painting designs on the belts, caps, and bats of a baseball club to which he belonged.

When Atlanta began to work back toward a normal prosperity, art became popular and the number of instructors rapidly grew. In 1882 the Art Loan Exposition, under the auspices of the Young Men's Library Association, brought to the city a large collection of paintings from all sections of the United States. So great was public interest that excursion trains were run from several Georgia towns in this region. The *Constitution* notes: " 'The Deliverance' by E.H. Blashfield, of Boston, is a large canvas and occupies a central position, around which cluster contributions from . . . other distinguished artists. Each picture is full of refined interest, and will delight the eyes of all who see them. . . . Mr. J. Carroll Beckwith sends his lovely ideal face of 'Azalia', which is beautiful in flesh color and exquisite drawing. . . . Mr. W.E. Herring, of this city, has kindly loaned 'Midsummer Night's Dream' by Ang. Riedel . . . this picture is valued at $10,000, and is one of unusual appearance, it being a little Cupid gracefully reposing upon a cloud and surmounted by three owls. . . . In the upper portion of the picture burns a beautiful flame, perfectly painted, which lights the figures dimly. The lights and shadows are perfectly managed and" —one may well believe!—"produces a wonderful effect."

During these years there were not many instructors in Atlanta who taught their pupils to paint from the living model. Usually the students copied from calendars and other pictures or at most did still-life oil or water color paintings from arranged fruits and flowers. Miniature painting was made so popular by the young ladies of Atlanta that often photographers employed painters to do this work, usually from photographs. Such miniatures of famous people are on permanent exhibition in the Department of Archives and History in Rhodes Memorial Hall.

Also on display at Rhodes Memorial Hall, as well as at the State capitol, are numerous portraits of Georgia statesmen produced by Atlanta artists who were popular during the last two decades of the century. Some of these canvases show an honest realism; others have a pompous rigidity, as though the clothes had been painted in first and the face inserted to order afterward. In at least one instance boldness and influence proved to be acceptable substitutes for talent: anecdotes are told of a woman who became locally known as a portrait painter by soliciting commissions from prominent citizens, hiring hack workers to copy the portraits from photographs, and signing her name to the portraits before they were delivered. This same lady also earned her living as a teacher, although her pupils state that after distributing materials she set them to work on elaborate lamp shades trimmed with roses and beehives without ever imparting a word of instruction. A far greater number, however, earned their way by honest work. Some of these, such as Adelaide C. Everhart, are still popular painters. Lucy May Stanton, who painted in Atlanta for a time, later won the medal of honor at the Pennsylvania Society of Miniature Painters Exhibition for her miniature of Joel Chandler Harris.

Sculpture during these years was for the most part rather elementary and imitative. Stonecutters produced much ornamental work in marble or granite in tombstones and in various memorial shafts and statuary. Oakland Cemetery has a striking example in T.M. Brady's Lion of Atlanta inspired by the famous Lion of Lucerne and erected in 1894 by the Atlanta Ladies Memorial Association to honor the unknown

Confederate dead. Bronze or marble busts of notable men constituted another popular form of art. Orion Frazee, a native of New York who came to Atlanta in 1885 and became well known both as a painter and sculptor, executed death masks of Jefferson Davis, Robert Toombs, Henry W. Grady, and other Southern celebrities. In the opening years of the twentieth century a Swedish sculptor named Ocherberg, who lived for a time in the city, carved numerous busts, including one of Joel Chandler Harris, upon which the famous writer is said to have placed his hat when he entered the house.

During the 1880's William Lycett came to Atlanta and opened an art school on Whitehall Street, where he and his wife gave lessons in oils and water colors and in china painting. The painting of plates and dishes was for years a popular pastime with Atlanta housewives, and examples of their white-and-gold handiwork still may be seen in many a cupboard and china closet.

An important step in the development of art in the city was taken when the Atlanta Art Association was chartered in 1905. This organization conducted an art school, gave funds for traveling exhibits, offered prizes, and arranged for lectures by nationally known artists. Meetings were held in bank offices and in various homes, while displays were set up in empty stores. In 1924, with the assistance of the Chamber of Commerce and of a member of the Art Association, J.J. Haverty, this organization secured its first exhibition of note from the Grand Central Galleries of New York. It was not until 1926, when Mrs. Joseph Madison High presented her home to be used as a museum, that the association acquired permanent quarters. A school to teach both fine and commercial art was opened immediately. In the following year a loan exhibit from Atlanta homes was sponsored by the association, and for the first time the public saw how many works of famous artists were in the city. Romney, Gainsborough, John Opie, Ralph Blakelock, Franz Von Lenbeck, Thomas Sully, Phillip Wouverman, George Inness, Ribera, Le Sidoner, Harpignies, David Tenier, and Jules Du Pre were among the artists represented. Since then loan exhibitions from various galleries have been arranged frequently at the High Museum by the director, Lewis Skidmore.

A strong influence on Atlanta art is exercised by several instructors, among the most important of whom are Ben E. Shute and Robert S. Rogers of the High Museum School of Art. Talented and progressive, Shute and Rogers have retained flexibility of expression by constant experimentation with fresh techniques, so that their work is as varied as it is dextrous. Ralph Britt, head of the Britt School of Art, is known not only for the soundness of his own craftsmanship but for his teaching. Maurice Seigler, instructor of drawing in the architecture department of the Georgia School of Technology, is known as a fresco worker, a portrait painter, and an outstanding draftsman of the human body. Although the prevalent green and purple tones are the most vivid feature of his paintings, even his work in oils is notable for the firm draftsmanship beneath the paint. Private individuals also have had vital influence. George Ramey, an architect and a gifted painter, has rendered invaluable service to art circles by the exhibitions which he has periodically arranged at the Carnegie Library.

One of Atlanta's best portrait painters is Marjorie Conant Bush-Brown, who works in an excellent traditional technique with modern expression. By careful under-painting, Mrs. Bush-Brown succeeds in rendering flesh tones of a glistening transparency, especially in her Negro studies, and her portraits are notable for their backgrounds which are boldly colorful yet kept subordinate to the subject. Elizabeth Paxton Oliver, too, has won honors for her Negro portraits, as well as for her animated and realistic bird paintings.

The favors of the public are well distributed among both the artists of longer standing and the newer ones. Charles F. Naegele has worked for many years at his portrait painting and has gathered a large following. Kate Edwards has long enjoyed widespread popularity for her portraits in oils; she has also received enthusiastic praise for her excellent drawings in white point. One of the most celebrated of the younger painters is Claud J. Herndon, who has excellent taste and a fine sense of decorative values in his portraits. Within the bounds of the strictly decorative, Athos Menaboni is eminent. Working on plaster, glass, or canvas to execute his brilliant murals, he intentionally keeps his figures flat, but they are vital because of their colors and the admirable arrangement of the patterns. Menaboni's bird paintings, which combine the delicate detail characteristic of Japanese work with a strongly anatomical quality, are in frequent demand for exhibitions by nationally known organizations.

Other examples of interesting work recently produced by Atlanta artists are Kitty Butner's colorful portraits, Wilbur G. Kurtz' illustrations of historic episodes, Cornelia Cunningham's pencil sketches, Catherine Nunnally's sensitively realized yet substantially executed figures, Mrs. A. Farnsworth Drew's striking murals and pleasing seascapes, Leroy Jackson's well composed water colors, Julian Binford's portraits and landscapes, and Lamar Baker's lithographs that are as widely celebrated for their strong social recognitions as for their finely patterned technique. Strongly contrasting work has been done by a talented daughter and mother. The faces in Mary E. Hutchinson's portraits have strength and dimension while retaining a decorative character almost equal to that of formal designs in a frieze. Her mother, Minnie Belle Hutchinson, paints abstractions with a gayly satiric realization, evoking an ironical emphasis by her seemingly innocent use of clear primary colors.

In Negro art Hale Woodruff is the most prominent instructor as well as one of the most original and powerful craftsmen. Painting in an uncompromisingly modern technique with a lavish use of strong raw colors, Woodruff has done memorable work in depicting the peasantry of Mexico and of his own people. His pupil Robert Neal has also been praised for the rhythm and gayety of his work even when he selects squalid backgrounds to render.

The statuary and monumental work of Fritz Zimmer, Steffen Thomas, and Joseph Klein have received wide notice, as have the sympathetic plastic studies of Mrs. Edward Donnelly. Outstanding in sculpture is Julian Harris, who in his work returns to the archaic principle of treating sculpture not dramatically but as an art of masses and their relation. Harris has made an important contribution to Atlanta art by his insistence on the close association between architecture and sculpture, and his bas-relief panels on the new State Office Building are indicative of this renascence.

Under the stimulus of growing public interest, Atlanta painters in recent years have been aroused to performances that express their own individual conceptions. The native characteristics of the State have been more zestfully realized in both landscape painting and portraiture, and the result has been productions that are more supple, informal, and audacious. Not only has new subject matter been discovered but newer techniques have been applied to the portrayal of old scenes with vigor and vivacity. Atlanta art is like a growing plant, strong, vital, and branching off in many directions.

The Arts

JULIAN HARRIS, ATLANTA SCULPTOR, AT WORK

"KATIE LOU," BY BEN SHUTE

"MAGNOLIAS AND MUSHROOMS," BY ROBERT S. ROGERS

"THE BREAKFAST," BY ROBERT S. ROGERS

ATLANTA THEATER GUILD PRODUCTION OF "THE BARKER"

GEORGIA TECH AND AGNES SCOTT STUDENTS IN GILBERT AND SULLIVAN'S
"H. M. S. PINAFORE"

"OUR TOWN," PRODUCED BY ATLANTA UNIVERSITY SUMMER THEATER

BIG BETHEL CHOIR

EMORY UNIVERSITY GLEE CLUB

HARMONY CLASS AT THE GEORGIA CONSERVATORY OF MUSIC

STATUE OF GENERAL JOHN B. GORDON ON THE STATE CAPITOL LAWN

CLASS AT THE HIGH MUSEUM SCHOOL OF ART

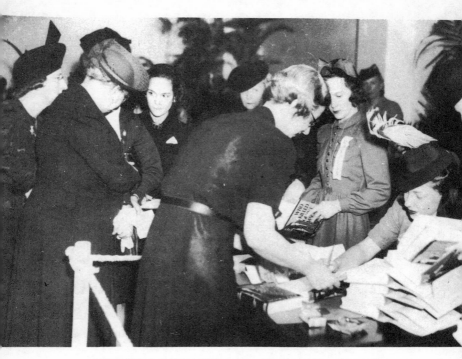

LITERARY AUTOGRAPHING TEA AT DEPARTMENT STORE

THE WREN'S NEST, HOME OF JOEL CHANDLER HARRIS

Almost the first music in the Atlanta vicinity came from the lusty throats of the railroad construction men in such simple airs as, "Joe, Crack Corn." Their only accompaniments were bird cries and the thud of axes, but when they went home in the evenings they sometimes twanged mouth organs or scraped fiddles. A little later, when wives and daughters came, these same fiddles were used for square dances. On Sundays the woods rang with old favorite hymns of Charles Wesley and others and with the Negro slaves' spirituals that presented a mixture of biblical and African imagery. Soon the musical and dramatic ingenuity of the people was aroused by local incidents—a log-rolling, a feud, or a romance—to the making of ballads, new verses being constantly added by different groups. Ballad making was popular until the War between the States brought a new collection of martial and sentimental songs, and even at present ballad singing is a regular feature of the annual fiddlers' convention at the city auditorium.

The settlers, though busy from daybreak to dark with their railroads, stores, and sawmills, were ambitious that their children should have better cultural opportunities. In 1857, ten years after the incorporation of the city, Mrs. J.A. Wright opened a school for young ladies where music was taught, and in the same year Carl F. Barth held music classes, and the firm of Barth and Nicolai sold pianos and stringed instruments. Instruction was principally for the girls of a family; a boy who played the piano had to be adept with fists as well as fingers if he escaped the charge of effeminacy. Vocalizing was more permissible, and many a manly baritone joined the sopranos in the evenings to render the sad love songs of the fifties.

By 1860 the Atlanta Amateurs, a mixed choral organization, was appearing before large audiences. Soon after the war broke out, this group was not only performing in its own city but, with the aid of free transportation offered by the Atlanta & West Point Railroad, was making trips to other Southern towns in order to raise funds for the Confederacy. Atlanta ladies, proud in Georgia homespun, were escorted by ragged soldiers home on leave to the old Athenaeum to hear these singers begin with the "Southern Marseillaise," continue with "Banks of the Blue Mozelle," "Cottage by the Sea," and other sweet songs, and wind up with the broadly satirical ditty on Abraham Lincoln, "Root, Hog, or Die." Sometimes benefits were given for a specific fighting force such as Captain (later General) John B. Gordon's "Raccoon Roughs." When General John M. Morgan escaped from his Union captors and came to the city, the Atlanta Amateurs gave him two benefits that netted him $250.

One of the most popular musical performers of the sixties was the pianist Blind Tom from Columbus, Georgia. Described as the "most amazing wonder of the age" and "a second Beethoven," Tom gave several concerts annually at the Athenaeum. Although virtually an idiot and knowing nothing of notes, he had amazing imitative powers and was able to reproduce perfectly any composition, however complex, which was played within his hearing. The most brilliant of his feats was the rendition of three compositions simultaneously.

After the war vocal music continued to be popular, but the new martial airs created a demand for brass bands. Stringed music also began to find a larger place—mandolin and guitar clubs and lady harpists delighted their audiences. When the impoverished citizens began to make enough money to refurnish their parlors, more of them began to include the piano as a necessary fixture. Atlanta music was not silenced even during the most humiliating days of Reconstruction and Northern military rule. Choral concerts were given at the Bell-Johnson Hall on Mitchell Street, and the Fulton Brass and String Band made the street crowds tap their feet in rhythm. In 1869 Will F. Clark is advertised as "giving instructions on the violin, guitar, harp, piano, and various other instruments." Clark, leader of the Gate City Silver Band, provided music for "parades, balls, private parties, serenades, etc., at reasonable rates."

Some of Atlanta's finest religious music during the 1870's was presented by the choir of old St. Philip's Episcopal Church, directed by Ludwig Harmsen, an accomplished Scandinavian pianist who had been in the city during the war. Old directories reveal that this decade brought many music teachers. In 1872 the city's first white orchestra was brought by Ferdinand Wurm, a man of remarkable linguistic and musical attainments, who had formerly taught at the university in Munich. Professor Wurm, who had taught Sidney Lanier to play the flute, performed on almost all instruments. His orchestra, the original members of which were the professor and his four sons, consisted of a first violin, second violin, bass violin, clarinet, and cornet. It was later enlarged, but for some years, in accordance with general musical custom, there was no piano. For more than 40 years Wurm's Orchestra played at weddings and receptions and on all kinds of public occasions. Sunday concerts were given in the dining room of the fashionable Kimball House, but only sacred music was played.

During this decade musical organizations were formed under the names of famous composers. The first of these, the Beethoven Society, met on the third floor of the old Georgia Railroad Depot at the foot of Alabama Street. Here this mixed group rehearsed choral selections with instrumental accompaniment, but public performances were presented in DeGive's Opera House on Marietta Street. Gaslight from chandeliers danced over brilliant audiences of men in tails and women in satins and velvets with long white gloves; the gas footlights flared on the tiers of singers, who were seated pyramid fashion with the various "leads" strategically distributed. The general taste of the time ran to songs about gravestones and severed hearts, but these choral societies insisted upon rendering good music. Although social prestige counted for something in these societies, they caused the breakdown of many old barriers. A strict father might protest when his delicately nurtured daughter was called upon to sing soprano to a bartender's tenor—but in the name of music it was usually allowed.

The Beethoven Society contented itself with solos, choruses, and occasional single scenes from grand opera; but the Rossini Club, organized in 1876, presented two or three entire operas, beginning with Balfe's *Bohemian Girl* in November of its first year. A few years later the Mendelssohn Society was established by a young Italian pianist, Alfredo Barili, who came to the city in 1880. A nephew of the famous singer Adelina Patti, he was for many years among Atlanta's leading music teachers and most distinguished musicians. As a composer he became known for the songs "There Little Girl, Don't Cry" and "Cradle Song" and for the piano compositions "Modern Minuet," "Miniature Gavotte," and "Butterfly Waltz."

The number of Atlanta's local musicians increased during the last years of the century. Brass bands and mandolin clubs continued to flourish, and a fiddlers' convention was inaugurated in 1885. More cultivated tastes were pleased by the concerts given by the Prather Home School for Girls and the Women's Exchange. But a perpetually increasing number of citizens demanded to hear the best internationally known musicians available. In 1883 alone, Atlanta audiences heard Minnie Hauk and Company, the Duff Grand Opera Company, Grau's English Opera Company, and the Theodore Thomas Orchestra. In 1895 Atlanta singers and pianists performed at the Cotton States and International Exposition, which drew great crowds to the hilly acres that later became Piedmont Park. Sometimes scores of gray-uniformed veterans burst into the rebel yell after "Dixie" or "Tenting Tonight" had been sung. The Damrosch Opera Company made Atlanta better acquainted with the heavy, dramatic Wagnerian pieces by the presentation of *Lohengrin* and *Siegfried,* and the New Orleans Opera Company gave the French musical dramas *Les Huguenots* and *Romeo and Juliet.* In 1898 the Atlanta Concert Association brought such famous artists as De Pachman, Rosenthal, Bloomfield-Ziegler, Mark Hambourg, Lillian Nordica, and Nellie Melba. Eleven years later, when the municipal auditorium-armory was opened, this body became the Atlanta Music Festival Association.

In the first year of the new century the Klindworth Conservatory was opened by Professor and Mrs. Kurt Mueller in the then fashionable residential section of Courtland Street near Cain. The Muellers soon became salient figures in the musical receptions that were given in the homes of Mr. and Mrs. John Pappenheimer and Colonel and Mrs. William Lawson Peel—lavish, brilliant affairs at which Atlanta's aristocracy mingled with the aristocracy of the music world. In 1905 the Muellers achieved an outstanding success when the conservatory presented a program of Brahms selections, then considered odd and difficult by most Atlanta audiences. Offering a 36-week scholastic year, the Klindworth Conservatory served Atlanta for years by capably teaching not only vocal and instrumental music but regular academic courses. In 1909 it was combined with the Atlanta Conservatory of Music, which had been formed two years previously, and under the latter name the combined organizations continued to function until 1938. Another group that was active in the formation of sound musical taste in the city was the Atlanta Musical Association, organized in 1908 with 15 or 20 charter members under the leadership of Bertha Harwood. In the following year the Schleiwen String Quartette, formed from the symphony orchestra of this association, made Atlanta still more widely known as a musical center when it toured under the Atlanta Lyceum Bureau.

That good music was becoming important to increasing numbers here is shown by the construction of the new $200,000 auditorium-armory, with a seating capacity of more than 5,000. In May 1909, shortly after its completion, the auditorium was opened by the most dazzling musical event up to that time—the Atlanta Music Festival, featuring Olive Fremstad, Geraldine Farrar, Giovanni Zenatello, Antonio Scotti, Ricardo Martin, and the Dresden Philharmonic Orchestra with its young stars Mary Lansing, contralto, and Albert Spalding, violinist. Five hundred local singers formed the chorus, and the four concerts were attended by more than 25,000. The Atlanta Music Festival Association installed a large pipe organ in the following year and presented Edwin H. Lemare in the opening concert. Percy Starnes, later selected as municipal organist, inaugurated regular

Sunday afternoon concerts which were continued by his successors, Edwin Arthur Craft and Charles Sheldon, Jr. Other well-known organists who gave recitals were Joseph Bonnet and Clarence Eddy.

The success of the festival of 1909 led the Atlanta Music Festival Association to the audacious plan of having an entire week of opera by the Metropolitan Opera Company of New York City as the festival of the following year. Despite the guarantee of more than $40,000 demanded by the company, this plan was carried out with overwhelming success. The greatest star of this week was Caruso, who sang in *Aida* and *Pagliacci,* but enthusiastic homage also was rendered to Farrar, who had won great popularity at her Atlanta debut the year before. Homer, Gadski, Amato, and other famous singers added to the luster of the occasion. At the end of the week the manager stated that "never before had the Metropolitan Opera Company sung to so many people or such an amount of money in one week." Until 1931 Atlanta was the only Southern city to feature the Metropolitan in a week of grand opera annually. After the success of the performances in Atlanta's Metropolitan Opera revivals of 1940 and 1941, it is believed that opera week will again become a regular date on the Atlanta calendar.

During the World War years, while the city auditorium was packed with young men in khaki shouting "Over There" at Sunday afternoon rallies, the serious music groups were working to bring the best vocal and instrumental performers to the city. In 1916 the Atlanta Music Club, organized the year before as the Woman's Choral Club, began its concert series, and two years later a succession of concerts that subsequently became the All-Star Concert Series was initiated. The Atlanta Symphony Orchestra Association was formed in 1922. A series of civic concerts with solo and orchestral selections was opened by the music club in 1927, and this organization has now joined with the Atlanta Philharmonic Society, formed in 1930, in sponsoring an annual series of these presentations.

In the first year of the new decade, Evelyn Jackson, then president of the Georgia Federation of Music Clubs, established the MacDowell Festival to honor the famous American composer Edward MacDowell. This festival was adopted by the entire Nation, the proceeds of the performance being used to provide funds for the Peterborough artists' colony founded by MacDowell. These years were notable also for the improvement of church music throughout the city. Charles A. Sheldon, Jr., organist at the Temple, became known for his traditional Jewish sacred music; Mrs. Victor B. Clark, at the Peachtree Christian Church, was the organist and director of the only Protestant antiphonal and chancel choir in the city; Joseph Ragan, organist and choir director at All Saints Episcopal Church, attracted large crowds by his Easter choral celebrations; the choir of St. Luke's Episcopal Church became known especially for the coloratura solos of Minna Hecker; and the Sacred Heart Roman Catholic Church became still more widely celebrated for its midnight mass music on Christmas Eve. These are only a few of the churches that still provide sacred music of good quality.

Both talent and appreciation for fine music are now abundant in Atlanta, although the city badly needs a greater number of capable instructors and strong leadership for fusion of the divergent factors. The All-Star and Atlanta Music Club concerts provide the two best regular annual musical series. Atlanta is known for at least two fine voices —Minna Hecker, coloratura, and Edward Kane, tenor. The Emory University Glee Club, less than 20 years old, has become celebrated under the direction of Malcolm H. Dewey for its excellent choral programs. Especially notable are its Christmas carol singing and its presentations of Negro spirituals, which are sung by the chorus without effort to emulate Negro mannerisms but simply as good music. Among the first college organizations to dispense with mandolin clubs and jazz bands, this group has made numerous successful tours including two in England. In 1940 this glee club, assisted by the Emory Little Symphony Orchestra, combined with the Agnes Scott Glee Club to present two successful performances of the Gilbert and Sullivan opera *Iolanthe*.

Atlanta offers numerous facilities for a sound musical education. The Griffith School of Music, organized in 1890 by Mrs. Mary Butt Griffith, has been continued by the same family for half a century. Providing instruction in virtually all branches of instrumental music, this school makes a specialty of classes in the Italian harp. The Atlanta Conservatory closed in 1938, but many of its former instructors are now teaching independently. The Georgia Conservatory of Music, which was opened in Atlanta in 1940, was short-lived, closing after only one year of operation. Well known among Atlanta's music teachers are Hugh Hodgson and Earle Chester Smith in piano, Elinor Whittemore King in violin, and Margaret Hecht in voice. Ruby Chalmers has served as an accompanist for several visiting artists. Annie Grace O'Callaghan, director of music in Atlanta high schools, has rendered excellent service to the city by her courses in general music and by periodic student performances of special choral, instrumental, and orchestral groups, and Ruth Weegand directs the grammar schools in a similar program of work. The WPA Music Project assists by giving frequent concerts in the schools.

Among numerous composers, Jane Mattingly, Elizabeth Hopson, and William O. Munn have received recognition for their children's music; Nan Bagby Stephens for songs for DuBose Heyward's play

Porgy and her own Negro drama *Roseanne;* and Bonita Crowe for her songs and piano pieces.

Atlanta in recent years has become known for Negro music, especially for *Heaven Bound,* written and performed by members of the Big Bethel Methodist Church. Utilizing many of the old spirituals in the form of the miracle play, this piece has attracted large crowds in many performances. Kemper Harreld, director of music at Morehouse College, has done notable work with orchestras and glee clubs in various Negro schools and in the field of Negro folk music.

The Theater

ATLANTA's early citizens had but little time for pleasure; work and sleep constituted a routine that was seldom broken. Cultural recreation, especially in the form of the theater, was not even remotely considered. By the early forties, however, the town had taken on some elements of permanency and citizens were beginning to have a few daily leisure hours. Word quickly spread along that "grapevine system" which has ever been the characteristic gossip medium of the show world and at once a stream of Punch-and-Judy shows and street performers were attracted to Atlanta. Local music clubs were organized and concerts of a sort were given. By 1850 a newspaper was already complaining that "concerts and sleight-of-hand performances have become stale from the frequency of their occurrence."

In 1854 Parr's Hall, located on the third floor of a brick building at the corner of Whitehall and Alabama Streets, was opened for the accommodation of traveling shows. Here William H. Crisp and his talented family began their first attempts at portraying the drama. In the same year Crisp persuaded James E. Williams, later mayor of Atlanta, to remodel the second floor of his feed store, between Pryor and Peachtree Streets on Decatur, into a theater. The resulting auditorium was called the Athenaeum and was reached by a narrow flight of stairs, at the top of which was a little box office. There were enough rude chairs and benches in the "parquette" and gallery to seat 700 persons, although Williams advertised the capacity as being over 1,000. The rear of the hall was given over to a shallow stage, the sliding curtains of which stopped just short of the walls to afford a little "dressing room" privacy. There was no back door and it was often necessary for the hard-put actors to make precarious rear entrances and exits by means of a long ladder which barely reached one of the windows. Candles gave the only illumination, and patrons endured uncomplainingly the odors of the feed grains stored in the lower floor, the snorting of horses in adjacent stables, and the acute discomfort of sitting for hours on rough, uncushioned benches. Nevertheless, it held all the mystery and enchantment that is the theater, and at every performance the house was packed by citizens who wept over high tragedy and laughed uproariously at low comedy. The Athenaeum became headquarters for Crisp and his family as well as for the traveling shows of the day.

William Choice, another amateur actor, organized the Murdock Dramatic Club in this same year and the company sprang into immediate popularity. Choice was an energetic and sensitive young man of exceptional talent who excelled in tragic roles. "As gentlemen," he stated in speaking of the aims of the club, "we promise we will not pander to perverted tastes, but the noblest thoughts of noblest men shall be presented." Typical plays were *The Gladiator, Pizarro,* and *William Tell,* all with strong male leading roles which provided Choice with excellent opportunities. The organization was exclusively male, but for such plays as *Poca-hon-tas* (*The Gentle Savage*) and *The Wife* professional actresses were employed. On occasion the Murdock Club supplemented the ranks of traveling companies which appeared in Atlanta. Among these were the companies of Maggie Mitchell who presented *Mazeppa,* and of the great tragedian Neafil, who appeared in *The Corsican Brothers.* Although he was immensely popular, Choice's career was brought to an untimely end when he murdered a creditor and was committed to the Milledgeville insane asylum in 1860.

Crisp and Choice followed the precedent established by traveling shows, that of presenting a serious drama followed by a short comedy, and drama or comedy alike carried explicit subtitles. Thus were combined such double features as *Lucretia Borgia* or *The Female Poisoner* and *The Happy Man* or *Paddy Among the Orientals.* So firmly entrenched was this pattern that the companies did not dare ignore the public expectations, but the comic relief was often cut to proportions which made it a mere sop to satisfy custom. Thus one billing of the day announced "Shakespeare's Beautiful Tragedy MACBETH in five acts, to conclude with MINNA, a Comic Song."

Comedy, however, was by no means eclipsed. On the contrary the Fulton Minstrels, the Campbell Minstrels ("The Campbells are Coming!"), or the Atlanta Amateurs could put on an entire evening's show of fun. Shortly after the disbanding of the Murdock Dramatic Club, William Barnes, who had played juvenile roles in Choice's company, founded the Atlanta Amateurs, an organization that seems to have been given more to musical extravaganzas than to plays, although short dramatic skits occasionally were given in the course of an evening's entertainment. Barnes' company became the most popular troupe of the era in Atlanta and, during the War between the States,

almost completely dominated the stage of the city. Scarcely a week
went by without a benefit performance for the soldiers, and the fame
of the Amateurs spread throughout Georgia and neighboring States.
So popular was the troupe that newspapers fairly gushed their praises,
and one enthusiastic critic overshot his meaning by declaring that
"these exhibitions are in every way *un*exceptional."

During the course of the war, William Crisp, then a major in the
Confederate Army, became lessee and manager of the Athenaeum as
well as operator of theaters in Mobile and Montgomery, Alabama.
His company, headed by his wife, continued to present plays, and
Major Crisp himself occasionally enacted roles while home on furlough. Once during his absence the city council threatened to close the
theater as a precautionary measure when the opposing armies approached too close to Atlanta and stray shells were falling in the city.
Mrs. Crisp, with ready acumen, immediately announced that hence-
forth every performance would be a benefit for the soldiers, a move
which so appealed to the patriotism of the citizens that council dared
not carry through the proposal.

During the war traveling companies seldom appeared in Atlanta,
but individual entertainers often contrived to get into the city. Thus
the Athenaeum billed such performers as "Mr. Nash Butler, in his
inimitable Comic Song"; "Mr. Dan May, The Ethiopian Deline-
ator"; "Madame Amelia Celeste, Rope Ascentioniste and Danseuse";
and "Wm. E. Yeaman, Blind Slack Wire Performer." The war aided
the growth of the theater in Atlanta rather than seriously deterring
it, and every company or individual was hard put to supply the demand
for entertainment. If, as rarely happened, one of the professional
groups was not putting on a nightly show, churches, social clubs, and
relief organizations would take advantage of the opportunity to call
on everyone who could sing or recite and put on a "benefit." Many
a shy maiden was thrust upon a stage on these occasions by ambitious
"mammas" and made to sing:

> Here's to the boys in Confederate gray,
> Vive la Compagnie
> Who never their country nor sweethearts betray,
> Vive la Compagnie. . . .

and so on for as many verses as fond relatives and friends could im-
provise. In those war-mad years the inevitable result was wild in-
discriminate acclaim, and it is not surprising that numbers of these
susceptible girls were dazzled by their easy success and believed themselves "stars." Ten years after the war many of these "Sweethearts
of the South" or "Dixie Darlings" could be found traveling the cheap
vaudeville circuits with little change in their routine, still singing

"Vive la Compagnie" and "The Girl I Left Behind Me," still trying to establish themselves by appealing to a fast-fading pseudo-patriotic emotionalism, still goaded on by stage-mothers who refused to recognize the fact that their daughters never had had, nor ever would have, any talent.

The behavior of the audiences during the latter years of the conflict hastened the closing of the Athenaeum. Soldiers on furlough, deserters, exchange prisoners, sports, and hoodlums filled the gallery at the Athenaeum and dictated the manner in which the shows should be run. They hissed, hooted, swore, hurled insulting remarks to the players, and generally upset the house. One of their favorite diversions was reaching out and tilting the candle chandeliers so that hot tallow poured down upon the heads of the parquet audience. For a while the Crisp family, the Waldron family, and such old experienced players as Edwin R. Dalton were able to carry on in the face of such rudeness. The papers took up the issue and council placed policemen on duty at each performance. The audiences, however, went from bad to worse, the police were hopelessly outnumbered, and arrests often led to bloody rows. The billing degenerated into cheap vaudeville catering to the vulgar audiences, and the theater was finally closed by order of the mayor, who called the place a "den of vice." The building was ultimately destroyed in the burning of Atlanta.

Within a year after the close of the war, Davis Hall was opened on Broad Street between Hunter and Mitchell. The stage of the hall had drop curtains and kerosene footlights, and the seating capacity of the auditorium was more than 4,000. For an entire summer the hall was managed by John Templeton, who played leading roles in his own stock company. Templeton's talents extended over a wide field from tragedy to broad comedy and it was nothing for him to step from the melancholy role of Hamlet to the slapstick character of Toodles, a comic afterpiece, in the course of an evening.

The popularity of Davis Hall was overshadowed in 1867 by the opening of the Bell-Johnson Hall on the northeast corner of Broad and Alabama Streets. This hall was used by various amateur groups, church societies, and fraternal organizations, as well as occasional professional troupes. One amateur group which often put on plays in this hall was the Concordia Association, composed of Jewish citizens who raised money for their many charities through these performances.

Various other little halls were opened in the town during the next few years, but all were completely eclipsed by the grandeur of the DeGive Theater, built by Laurent DeGive and opened in 1870 on the northeast corner of Broad and Marietta Streets. It was the first building to be constructed specifically for theatrical purposes and immediately became a show place of the city. The facade featured tall iron columns placed flush with the edge of the sidewalk and supporting a broad iron balustraded veranda in the French manner, upon which the theater's patrons gathered between acts for refreshments. The management brought all of the currently popular plays and operas to the theater, and many famous actors and actresses appeared in response to Atlanta's demand for a higher type of entertainment. Sarah Bernhardt played *La Tosca* here, Fanny Davenport starred in *Cleopatra,* and Joe Jefferson performed his famed *Rip Van Winkle.* Edwin Booth, Richard Mansfield, Julia Marlowe, the famed Polish tragedienne Modjeska, and the comedians Al G. Fields and Lew Dockstader were among other celebrities who walked the DeGive boards.

Many amusing incidents are told concerning the noted players of those days. On one occasion Richard Mansfield had been requested to present a double bill featuring parts of *Dr. Jekyll and Mr. Hyde* and *Parisian Romance.* Strong-willed genius that he was, Mansfield declared that he would not mutilate the plays but would present them both in full. He did, the curtain going up at eight in the evening and coming down at two in the morning. During a presentation of *Richard III* the act was disrupted by the appearance on the stage of an unexpected character in the person of a large Negro woman who waddled over to an amazed queen and announced, "Lady, here's yo wash!"

The name of the DeGive Theater was early changed to the more dignified one of DeGive Opera House. The building was the town's most popular show place for two decades, a period that old timers regard as the golden age of the theater in Atlanta. The city was in a strategic position, "breaking" the circuit from New York to New Orleans, and virtually every important company played the various theaters. The "star system" was becoming more the order and impresarios, such as Charles and Daniel Frohman, were taking leases on theaters throughout the country. Thus the DeGive Opera House and two newer but smaller houses, the Orpheum and the Edgewood Theaters, were assured of year-round bookings through their various lessees. The most popular plays of the 1880's were *The Lady of Lyons, Toodles, Camille, The Spectre Bridegroom, East Lynne, Slasher and Crasher, Jenny Lind, Under the Gaslight, Ten Nights in a Barroom,* and all of Shakespeare. French tragedies never failed to attract a full house and were surpassed in popularity only by American comedies. This, too, was the heyday of chautauqua and of the big tent shows or circuses, one of which, in 1882, brought to Atlanta the first electric light to be exhibited in the city.

The Crisp family had grown in local favor and was still holding forth after a most successful tour of the West. Several other amateur groups had come into being. Foremost of these was the Atlanta

Dramatic Club, which is still remembered for its unique presentation of *Julius Caesar* at DeGive's. After ninety rehearsals the actors still lacked much in stage presence and timing, and the audience was treated to such incidents as a belated clock striking the hour several seconds after one of the conspirators had remarked upon its chiming, the collapse of a section of scenery carrying to the floor with it a grief-striken supernumerary weeping for the dead Caesar, and another confused "supe" referring to Brutus as "a noble vessel full of *beef*" instead of grief. Cassius, in reply to his question "Am I not stayed for, Cinna?" received the answer, "You bet your sweet life!" Caesar himself seems to have suffered the most indignities, however, for an over-enthusiastic Anthony stepped on his stomach during the famed oration. A few minutes later when Anthony was broken-heartedly pointing out the wounds on Caesar's body to another character, he inadvertently touched Caesar's neck, whereupon that deceased gentleman, being posthumously ticklish, burst into laughter and convulsed an already hysterical audience.

In 1893, Laurent DeGive surprised Atlanta by building the Grand Theater on Peachtree Street. Despite predictions that the venture would bankrupt the DeGive fortunes and the objection that the building was too far from the center of town (then around Alabama Street), the theater was an immediate success and became the leading house for celebrities of the day. The galaxy of headliners included Sir Henry Irving, Ellen Terry, Maude Adams, John Drew, Anna Held, Lillian Russell, Maxine Elliott, Otis Skinner, and William Faversham.

With the opening of the Grand Theater the old DeGive house rapidly fell to second place. Jake Wells obtained control of it and renamed it the Bijou. There he brought Little Chip, Mary Marble, the Fanchonettis, Hoffman, and a host of others who afterwards became celebrities in the theatrical world. He also established a stock company that was very successful for a time. But the better patronage soon deserted the old theater for the attractions of the Grand, and the stock company gave way to cheap vaudeville and burlesque. Censorship stepped in and the house was often closed. Around the turn of the century an attempt was made to re-establish a stock company, but the venture failed, the property was sold, and finally the Bijou was torn down to make way for an office building.

Meanwhile Atlanta had grown to a town of more than 100,000 people. More and more shows were coming South on the New Orleans-Texas circuit, and new theaters for their accommodation were built. Two of the most important of these, the Lyric and the Forsyth Theaters, were "big time" vaudeville houses, presenting such "headliners" as Anna Held, Eddie Foy, and the young Buster Keaton. The

Atlanta Theater, opened in 1911, was strictly a legitimate house, bringing to the city stars of the caliber of George Beban, Robert Mantell, and Minnie Maddern Fiske.

The rapid development of the cinema industry on a large scale between 1905 and 1915 resulted in the erection of many motion picture houses. Atlanta's first movie had been shown at the Cotton States Exposition in 1895, but the venture was a complete failure. With the turn of the century, however, the improved technique of making and projecting films captured the public interest, and several motion picture houses were opened. Many Atlantans remember the years Dave Love and his orchestra held forth at the Criterion Theater, during which time he introduced the playing of classic overtures between showings of the feature picture, an entertainment pattern that was copied by other Atlanta theaters and maintained for more than a decade. During this period, too, the Metropolitan Opera, which had made its first appearance in the city auditorium in 1910, was returning annually for a week's presentation of the greatest operas. Atlanta was becoming famed as the musical, as well as the theatrical, center of the South.

The Howard Theater, later known as the Paramount, was opened in 1920 as the first "million dollar theater" to be erected in the South. Though ornate, the decorative details were in good taste and exhibited but little of that rococo garishness which characterized later Atlanta theaters. For years the Howard orchestra, conducted by Enrico Leide, staged elaborate prologues and overtures with Virginia Futrelle as prima donna and danseuse.

During this decade the Atlanta Theater became the leading outlet for the legitimate stage in Atlanta. Virtually every theatrical celebrity of the day appeared here. In addition to occasional road shows presenting the current New York plays, there were several successive stock companies which kept the house open throughout the year. Louise Hunter appeared here for several summer seasons of light opera.

The Metropolitan, the Georgia (now the Roxy), and the Capitol were also erected during the 1920's, Atlanta's boom period. In 1926 the management of the Atlanta Theater built the Erlanger, which immediately became the city's leading legitimate theater and took over the presentation of the better road shows and stock companies. For several years virtually all the other theaters ran on a year-round schedule, featuring both stage and screen entertainment. DeGive's Grand was leased by the Marcus Loew interests as a house for that vaudeville chain, the old Forsyth featured big time Keith-Albee vaudeville which was later moved to the new Georgia Theater, while the Paramount presented the spectacular Fanchon-Marco shows. Every house maintained its own orchestra, playing not only in the pit but often as a part of the entertainment unit on the stage. Even the legitimate theaters were almost continually open.

Then came the depression with its disastrous effects upon the entertainment industries. All legitimate houses were dark, stage shows were discontinued and orchestras were dismissed, and the "canned music" of the talkies took their place in the few movie houses which remained open. The Metropolitan Opera discontinued its annual appearance at the auditorium and theater patronage reached an all-time low. For a time the Fox Theater, an elaborate house erected at the beginning of the depression, was able to maintain a fair imitation of the former spectacular stagings of the 1920's, but it quickly fell into the depression pattern and became solely a movie house.

Strangely enough, the lean years, which had drastically curtailed all other stage entertainment in Atlanta, gave new impetus to the amateur theatrical movement. Several of these groups had been organized prior to the depression. These included the Blackfriars Dramatic Club of Agnes Scott College organized in 1915, the Playcrafters and the Little Theater Guild in 1924, the Emory University Players and the Drama Guild of the Studio Club in 1928, the Atlanta University Players (Negro) in 1929, and the White Barn Theater in 1930. Of these, the Blackfriars, the Emory Players, and the Atlanta University Players were the most successful and are still producing. The Blackfriars won third place in competition with other university theaters in 1924 and, in 1928, won first prize in the International Little Theater Tournament of unpublished plays held in New York City. The group covered the field of drama from early Greek literature to plays with modern plots and backgrounds. The Emory Players, who have obtained an enviable position among local amateur groups, specialize in the presentation of contemporary plays. The Atlanta University Players have received national recognition through many favorable notices in stage publications. Their repertoire runs the gamut from Greek drama to modern plays of Negro life, spanning the gap with an occasional Shakespearean production.

Newer groups include the Atlanta Children's Theater Guild, organized in 1934 by the Junior League; the Children's League of the Studio Arts Club, founded in 1935; the Atlanta Players Club, formed in 1935; and the Atlanta Theater Guild, which staged its first production in 1936.

In January, 1937, the local unit of the Federal Theater Project presented its first play at the Atlanta Theater under the auspices of the Works Progress Administration. In the fall of 1938 it moved to the Erlanger Theater. During the two and one-half years of its existence the Federal Theater Project offered a wide variety of plays ranging from Christopher Marlowe's *Dr. Faustus* to such contemporary drama as *Boy Meets Girl* and *Excursion*. From time to time professional actors were sent from the central casting office in New York to strengthen the presentations of the local unit.

In the past few years there has been a surprising increase in the number of neighborhood motion picture houses in the city and there are two open-air theaters for motorists who do not wish to leave their cars. Vaudeville has returned to a few houses, and even those theaters which seldom present stage shows are offering double-feature movie billings in an effort to stimulate patronage. The Erlanger is Atlanta's only legitimate house today. In the past two years many New York successes have been presented here, starring such celebrities as Katharine Cornell, Maurice Evans, Tallulah Bankhead, Alfred Lunt and Lynn Fontanne, Katharine Hepburn, and Victor Moore.

Literature

ATLANTA, less than a quarter of a century old at the outbreak of the War between the States, had virtually no literary life before that time. The older and quieter Georgia cities with their aristocratic plantation tradition regarded this community as a lusty *parvenu,* a hearty, pushing, rapidly growing railroad town whose citizens knew nothing of the arts. Nor did the energetic railroad builders and merchants take exception to this opinion, for they were too busy in the pursuit of prosperity to have much time for books.

In 1864 the besieged city fell before General Sherman's Union forces and was left in ruins. From that time until well into the 1870's, any incipient literary growth was atrophied by the poverty and humiliation of the Reconstruction Era. Yet these disasters brought enrichment, for they razed barriers between the social classes and thus not only cleared broader vistas for writers but removed many inhibiting customs, so that dilettante authors ceased to scribble and became professional craftsmen. Of even greater immediate importance was the wealth of subject matter provided by the war, which many had experienced at first hand. In the last quarter of the nineteenth century, Atlanta writings on war and reconstruction ranged from the eloquent conciliation addresses of Henry W. Grady to the sincere but sometimes embittered accounts of Myrta Lockett Avary, whose *Dixie After the War* has had a recent reissue.

Talent had to take a practical turn. Writers, forced to work for a subsistence, did not write for their own pleasure but became affiliated with newspapers or political publications. From its beginnings, Atlanta literature has been vitalized by its journalists. In the 1880's and 1890's several gifted columnists brought forth work that later became a permanent part of the city's literature. The gentle, diffident Joel Chandler Harris adapted his enormous store of African lore to his Uncle Remus tales in which the aged Negro tells the little boy of delightful animals—Br'er Rabbit, Br'er Fox, Sis' Cow, and the wonderful Tar Baby. Bill Arp (Major Charles Smith) got out his column of humorous, designedly rustic common sense. William Henry Peck, after long journalistic experience in New York, moved to Atlanta in 1875 and wrote news articles and also numerous novels of the romantic cloak-and-sword variety. While not inventing machines Benjamin Franklin Sawyer wrote editorials and novels, his domestic chronicle *David and Abigail* reaching a large audience. Francis R. Goulding, living at Roswell 12 miles from Atlanta, wrote *The Young Marooners,* a popular book for boys that became the forerunner of the newer juvenile stories by Atlanta writers such as Madge Alford Bigham, Eva Knox Evans, and Elizabeth Downing Barnitz.

Although there was still much verse of the autograph-book type, some poets began to bring in a more individual quality. James Barrick's sonorous stanzas may seem old-fashioned now, but they do not lack dignity. Of more lasting popularity was Frank L. Stanton, who was of the homespun school of Eugene Field and James Whitcomb Riley, Stanton's friend and correspondent. Known most widely for his words to such popular songs as "Mighty Lak a Rose" and "Just A-Wearyin' For You," Stanton occasionally wrote verse about Georgia life that was virile and even grim. The erudite, solitary Thomas Holley Chivers lived in Decatur near Atlanta, corresponding with Poe, charging him with plagiarism, and brooding over his own metric innovations that were to last longer than his poems.

During the early years of the new century, Atlanta brought forth no new writers of first rank. Apparently the city had found its economic footing and had rebuilt itself into a thriving commercial community with little creative impulse. Cultural groups studied the European writers, and less serious readers also seemed to prefer stories about foreign lands if the narrative was colored by a light, pleasing romance. Neither realism nor regionalism was popular in fiction. Atlanta verse also, like that of the Nation, was on the whole lifeless during these years. The only spark was lighted by the national drama league, which awoke considerable enthusiasm for the writing and production of plays. The force of this movement was shattered by the First World War, but some of its Atlanta workers became celebrated playwrights after the war.

This war, although far away in material distance, had powerful intellectual and moral effects. During the 1920's Atlanta literature entered a relentlessly analytical era. New standards of form and style were established, but first the old values were scrutinized and sometimes discarded. Cynical and violent the new writers sometimes were, but they were attaining a refreshing pungency. Laurence Stallings, injured in the war, caused a Broadway sensation with his play *What Price Glory,* whose lusty humor and outspoken language revealed the author's scorn for all romantic idealization of warfare. Dramatists of a gentler outlook awakened to the abundant subject matter near to hand and began to write plays whose principal theme turned on folklore or rustic convention. Nan Bagby Stephens' *Roseanne,* dramatically sound and psychologically arresting, challenged hitherto indifferent Eastern audiences to interest in the Southern Negro. Lula Vollmer had a successful New York run with her mountaineer play, *Sun-Up.* Novelists also became sympathetically aware of Georgia's peasantry, as did Fisewood Tarleton, who lived near Atlanta and wrote of passionate, primitive men and women in his *Some Trust in Chariots* and *Bloody Ground.*

The critical faculties of the post-war writers sometimes veered toward satire. Frances Newman, who had won distinction as a book reviewer, published *The Hard Boiled Virgin,* the highly stylized and ironic study of a frustrated woman, and *Dead Lovers Are Faithful Lovers,* equally polished in technique and depicting a modern triangle love story. Isa Glenn's early novels, such as *Heat* and *Little Pitchers,* also are full of an amused and not wholly severe disillusionment. With *Cora Potts,* Ward Greene began to publish a series of savagely naturalistic but engrossing novels of Southern life in the bootleg age. Drawing on his abundant reportorial experience, Greene frequently selects as his main characters the denizens of the underworld and police court. Other journalists, some of whom paused only briefly in the city, put analysis and dissection into newsprint. Of this number were Pierre Van Paassen, William Seabrook, Don Marquis, Roark Bradford, W.E. Woodward, Morris Markey, Ward Morehouse, and Roy Flannagan.

Equally striking was the poetic renascence that sprang up late in the 1920's. A very young Atlanta poet, Ernest Hartsock, nettled by H.L. Mencken's jeers at the South as a "Sahara of the *beaux arts,*" joined with his friend Ben Musser in establishing the magazine *Bozart Contemporary Verse* and began to publish the work of local and national poets. The standard of acceptance was very high. Interest was heightened by Thornwell Jacobs, president of Oglethorpe University and himself a writer of verse, who created a chair of poetry at his college and appointed Hartsock to occupy it, which he did until his untimely death in 1930. Some of the group who were writing verse at that time have since become widely known, and three of them —Ernest Hartsock, Daniel Whitehead Hicky, and James Warren, Jr. —have won the annual award of the Poetry Society of America.

No commentator has advanced a completely satisfying reason for the large number of poets in this city. Ruth Elgin Suddeth's anthology, *An Atlanta Argosy,* shows the work of more than 30, but there are many more writing verse. The anthologist Richard Moult has stated that of all American cities only New York has contributed as many poems to his pages as Atlanta. It has been suggested that this large number has risen in half-conscious rebellion against the prevailing commercial atmosphere. Others account for it by mentioning Atlanta's hills, trees, and streams that are so readily adaptable to nature poetry.

But Atlanta's leading poets are not nature poets in the restrictive sense. Ernest Hartsock, generally recognized as Atlanta's most distinguished modern writer of verse, was concerned with philosophic rather than visual recognitions, and his best known work, "Strange Splendor," is so full of the excitement of cosmic speculation that abstractions seem to swirl into tangible, dazzling material shapes. Marguerite Steedman also contemplates the mysteries of faith and creation in poems that are somber but frequently full of imaginative power. Daniel Whitehead Hicky and Gilbert Maxwell, pre-eminently lyric, are concerned with nature not in a purely descriptive sense but in relation to the moods of man—his love, his spiritual isolation, his awareness of his own mortality. Minnie Hite Moody, Mary Brent Whiteside, and Anderson Scruggs use earth and sky as a background for meditative utterances, and Agnes Gray's delicately fashioned sonnets have an emotional import beyond the clear images themselves. Lola Pergament, who constantly seeks new technical forms to embody her thoughts, is notable for the intellectuality of her workmanship, especially in her use of the intrinsic, not the loosely derivative, value of words. James E. Warren, Jr.'s, verse, though deeply felt, is very scholarly, often with a foundation of history under its impressions. It is interesting to note that these writers are arrested by different aspects of Georgia's landscape—Hicky by the coast, Scruggs by bare autumn fields, Mrs. Moody by city lanes and back yards, and Maxwell by the hidden, sometimes menacing, drama in the small towns. Most of this group were writing verse in the 1920's and are writing now; most of them have at least one published volume.

In recent years Atlanta has produced almost every kind of prose writings. Outstanding examples of non-fiction are Walter Cooper's histories of Fulton County and of Georgia, Haywood Pearce, Jr.'s biography of Benjamin H. Hill and Vann Woodward's of Thomas E. Watson, Walter Millis' relentless exposure of propaganda, *Road to War,* and Arthur Raper's two fearlessly liberal inquiries into Southern social conditions, *The Tragedy of Lynching* and *A Preface to Peasantry.* Virginia Pettigrew Clare has written an admirable critical biography of the South Carolina poet Henry Timrod in *Harp of the South.* The Writers' Project of the Work Projects Administration has prepared guide books of the state and of several Georgia cities.

A number of prominent newspaper writers have published their experiences and observations in book form, Mary Knight in *On My*

Own and Mildred Seydell in *Chins Up*. Mrs. Seydell has also written a novel of marital and parental responsibilities, *Secret Fathers*. Thomas Ripley has been highly successful in his chronicle of Western "bad men," *They Died With Their Boots On*. *Fire in the Sky*, Tarleton Collier's novel of a woman's development, contributes a view of sharecropper life, which, instead of employing the traditionally brutal realism in its technique, is rather compassionate though clear-sighted. Thomas Stokes, winner of the Pulitzer Prize for distinguished American reporting in 1939, presents a vivid picture of the Atlanta of his boyhood in *Chip Off My Shoulder*.

Fiction has slid imperceptibly from a period of criticism into one of creative abundance. The novel covers an almost illimitable range: from Parker Hord's novel of the biblical King David, *A Youth Goes Forth*, to the clever, urbane mystery stories of Alice Campbell, Linton C. Hopkins, Dorothy Ogburn, Beatrice Jefferson, and Medora Field; from Thornwell Jacobs' romance of old Charleston, *Red Lantern on St. Michael's*, to Don Prince's satiric fantasies, *Tom* and *Swoop*. In *Fox in the Cloak* Harry Lee uses his gift of dispassionate, clear-cut narrative to reveal another picture of Atlanta, a city of department stores, beer parlors, movies, and middle-class homes, amid which the young artist struggles for the right to create according to his own standards. Samuel Tupper, Jr., and Minnie Hite Moody have written novels of the domestic type, Tupper gayly or dramatically and Mrs. Moody with the haunting quality of emotion that distinguishes her verse. Tupper's *Some Go Up* and *Old Lady's Shoes* are both about Atlanta society, but Mrs. Moody's more numerous books, including *Death Is A Little Man* and *Towers With Ivy*, cover American life from the South to the Middle West. Her latest book, *Long Meadows*, is an ample, well-documented chronicle of her own family, beginning with its immigration from the Netherlands in the eighteenth century and ending with its participation in the War between the States.

In 1936 a young Atlanta woman published a historical novel that broke all previous sales records, won the Pulitzer Prize, and found what is generally agreed to be a permanent place in universal literature. Numerous qualities of Margaret Mitchell's *Gone With the Wind* explain its extraordinary popular success. Although the story is told from the viewpoint of noncombatants, it is a shrewd and graphic account of the campaign leading to the destruction of Atlanta by General Sherman's Federal troops in 1864. By skillful distribution of battle pieces throughout the narrative, the author never lets them interrupt the superb sweep of her long story from beginning to end. Most important of all, she has created two characters of such vitality that they promise to be known permanently: Scarlett O'Hara, the heroine, who emerges embittered but dauntless from many tragic episodes of war and reconstruction; and Rhett Butler, the debonair and ruthless man who loves her. These two are not only compelling as individuals, but to many people they embody the indomitable spirit of Atlanta that lifted it to growth and riches after the war.

The success of this book has stimulated Atlanta authors to further strenuous efforts that already have shown remarkable results. Although the writers in the city are constantly becoming more numerous, they do not form a group or attempt to establish any particular school of writing. Each follows his own aspirations and the result is an animated variety. Most of them have been writing too short a time to have had more than one book published, but others are following rapidly.

Atlanta literature, like Atlanta, is young and vigorous. Its writers have few models of their own section to set them a regional tradition, and most of its best historical works have been produced in the twentieth century, with a keen, modern viewpoint turned upon historical events. Unlike the older Southern cities, it cannot look back deeply into the past, but it has an exciting present sustained by many writers —historians, novelists, dramatists, poets—who have made it one of the leading Southern centers for books and writers. The present period of fertility is too new for anything but surmise regarding its permanence. It is significant, however, that in recent years several large Eastern publishing houses have established branch offices here. Literary traditions are not being followed, but made.

Most of the Negro writers who have lived in the city have been members of the Atlanta University group. Their race has strongly influenced their literary development, and their writings have been predominantly on racial, social, and educational problems. But, although their field is less broad than that of the white writers, they have frequently performed with intensity and penetration within the range of their chosen subjects. In recent years some of them, the poets in particular, have written with a graceful and whimsical lightness. The greater part of the group, however, has continued to treat the racial question with a serious, often somber, dignity.

Walter F. White, known nationally for his efforts for the improvement of Negro political and social conditions, first received literary notice for his novel *The Fire in the Flint,* which depicted the struggle of a sensitive, talented Negro physician to practice in an intolerant community. This was followed by *Rope and Faggot,* a sincere and uncompromising study of lynching. William E. Burghardt DuBois also is known principally for his social writings, and such books as his *The Souls of Black Folk* are remarkable for their richly ornamental style and their tragic power of emotion. Edward Randolph Carter writes of the Negro from a decidedly theological and educational view-point in *Our Pulpit* and *Black Side of Atlanta*. Helen A. Whiting has brought wide knowledge and keen discernment to her fictional and non-fictional studies of the Negro.

The poets, though less intense, sometimes show a greater variety. Alexander Henry Jones' verse has a pastoral and religious tone; Georgia Douglas Johnson, while writing about her own race in her poems and in her play *Blue Blood,* has a strong sense of its amusing side; and Thomas Jefferson Flanagan writes verse whose appealing charm is often flavored with humor. Maude McGehee, a Negro nurse, has become known for her pleasant short verses about everyday Negro affairs.

One of the most distinguished Negro writers who has ever lived in Atlanta is the critic and anthologist William Stanley Braithwaite, now an instructor in Atlanta University. Braithwaite, who won the Spingarn Medal in 1918, has produced criticism of poetry and prose and has become celebrated for his books of essays. *The Book of Georgian Verse* and *The Book of Victorian Verse* are good examples of his work.

The number of Negro writers in Atlanta is constantly increasing, and there is some indication that better social conditions are bringing a more broad and serene outlook as well as a greater boldness of utterance. The Negro writers in Atlanta have risen too suddenly to have attained the gracious ripeness that is indicated for the future, but their work is full of vitality and skill.

Part Two

POINTS OF INTEREST

1. The STATE CAPITOL (*open Mon.-Fri. 8-4; Sat. 8-12*), occupying the block bounded by Capitol Ave. and Washington, Mitchell, and Hunter Sts., is an imposing structure modeled after the National Capitol, with domed cupola, Corinthian entrance portico, and broad balanced masses. Contrasting with the gray Indiana limestone is an encircling green lawn planted with many trees, and in summer white magnolia blossoms give out a heavy perfume. On the lawn are various bronze statues of men prominent in the State's history: G. Moretti's and I. Dean Dumley's full-length figure of Joseph E. Brown, Georgia's hot-headed governor during the War between the States, here shown with his wife in a tranquil daguerreotype pose; Joseph Klein's statue of the fiery agrarian Senator Thomas E. Watson, with upraised fist in an attitude of oratorical eloquence; and Solon Borglum's graceful, spirited equestrian figure of General John B. Gordon, a member of Robert E. Lee's staff and later the first Georgia governor to hold office in the present capitol. Surmounting the dome is a bronze female figure, holding a torch in one hand and a sword in the other and, from the ground, somewhat resembling the Statue of Liberty.

Inside, the various State offices are arranged about a galleried rotunda finished in white Georgia marble and rising three full stories to the dome. Throughout the interior are placed numerous statues and memorial plaques including busts of Benjamin H. Hill, one of Georgia's most notable Confederate statesmen, and Moina Michael, originator of the "Poppy Day" method of soliciting funds for the benefit of the World War veterans. Flags, documents, and other relics of the War between the States are displayed on the lower floor by the United Daughters of the Confederacy, while exhibits of the State's resources are shown in the corridors of the upper floors.

When the legislature is in session the capitol swarms with life. In the chambers of the senate and house, galleries are crowded with farmers, businessmen, and members of various civic groups, while below them on the floor debates are thundered forth. By the soft drink stand in the third floor corridor other listeners stand before the radio loudspeaker to hear the broadcast of the debates.

Atlanta in 1868 became the fifth capital of Georgia after this honor had been bestowed successively upon Savannah, Augusta, Louisville, and Milledgeville. The city agreed to provide the State with office space free of charge for ten years, and after considerable controversy an unfinished opera house on the southwest corner of Forsyth and Marietta Streets was rented from Edwin N. Kimball to be used as a capitol. This building was a handsome brick structure with mansard roof, marble vestibule, and walnut-banistered marble stairs. The first legislative session in this building convened on January 10, 1869. Several weeks later a lavish reception was given here by the Kimball brothers, among the guests being Rufus Bullock, the extravagant carpetbag governor who had advanced Kimball $54,500 for the installation of heat, lighting, and furnishings. From their quiet homes along Marietta Street, conservative citizens looked on in helpless resentment as the carriages clattered up to the brilliantly lighted entrance.

Later in the year Edwin N. Kimball transferred the capitol property to his brother H.I. Kimball, who proposed that the State purchase it from him. After turbulent debates in the senate a transaction was made whereby Kimball was to receive $250,000 in State bonds and $130,000 in municipal bonds, making a total price of $380,000. When the purchase was agreed upon in October, 1870, the general assembly required the appointment of a committee to see that the $54,500 advanced by Bullock was returned. But the committee appointed in 1872 to investigate Bullock's administration did not find that this was ever done. Kimball, when deeding the property to the State, declared it to be unencumbered. The committee of 1872 found in the executive department files, however, an agreement by Kimball guaranteeing payment of a $60,000 mortgage held by the Northwestern Mutual Life Insurance Company and indicating that he had given Bullock as security the certificate for the $130,000 in city bonds. Refusing to pay off the mortgage, the legislature promised agitation to secure return of the capital to Milledgeville, whereupon the city paid it and the interest. The mortgage was then transferred to the city and held uncancelled until the State made plans for the erection of the present capitol. This affair and other charges of extravagance and corruption were contributory causes of Governor Bullock's resignation and flight from the State in 1871.

At the time the capital was removed from Milledgeville to Atlanta, there was considerable dissatisfaction in some sections of the State because it had been accomplished when the Federal military regime and Republican government were in power. In 1877, after the Democrats had regained control, it was decided by referendum that Atlanta should remain the capital. Immediately the legislative body began to discuss plans for a new building, for Kimball's opera house, handsome as it was, was inadequate for the increasing number of legislators. Because of the excesses of the Bullock administration financial committees were cautious, and debates on appropriations went on for years. After many bids had been submitted, Edbrooke and

Burnham, of Chicago, were chosen as architects, and construction was begun on the city hall lot which Atlanta had given to the State for a capitol site. The cornerstone was laid on September 2, 1885, and the capitol was completed on June 15, 1889, one of the few buildings of such scope to be finished within the amount appropriated.

The STATE LIBRARY (*open Mon.-Fri, 9-4; Sat. 9-12; books must be used in Library*), on the third floor, contains a large collection of Georgia material. The 79,000 volumes in the library include many rare books and an excellent historical collection, the nucleus of which was bequeathed to the State during the 1880's by Edward DeRenne, son of the founder of the famous library now a part of the University of Georgia in Athens.

2. The STATE OFFICE BUILDING, Mitchell St. opposite the capitol, is a six-story edifice of marble, granite, and cream brick, designed by Augustus E. Constantine. In striking contrast to the white marble facade are six bronze relief figures, historical and symbolic, embossed on black marble spandrels. These figures are the work of Julian Harris, a well-known Atlanta sculptor.

Housed here are the State departments of education, labor, health, and public welfare. The capitol had become so overcrowded in recent years because of expansion in governmental services that some of the departments had been forced to take over old dwellings on the square for working space. With the aid of a Federal grant of $365,000, the new building was completed in 1939 at a total cost of $815,000.

3. The ATLANTA CITY HALL (*open 8 a.m. to 4:30 p.m. except Sat. afternoon and Sun. Observation tower open 9 to 11 a.m. and 2 to 3 p.m.*), SW. corner Mitchell and Washington Sts., stands out boldly on Atlanta's skyline, a commanding edifice that towers above a broad expanse of smooth green lawn. Erected in 1929 at a cost of more than $1,000,000, the 14-story building follows the modern "business Gothic" design embodying the setback architectural principle with the shaft tapering upward from a broad base to the small observatory. Marble, granite, brick, and terra cotta, all of which are Georgia products, have been used in the exterior construction; and when the sunlight is bright, the terra cotta imparts a pale amber hue to the entire mass. The lobby, with its ceiling of elaborately carved and gilded wood, is finished in travertine and marble in varicolored effect. In the rear are four bronze elevators. Inscribed on each elevator door is the seal of the borough of Atlanta, a phoenix representing the city's valiant rise from the ashes, and the inscription "Resurgens, 1847-1864, Atlanta, Ga." G. Lloyd Preacher & Company, Inc., were the architects.

Atlanta's first city council meeting on February 2, 1848, took place in a store, since no official quarters had been selected. Further meetings were held in commercial buildings rented or borrowed for the occasion until 1854, when Atlanta's first city hall was constructed. The site chosen was the block now occupied by the State capitol. The first city hall, which also provided space for county offices, was a brick building of two stories, fronted by Doric columns and topped by a cupola and weather vane. Citizens in homemade fancy dress costumes came to the ball that was given to commemorate the opening.

In 1879 Atlanta presented the State with this lot as a capitol site. Considerable time elapsed before plans for the capitol were completed, but in October, 1884, the municipal government made way and moved its quarters to the Chamber of Commerce Building at the northeast corner of Pryor and Hunter Streets. The first floor of this four-story brick structure was occupied by the city officials as tenants until 1901, when the entire building was acquired by paying $7,500 to the Chamber of Commerce for its equity and assuming a $30,000 mortgage.

This structure continued to serve as the city hall until 1910, when Atlanta bought a four-story brick building, formerly used as a post office, at the northwest corner of Marietta and Forsyth Streets. Mayor Robert Maddox, wealthy and public-spirited, financed this purchase by giving in full payment his personal check for $70,000, which was repaid him within the following two years. Here the departments of the city government were housed until 1929, when the present building was erected.

4. The CHURCH OF THE IMMACULATE CONCEPTION, SE. corner Central Ave. and Hunter St., is the oldest church building in Atlanta, a landmark of the formerly handsome residential section around Capitol Square. Constructed of painted red brick, the building is of Gothic design with a square tower and a three-arched main entrance topped by a balustrade. The vaulted interior gives an effect of restful beauty because of its excellent proportions and because of the soft light filtered from outside through stained-glass windows. The dominant feature is a white marble altar, installed by the women of the parish in 1879.

The first members of the congregation, Irish laborers who were brought here to construct the railroads, received mass from missionary priests from the Savannah diocese. The earliest entry in the records of the parish is that of a baptism administered on August 9, 1846, probably in a member's home, for the first Catholic church was not erected until 1848. When General Sherman's Federal troops destroyed Atlanta in 1864, they were about to burn this building; but the priest, Father O'Reilly, walked boldly to the head of the line and announced that if his church was fired every Roman Catholic in Sherman's army must leave the ranks. Since the regiment was composed largely of Catholics, the church was spared. The small frame structure on this site, though damaged by shells that had exploded about it during the siege, continued in use until 1869, when the present building was erected.

Each year on April 28 the Church of the Immaculate Conception is crowded by the Irish Horse Traders and their families, who come to Atlanta on that date to hold funeral services for those of their number who have died during the year. The first of these families, mistakenly believed by some to be of gypsy origin, came to America in the 1850's and set up a livery stable in Washington, D.C. The first

Downtown

STATE CAPITOL

BROAD STREET IS IN THE MIDST OF THE CROWDED BUSINESS DISTRICT

MILES OF RAILROAD TRACKS RUN BENEATH THE VIADUCTS OF THE
BUSINESS SECTION

NARROW STREETS FORM A ZIGZAG PATTERN—PEACHTREE AND IVY STREETS

STATE CAPITOL—1868

ATLANTA DURING CIVIL WAR

THE CITY HALL TOWERS HIGH AND MODERN A BLOCK FROM OLD CAPITOL
SQUARE

THE POST OFFICE ANNEX SHOWS THE NEWER ARCHITECTURAL TREND

BUSINESS OFFICES STAY OPEN LONG AFTER DARK

AT MARIETTA AND FORSYTH STREETS STANDS A MONUMENT TO HENRY W. GRADY, PERSUASIVE ADVOCATE OF AN INDUSTRIAL "NEW SOUTH"

WHITEHALL STREET AT RAILROAD TRACKS—1865

LOOKING TOWARD FIVE POINTS—1867

traders prospered, and others followed until eight families were established in America: the Rileys, McNamaras, Carrolls, Sherlocks, Garmons, Costellos, Dartys, and O'Haras. As time passed, some of them became itinerant traders, ranging over the country in covered wagons with their horses and mules on leads.

One such band, led by Pat O'Hara, first halted to establish headquarters at Nashville, Tennessee, but these restless Irishmen soon changed their minds and pushed southward. Settling for a time in the new, bustling city of Atlanta, they purchased large tracts of land and sometimes made fortunes as property values expanded with the rapidly growing municipality. Later most of them moved on, but the burial of John McNamara, a leader of the clan, in Oakland Cemetery in 1881, had established a strong tie that resulted in the custom of bringing their dead here each year for burial. When Oakland Cemetery became overcrowded, lots were purchased in the newer and more spacious West View. The memorials to their dead are usually massive and ornate, bearing decorations that range from stately guardian angels in marble to the inset photographs of a deceased trader and his still surviving widow.

The descendants of the eight original families, numbering about 10,000, now travel by automobile with household goods in trailers and horses in large vans. But, despite such modern appurtenances, many old customs prevail. Encampment is made in tents, as in the early days. In order to preserve their cherished tribal entity, the traders have made strict rules to keep marriage within the bounds of the original families, and only rarely have these rules been disobeyed. Nevertheless, they justly pride themselves on being good American citizens and have proved their loyalty by always enlisting readily in time of war.

Except for Nashville, Atlanta is the only city to which the clans come for their annual reunions, which are held for business conferences and betrothals as well as funerals. On the morning of April 28 the Church of the Immaculate Conception is a scene of unforgettable contrast. The dim gray background of the old church, the solemnity of the Roman Catholic service, the reverence of the worshippers, and the black veils of the widows throw into high relief the cries of restless children and the vigorous beauty of black-haired, blue-eyed Irish girls in the finery of bright dresses and costume jewelry.

5. A STONE MILEPOST marked *zero,* surrounded by railroad ties beneath the Central Avenue viaduct, designates the eastern terminus of the Western & Atlantic Railroad, which the State legislature authorized to be built in 1836 to connect Georgia by rail with Tennessee and the West. The original surveyor's stake driven in the fall of 1837 was probably somewhere near the Broad Street viaduct, and it was not until 1842 that the dense, swampy undergrowth was cleared and the track extended to the point where the marker stands.

On July 11, 1842, Samuel Mitchell, who owned Land Lot 77, donated five acres to the State for the use of the Western & Atlantic Railroad. When streets had been laid out, this tract, which came to be known as the State Square, was bounded by Alabama, Pryor, Decatur, and Loyd (Central Avenue) Streets. In 1844 the Georgia Railroad acquired a tract adjoining the State Square at Pryor Street, and in 1846 Mitchell deeded to the Macon & Western Railroad additional land adjacent to both the Georgia Railroad block and the State Square. These three tracts formed a plot two city blocks square in the heart of town, and thus the three railroads met at one point.

In the first years of Atlanta's existence as a city, the Western & Atlantic Railroad office stood on the northern section of the State Square between Decatur Street and the tracks. Sometime after the union passenger depot was erected early in the 1850's, this building was removed, and the city and State decided to convert the unused plaza into a public park. Since failure to use the property for railroad purposes might cause it to revert to the Mitchell heirs, a dummy track was laid into the middle of the plot. Sand walks were laid out, grass and shrubs were planted, rustic benches were placed under the trees, and a high white fence was built.

During the Battle of Atlanta, when the 11 hospitals were overflowing, this park was used for the care of the wounded. Large tables for surgical treatment were set up under the trees; the wounded were brought in and stretched out on the grass until Noel D'Alvigny and other overworked doctors could tend them. On the edge of the park General John B. Hood sat his horse in readiness for action while he received reports from the battlefields and gave orders to aides who dashed away on swift horses toward the sulphurous smoke clouds overhanging the eastern part of the city.

During the Reconstruction Era the Mitchell heirs sued on the grounds that the land was not being used for railroad purposes. By a compromise in 1870 the heirs paid $35,000 to the State and received title to the greater part of the property, and in the same year the park area was divided into city lots and sold.

6. The FULTON COUNTY COURTHOUSE, SE. corner Pryor and Hunter Sts., is a nine-story building constructed of terra cotta and Georgia granite, with a row of fluted engaged columns that rise to the height of five stories above the three arched entrances. Fulton County maintains here seven branches of the Superior Court, five branches of the Civil Court, two branches of the Criminal Court, and one Court of Ordinary, in addition to the various administrative offices of the county agencies. The marble halls of the interior are usually crowded with white and Negro citizens making tax returns, attending sessions in one of the 15 courtrooms, securing licenses, recording transactions, or idly standing in groups discussing politics.

Plans for the construction of this courthouse were made as early as 1907, when a tax was levied and produced more than $100,000. Additional funds were raised in subsequent years, and A. Ten Eyck Brown, an Atlanta architect, was engaged to make a study of courthouse construction in the leading cities throughout the country. Brown later drew the design in collaboration with Morgan & Dillon, a local architectural firm. The building, which cost more than $1,500,000 complete with furnishings, was begun in August 1911, and was ready for occupancy in August 1914.

Fulton County covers an area of 548.25 square miles along the Chattahoochee River, with an extreme length of 60 miles and a width varying from 2.5 to 20 miles. Although it ranks twentieth in size, a population of 392,886 makes it the most thickly settled county in the State. In addition to Atlanta, the county contains eight incorporated towns (Alpharetta, College Park, East Point, Fairburn, Hapeville, Palmetto, Roswell, and Union City) and many thickly populated suburban areas. Administrative affairs are directed by a board of five commissioners who are chosen for four-year terms by popular vote.

Outside the environs of industrial and commercial Atlanta, there is in Fulton County an extensive agricultural region of red-clay soil interspersed with ridges and bottoms of fertile gray loam. On more than 3,000 farms 4,500 growers, 65 per cent of them tenants, raise "everything from cotton to orchids." The county ranks twelfth in the State in the production of cotton, which is the leading money crop. Corn, covering the greatest acreage, is second in importance, while truck produce ranks third. Dairy products and poultry find a ready market in Atlanta, and, in order to provide food for livestock, many acres are planted in peas, alfalfa, velvet beans, and other hay-producing crops. There are still many wooded tracts, although the development of residential suburbs has been rapid.

Most of the land included in Fulton County was opened to settlement in 1821, when the chiefs of the Creek Nation ceded this territory to the Federal Government in a treaty signed at Indian Springs. The following year the area was included in the newly created DeKalb County, and a few men cleared land for widely scattered farms. In order to encourage settlement further, the inferior court ordered roads cut through the region to connect these isolated settlements with established trading posts.

After building houses and planting crops, the first activity of the early citizens was the organization of churches. The first was the Mount Gilead Methodist Church, organized in the southern part of the county on April 24, 1824, and the second was the Utoy Baptist Church, organized near what is now Fort McPherson on August 15 of the same year. The Utoy Church joined the Yellow River Baptist Association in 1825 and immediately became prominent in the affairs of that religious body.

During the 1840's the settlement around the terminus established for the railroads grew rapidly. Immigrants came from other sections of Georgia, from North and South Carolina, and even from such distant States as Pennsylvania and Maine. Many of these were industrial men who lived in town and bought near-by farms to supplement their business enterprises, while others were farmers who settled well away from the railroads.

This influx of people soon created the need for a county seat more accessible than Decatur, which was reached with difficulty over poor roads. Consequently Fulton was created from DeKalb by a legislative act approved on December 20, 1853, and amended on February 21, 1856, when one land lot was transferred back to the parent county. Atlanta was made the seat of the new county. The commissioners, without funds to build a courthouse, acquired administrative offices in the city hall which was at the time being erected on the site of the present State capitol.

Fulton County shared little in the antebellum civilization that prevailed in the plantation belt of the coastal plain. Urban life was primarily commercial and centered about the railroads. The rural section was settled chiefly by owners of small farms and by tenants who cultivated the farms of the townspeople. The first census of the county (1860) reported a population of 14,427, of which only 2,955 were slaves.

After the War between the States the population increased at a phenomenal rate. Business enterprises multiplied as Northern capitalists recognized the commercial advantages of Atlanta, and the transfer of the State government from Milledgeville in 1868 attracted still more newcomers. By 1880 the population was 49,137, and the county officials, cramped by limited quarters in the city hall, felt that the county was sufficiently prosperous to erect a courthouse. Consequently, a red-brick structure was begun on the site of the present courthouse in 1881 and completed the following year.

Industry and commerce far outstripped agricultural development despite the fact that a series of land transfers greatly augmented the area of the county. The first such boundary change was made in 1872, when 6 land lots were added to Fulton from Campbell County; a second was effected in 1916 by the addition of 11 more lots from Campbell; and a third was made in 1927 when 35 lots were transferred from Milton County. The most substantial increase, however, took place on January 1, 1932, when all of Campbell and Milton were absorbed into Fulton County. This merger so isolated the Roswell district of Cobb County that it too was incorporated in Fulton during the latter part of the same year. The total acreage gained was 361.25 square miles: 211 from Campbell, 145 from Milton, and 5.25 from Cobb.

Throughout this period industrial development continued at a rapid pace. Many factories were built and assembly and distribution plants were established within Atlanta and its suburbs. Although the courthouse had been fashioned to "serve forever," the enlarged functions of government soon made the facilities of the building inadequate. In 1911 the county records were moved into rented offices in the Thrower Building and remained there until the present courthouse was erected on the site of the old.

Recommendations have been made in recent years for combining certain city and county departments to avoid duplication of services, but no such changes have been made. The two governments operate as entirely separate entities in their neighboring buildings.

7. An OLD LAMP POST, NE. corner Whitehall and Alabama Sts., has stood in this same location since it was first lighted with gas on Christmas Day, 1855. It is one of the original 50 ornamental iron street lamps which the city ordered installed that year at a cost of $21 each. During the siege of Atlanta in the summer of 1864, the first shell that exploded in the business section of the city struck this post, piercing its base and breaking the shaft into three pieces. The pieces were preserved, and the post was later repaired.

A bronze tablet, relating the history of the post, was placed on the base in 1919 under the auspices of the Old Guard and the Atlanta Chapter of the U.D.C. In December of 1939, for the world premiere of *Gone With the Wind,* a gas connection was again installed so that the old lamp might burn with a perpetual flame as a memorial to the traditions of the South.

8. The KIMBALL HOUSE, 33 Pryor St., SW., a large stone-trimmed brick hotel extending the entire breadth of the block between Decatur Street and the railway viaduct, is an arresting landmark of old Atlanta. A rambling edifice of 440 rooms built at a cost of $650,000 in 1885, the Kimball House was once the largest hotel in the South and a symbol of Atlanta's hospitality. Its turrets, vari-shaped windows, and flat Saracenic ornamentation are characteristic of this lavish, ornate decade when prosperity was first beginning to return to war-ravaged Atlanta.

In the marble lobby is an old silver water cooler and a table which survived the burning of the former Kimball House. Rising to the top floor is an open banistered well, an architectural feature characteristic of many buildings erected in the past century but now almost obsolete. Much of the woodwork is of solid mahogany, and its dark rich tone lends an impressive dignity that is heightened in some of the rooms by stained-glass windows. Several public halls contain elaborate chandeliers—one with more than 50,000 pieces of cut glass—and have beautiful inlaid floors. A brick fireplace with an enormous mahogany mantel extends almost the entire width of the ballroom.

In recent years a few interior and exterior details have been altered, but in all essential respects the hotel appears as it was when first opened. The "Presidential Suite" has been maintained almost as it was when occupied by Presidents Cleveland and McKinley. Old registers show the names of other distinguished visitors who have enjoyed the hospitality of the Kimball House, and for many years this hotel provided the background for the most important social and public gatherings of the city.

Since 1846 this site has been used for inns. In that year Dr. Joseph Thompson erected on the lot the town's first real hotel—a two-story brick structure—and named it the Atlanta Hotel. The building stood diagonally across the street from the railroad depot and quite naturally attracted every visitor to the city. President Millard Fillmore was a guest here in 1856. The Atlanta Hotel was destroyed in 1864 by General Sherman before he left the city to begin his march to the sea.

During Reconstruction Atlanta's quick expansion attracted the attention of many Northern capitalists. One of these was H.I. Kimball, a native of Maine who had made his fortune as an associate of George M. Pullman, the railway car magnate, in Chicago. Kimball came to Atlanta in 1868. A born opportunist, he quickly became the city's leading financial figure. As a promoter, real estate operator, financier, and semiofficial agent of the notorious post-war Governor Bullock, Kimball had interests so extremely complicated by apparently conflicting motives of philanthropy and personal profit that it was difficult to judge his aims.

He was quick to urge the legislature to move the seat of State administration from Milledgeville to Atlanta, and, when the move was made, was equally quick to sell the State his newly erected opera house for a capitol. He led the movement to convert the central city park into a business block, arguing that the sale of the lot and the tax on improvements would swell the municipal treasury. When the opposition gave in, he bought the park area himself and began the construction of business houses. In the meantime he bought the Atlanta Hotel site, planning to erect a new hotel, and immediately set about agitating for the construction of a new Union Depot which would be a credit to the city and which, incidentally, would be located across the street from his proposed hotel. In addition to these activities, Kimball found time to promote seven railroads in various parts of the State. His philanthropies were many and he contributed large sums to educational and charitable institutions.

In 1870 he opened the first Kimball House, a magnificent $500,000 six-story brick structure which at that time was the largest hotel in the South. Dominating the city's skyline, the Kimball House soon became to many a synonym for Atlanta. The hotel was particularly favored by the members of the Georgia legislature who gathered in its rooms for informal night sessions, and it was commonly said that more bills were really passed in the Kimball House than in the State capitol a few blocks away.

But the tide of Kimball's fortunes turned. He lost controlling interest in the hotel even before it opened and, in 1872, because of over-expansion and a growing Nation-wide depression, the rest of his Southern financial empire collapsed. Virtually bankrupt and in failing health, he returned to Chicago, the scene of his early successes, but here he met another disaster in the great fire that swept the city and destroyed his property holdings.

Businessmen of Georgia and the South, who had lost money in the Kimball ventures, arose to accuse him of the illegal manipulation of State and privately owned bonds. Kimball's background, political affiliations, and financial associates, all of which had been overlooked so long as his enterprises paid large dividends, now were made added points of condemnation.

Suddenly in 1874, with his health restored and at least part of his fortunes regained, Kimball reappeared in Atlanta to defend himself. At his request Governor James Milton Smith appointed Judge Linton Stephens to investigate his activities. The judge cleared Kimball, and a grand jury, convened to sit on the case, refused to indict him although several of his business associates were brought to trial. A vindication ball planned in Kimball's honor by leading Atlanta citizens was called off when he refused to attend, stating that he could not accept any public demonstration of trust and respect until the people of Georgia were entirely convinced of his innocence. Inasmuch as there had been no legal indictments made, there was no possible legal redress or vindication.

Time, however, did what his friends and the processes of law could not do. So great was his personal magnetism and executive ability that within a few years Kimball was again directing civic enterprises. He purchased Oglethorpe Park as a fair ground for the city and got himself appointed director general of the International Cotton Exposition which was held there in 1881. He established the annual North Georgia Fair on this same site, organized the Atlanta Cotton Factory, secured the International Commercial Convention for the city, and took part in many other ventures.

At 4:40 on the morning of August 12, 1883, the Kimball House caught fire and burned to the ground in one of the most spectacular fires in the city's history. Virtually everyone in town left his bed and rushed to the scene, standing in dumb horror as the symbol of a city was destroyed before their eyes. Fortunately no lives were lost nor was anyone seriously injured, but the sight of the blackened ruins cast a pall of depression over the city.

Kimball, who was in Chicago at the time of the fire, immediately returned to Atlanta and organized a stock company to undertake rebuilding. In this he was successful and the present Kimball House was opened in 1885. Kimball, completely restored to public favor, made his home in Atlanta until his death in 1895.

9. The JOEL HURT PARK, occupying the block bounded by Gilmer and Courtland Sts. and Edgewood Ave., is a vivid green triangle in this section of high buildings and crowded traffic. Twenty-one full-grown trees, including live oaks, magnolias, sugar maples, willows, and water oaks, have been placed about the grounds, as well as scores of evergreen shrubs. A large fountain is illuminated at night by a battery of multi-colored lights that play constantly over the spouts and veils of water. The combination of changing water patterns and colors—from lilac and blue to rose—complete their cycle in about 20 minutes.

The site of this city park and a sum of $50,000 were acquired in 1940 in exchange for the old city hall property at Marietta and Forsyth Streets. The park was constructed with the aid of funds from the Work Projects Administration and the Hurt Memorial Association. William C. Pauley landscaped the park as a setting for the Joel Hurt Fountain, designed by the Atlanta sculptor Julian Harris and presented to the city by the Emily and Ernest Woodruff Foundation.

10. The MUNICIPAL AUDITORIUM, NE. corner Courtland and Gilmer Sts., now (1942) faces the street with a bare three-story brick wall streaked and blackened by a fire that destroyed the entire front of the building on the evening of November 11, 1940. In the gutted portion were Taft Hall, a convention room with a seating capacity of 500, and the assembly rooms and armory for the State military forces. A temporary walkway bridges the ruins and leads to the doorway of the auditorium.

The main hall, which has a seating capacity of 5,163, was virtually undamaged and is still in use. Its horseshoe-shaped arena is surrounded by boxes, a dress circle, and a balcony, all reached by broad ramps leading up from the foyer. The console of the large Austin organ, which was installed by the Atlanta Music Festival Association in 1911, is at the rear of the stage, but the 6,000 pipes, ranging in length from a few inches to 32 feet, are entirely hidden in the ceiling. The sound is emitted through grilles 80 feet long above the orchestra pit.

Plans for the structure were begun in the fall of 1906, when the abandonment of a projected exposition left unexpended the public funds that had been raised for sponsoring it. At a mass meeting a resolution was adopted to urge the building of a city auditorium, and a committee of 25 was appointed to present the proposal to the mayor and council. Since the city charter prohibited officials from assuming obligations that would extend beyond the year in which they were made, the Atlanta Auditorium-Armory Company, a private corporation, was organized on February 7, 1907, to issue bonds in the amount of $175,000. These were sold to an insurance company, and the city was then able to assume the contracts annually and redeem the bonds from surplus funds in the treasury. The plain red-brick building was completed in 1909 at a cost of $192,000.

During the years 1936 to 1938, more than $600,000 was spent by the city and the Works Progress Administration in completely remodeling and redecorating the theater part of the building. John Robert Dillon, the Atlanta architect who designed the building originally, drew the plans for the remodeling.

Since its erection the auditorium has served as the setting for a wide variety of entertainment and for many colorful events in the history of the city. Recorded on its calendar are concerts, operas, political rallies, flower and automobile shows, graduation exercises, boxing and wrestling matches, basketball tournaments, roller skating derbies, dances, and even circuses sponsored by local organizations.

The capacity of the building has been taxed many times. From 1910 until 1930 the Metropolitan Opera Company of New York produced annually at the auditorium a series of operas, and an audience of more than 5,000 at a performance was not unusual. When Caruso sang in Atlanta for the first time in 1910 in a presentation of *Aida,* he faced an audience of more than 7,000, for all available standing room was sold before the crowds could be turned away from the box office. Another unusually large crowd was that which assembled to hear Franklin D. Roosevelt speak during the presidential campaign in 1932. Among other events that have attracted large numbers were the meetings of the Baptist World Alliance in the summer of 1939 and the ball celebrating the premiere of the film production of *Gone With the Wind* in December of the same year.

11. WOODROW WILSON'S LAW OFFICE, 44½ Marietta St., is a small, second-story room at the head of a narrow flight of stairs that leads directly from the street. Wilson's occupancy is commemorated by a bronze tablet on the Forsyth Street wall of the building and a framed feature story from the Atlanta *Journal* on the wall of the office.

Here, in the summer of 1882, immediately after he had received his license to practice as an attorney-at-law, Wilson was admitted to partnership with E.I. Renick, under the firm name of Renick and Wilson. But clients were scarce, and the young intellectual whiled away many empty hours watching from his office window the crowds that milled about the temporary State capitol across the square. Sometimes he sat in the galleries of the house and listened to the debates on the floor, afterward describing the representatives in letters to his friends as "country lawyers, merchants, farmers, politicians, all of them poor, many densely ignorant. . . ." In September 1882, Walter Hines Page, who was traveling throughout the South for the New York *World,* called at Wilson's office, and the two men were attracted to each other instantaneously by the similarity of their ideas and tastes. It was Page who excited Wilson with enthusiasm for study at Johns Hopkins, and in the fall of 1883 the young lawyer gladly left "slow, ignorant, uninteresting Georgia" for the more congenial atmosphere of the university.

12. The HENRY GRADY MONUMENT, Marietta and Forsyth Sts., was unveiled on October 21, 1891, as a memorial to Henry Woodfin Grady, renowned throughout the Nation as an orator and journalist. The ten-foot bronze statue, posed as if delivering an address, stands upon a massive pedestal of Georgia granite, which is inscribed with quotations from the orator's speeches. Draped female figures seated on each side of the pedestal represent *Memory* and *History.*

Henry Woodfin Grady, born in Athens, Georgia, on May 24, 1850, was only a schoolboy when his father was killed near Petersburg, Virginia, in the early days of the War between the States. He was graduated from the University of Georgia in 1868 and spent the two succeeding years studying law at the University of Virginia, where he won many honors for his oratory. When he returned to Georgia he married his boyhood sweetheart, Julia King of Athens, and moved to Rome, where he began his newspaper career on the Rome *Courier.* Soon he became owner and editor of the Rome *Commercial,* but the town was hardly large enough to support more than one newspaper, and the *Commercial* went into bankruptcy. Grady then moved to Atlanta and bought an interest in the Atlanta *Herald,* a paper that soon became very popular because of its expensive advertising stunts. Too much money was invested in this venture, however, and Grady lost heavily when the paper failed. After another failure on the Atlanta *Capital,* he secured an appointment as Southern correspondent for the New York *Herald,* a position that he filled brilliantly for five years. In 1880 he bought one-fourth interest in the Atlanta *Constitution* and developed this paper into a strong political factor not only in Georgia but in the entire South.

Handsome, emotional, and eloquent, Grady was a powerful force in the political and social life of the South. The dominant theme in all his writing and speaking was the rehabilitation of the Southern States through industrialization, and he popularized the term New South to emphasize the difference between the industrial economy that he championed and the old agrarian order. His magnetic personality and his moving pleas for a reunited Nation were influential in overcoming much sectional bitterness and restoring friendship between the North and the South in the years after the war. The speeches that brought Grady most acclaim were "The New South," addressed to the New England Society of New York City in 1886, "The South and Her Problem," delivered at Dallas, Texas, in 1887, and "The Race Problem" before a Boston audience shortly before his death on December 23, 1889.

Soon after his death a fund of $20,000 was raised by voluntary contributions from all parts of the country, and Alexander Doyle was commissioned to design a monument. Governor W.J. Northen of Georgia and Governor David B. Hill of New York presided over the impressive ceremony of unveiling the statue before a crowd estimated at 50,000.

13. The CANDLER BUILDING (*open*), 127 Peachtree St., NE., built 1904-06, was Atlanta's first skyscraper. So impressive were its 17 stories of Georgia white marble, rising high above the surrounding buildings, that "as tall as the Candler Building" was for several years a popular local simile.

Economy was apparently no item in the plans for a structure that was intended to be the finest and best equipped office building in the South. Excavations prior to laying the foundation required six months of blasting into the stratum of solid granite which underlies a large part of Atlanta. Installed in the first basement were luxurious baths and a swimming pool 20 feet long by 16 feet wide. The second basement contained a hydraulic power plant which for many years provided the current for the building.

The ornamentation is elaborate even for a period that was characterized by lavishness in architecture. For the execution of the artistic details Candler imported sculptors from Italy, France, England, and Scotland.

Marble was used for wainscoting and floors throughout all the corridors, and the two 26-foot pillars at the Houston Street entrance were cut from single blocks. A series of panels carved across the three sides of the building represents sculpture, art, literature, music, natural history, astronomy, statesmanship, agriculture, and steam power. Plaques bear the portraits of famous men carved in high relief, and marble atlantes support the imposing arch on both the Peachtree and Pryor Street entrances.

From the lobby a grand staircase constructed of Amicalola marble winds upward to the second floor and downward to the first basement. The broad marble rail ends with a flourish in the form of a dolphin. The elaborately carved frieze along the stairway portrays in high relief Alexander H. Stephens, Charles J. Jenkins, General John B. Gordon, General Joseph E. Wheeler, Sidney Lanier, Joel Chandler Harris, and Eli Whitney. In two niches are busts of Asa G. Candler's parents. Interesting embellishments include the marble alligators above the drinking fountains, the bronze birds that support the marble stairway, the bronze mailboxes bearing Latin mottoes, and the grillwork on the stairway that leads through the upper floors.

The southern portion of the lot on which the Candler Building stands is the site of old Wesley Chapel, a small structure of sawn planks that was erected in 1848 by the trustees of the First Methodist Church. During the War between the States the Confederate Government confiscated the northern part of the lot as a location for the headquarters of the Confederate Commissary Department. When the United States Government sold the captured Confederate property after the war, the congregation of the First Methodist Church purchased this adjacent site and in 1870 began construction of a tall-spired brick and stone edifice, which for many years was one of the leading houses of worship in Atlanta. About the turn of the century the expanding membership and the encroaching commercial houses of the growing city prompted the congregation to buy land farther out Peachtree Street and erect a larger church. The Candler Investment Company acquired the property in 1903 and engaged George E. Murphy to draw plans for the office building. Several changes have since been made in the lower floors to meet the needs of tenants.

14. The GRAND THEATER (*open*), 157 Peachtree St., NE., is the oldest theater building now standing in Atlanta. Soon after the War between the States several theaters were opened and operated successfully, but they were all completely outmoded when Laurent DeGive opened his elaborate Grand Theater on February 10, 1893, with a presentation of *Men and Women* by DeMille and Belasco. Atlanta society in full dress attended the opening performance, applauded enthusiastically the laudatory speeches of prominent citizens, and praised the luxurious appointments of the new opera house, "one of the finest theaters in the world." The cost of the building, which

was designed by McElfetrick & Sons of New York, was estimated at $250,000, and its seating capacity of 2,700 made it the third largest theater in the United States. Among the decorations particularly noted in the columns of the *Constitution* were the marble-tiled entrance, the stained-glass doors, the frescoes in pink, blue, and gold with many cupids and flowers, a picture in the dome of "lassies dancing and twining floral chains," the curtain portraying Shakespeare reading a play to Queen Elizabeth, and the silver rails and rich golden-brown velour draperies of the 22 boxes. More practical equipment included electric lights, a central heating plant, a check room for coats, and lounges for men and women.

Laurent DeGive, a distinguished Belgian, came to Atlanta in 1860 as a young man and in 1870 opened a successful opera house on Marietta Street. When he began building the Grand, many people predicted that he would lose his fortune in so extravagant a venture, saying that it was too large for Atlanta and too far from the heart of town, which was then centered around Alabama Street. On the contrary, the Grand had an immediate success and retained its pre-eminence over a long period despite the competition offered by later theaters.

It was here that the illustrious Sir Henry Irving appeared as Shylock in the *Merchant of Venice,* with Ellen Terry as Portia and Ethel Barrymore as Jessica. Julia Marlowe, E.H. Sothern, and Robert Mantell also played Shakespeare here, and Maude Adams starred in Barrie's immortal story *Peter Pan.* Joe Jefferson in *Rip Van Winkle* brought tears and laughter across the footlights, and William Faversham pleased his audiences in the old melodrama, *The Squaw Man.* Other celebrities who appeared at the Grand included John Drew, Fanny Davenport, Anna Held, Lillian Russell, Otis Skinner, Emma Calve, and Maxine Elliott.

When the Erlanger Theater was built farther out on Peachtree Street in 1926, legitimate drama was booked there, and the Grand was leased for 60 years by Loew's, Inc., as a motion picture house. This severed the DeGives' long connection with the theater in Atlanta. During the summer of 1932 the entrance and auditorium of the old building were completely remodeled and redecorated in modern design by Thomas W. Lamb, Inc., New York architects. The first floor facade and the doors are made of aluminum, and the walls are lined with marble. The passage from the street to the foyer is laid in squares of rubber matting, made of brightly colored strips pressed into a geometrical design.

On December 15, 1939, the Grand witnessed a brief return of its former glory when the premiere of *Gone With the Wind* was shown here. Again Atlanta society, in full dress, attended the old theater in company with cinema stars and other visiting celebrities to applaud the film production of the famous book and to pay honor to its Atlanta author, Margaret Mitchell.

The seven-story brick office building, through which the foyer of the theater runs, was erected in front of the auditorium building and opened for occupancy in 1894. Nixon and Lindsey were the architects. The name DEGIVE and the family coat-of-arms are carved across the front of the building, which shows Romanesque influence in its arched bay windows and the elaborate ornamentation of its stone trim. For many years the DeGive family lived in an apartment on the second floor.

15. The CARNEGIE LIBRARY (*open weekdays 9-9, children's department 9-6; Sun., reading room only, 2-6*), 126 Carnegie Way, NW., is housed in a rectangular, two-story building of Georgia marble designed by Akerman and Ross of New York and opened to the public in 1902. Tall engaged double columns with Ionic capitals frame the recessed entrance, which is arched to match the large windows across the facade. Beneath the dentiled cornice the names of classical writers are cut into the stone. From the lobby a broad marble stairway curves upward to the second floor. Covering the entire south wall of the reference room is a large mural, *The Dawn of Learning,* painted by Mrs. Farnsworth Drew, an Atlanta artist.

Prior to the War between the States Atlanta had no regular library service, although a few booksellers lent volumes at a low weekly rental. In December 1866, when Atlanta's young men had little money for entertainment, a group of them petitioned in the *Atlanta Daily New Era* for a reading room that would afford them intellectual improvement along with bodily warmth. The plan for a subscription library originated with Darwin Jones, a teller of the Georgia National Bank who had recently come south from Milwaukee. Citing examples of such institutions in Northern cities, Jones aroused other public-spirited young men, and a meeting was called in July 1867, which led to the formation of the Young Men's Library Association with an original membership of 47. A small room on Alabama Street was rented for $3 a month, and $15 was spent on shelving.

Unceasing financial difficulties were met with the proceeds from concerts, bazaars, lectures, and even spelling matches. Some additional income was realized in 1873, when young women were first admitted to membership. Funds were checked vigilantly; one librarian was asked to resign because of "faulty bookkeeping" as well as his candid habit of annotating the financial status of members on the books which were later read by the indignant subjects themselves. In 1883 an art loan exhibition, sponsored by the association, aroused unprecedented local enthusiasm for painting and brought a profit of $800. Lighter entertainment on this occasion was provided by *tableaux vivants* and a chess game with live pawns. Though never forgetting the high purpose of their enterprise, the members kept up their spirits by many gayeties, including frequent oyster suppers at Pease's Bar on Decatur Street.

The library was moved several times as it grew more popular and required more commodious quarters. In 1892, Eugene Mitchell, the president of the organization, suggested plans for securing a gift from Andrew Carnegie. In 1899 the famous philanthropist gave $100,000 for the construction of a building with the stipulation that the city provide a site and maintain the library at not less than $5,000 a year. In 1902 the Carnegie Library of Atlanta, the eleventh such institution to be established on the Carnegie plan, was opened in its present building. Anne Wallace, the first librarian under this system, was founder of the Georgia Library Commission, which extends service to rural areas.

In 1924 the Young Men's Library Association was officially dissolved and its records given to the Carnegie Library. Despite the depression of the 1930's, old services have been extended and new ones introduced. The library now owns approximately 190,000 volumes and maintains ten branches, two of which are for Negroes.

16. MARIST COLLEGE, junction Peachtree and Ivy Sts., is a military day school conducted by the Marist Order of the Roman Catholic Church. The plain, stone-trimmed red-brick building stands adjacent to the Sacred Heart Church with its Romanesque arches and elaborate clustered pillars. Priests and dark-robed nuns are familiar forms in this neighborhood, a sober contrast to the lively Marist boys in their horizon-gray uniforms. During school hours long lines of cadets drill on the level parade ground, and sometimes the sharp crack of rifles is heard from the target practice range.

Established in 1901, the school has no college department but offers courses in its junior and senior high schools providing sound preparation for entrance into any college or scientific school. Although the school functions under the auspices of the Marist Order, it is nonsectarian in its operation and its 200 students come from many denominations.

Cadets are under military discipline from assembly to dismissal, and a minimum of five hours a week is required for drill and military exercises. Under the command of a retired officer of the United States Army, this department offers the course of training prescribed by the War Department for junior divisions. Since 1917 a Reserve Officers' Training Corps unit has been established here, thus enabling graduates to obtain army commissions after four years in Marist College and one season in an R.O.T.C. camp. Another popular feature of this department is the band, which is composed of volunteer cadet musicians.

Marist maintains an excellent record in sports, and its football, baseball, basketball, golf, and swimming teams are prominent in all local interscholastic meets.

17. BALTIMORE BLOCK, Baltimore Place between West Peachtree and Spring Sts., is a row of brick houses which, occupied as residences by fashionable society during the eighties and nineties, has recently become a miniature Greenwich Village for Atlanta artists and writers. The three-story dwellings were erected in 1885 by a Baltimore investment corporation known variously as the Baltimore Land Company and the Atlanta Land and Annuity Company. According to the old Baltimore real estate system, the land was leased from its

original owner for 99 years and houses sold for the duration of the lease. Construction followed the Baltimore pattern of joining separate units in one continuous front set flush with the sidewalk.

Although the carved white cornice extending across the joined facades gives the impression of a single building, the dwellings are actually separate, with 18 inches of air space between the brick walls. The uniformity of the stoops and deeply recessed entrances is relieved somewhat by minor variations: some of the stoops have stone steps and others have brick steps with iron railings; some of the glass transom lights above the doors are rectangular, while others are fan-shaped. Grilles protect some of the basement windows, and the ironwork is repeated in a second-floor balcony that runs the width of several of the middle houses.

Early in the 1880's commerce had broken into the formerly desirable residential sections around Capitol Square, causing many of Atlanta's leading families to move farther north to Peachtree and its side streets. Some of them, attracted by the trim, compact dwellings of a type so new to the city, established themselves on Baltimore Block and made it a fashionable neighborhood.

Each house was occupied by only one family; the first floor was taken up by a dining room and a large and a small living room, while the second and third floors each had two large bedrooms, adjoining dressing rooms, and a large apartment used either for storage or by the seamstress on her biennial visits to deck out the ladies of the household. Following the plan of English town houses, the kitchen was in the basement, with back stairs leading up to the dining room. A system of central heating, one of the first in the city, was effected by placing a Baltimore heater in each fireplace on the lower floor with vents running to the rooms above. The plan for each house was identical except for "pairing off" by opposite arrangements of hallways and fireplaces.

Into the new century this row remained the habitat of the leisurely and elegant generation which had made it popular. Every afternoon of pleasant weather smart carriages clattered over the stone blocks of this street, for it had one of the first cobblestone pavements in the town. So arresting was this line of Georgian facades that Atlanta showed it to visitors as one of the leading sights.

But, as the twentieth century advanced, new commercial buildings closed rapidly about Baltimore Block and drove its residents still farther northward. Asa Candler, the affluent and public-spirited Coca-Cola king, attempted to buy the entire block for the establishment of a medical center, but this project failed because one owner refused to sell. In the years immediately following, the units were rented for various purposes to short-term tenants, but quality continued to decline until some of the houses stood vacant, their gaping doors inviting only vagrants to the shelter of the cobwebbed rooms.

During the depression a group of artists, in search of inexpensive quarters, rented space here and opened studios. Rent was low and remodeling had to be done at the tenant's own expense; some made only minor necessary changes, while others decorated with gay. colors, painting the fronts white and the doors deep blue or Chinese red. Window boxes and trellised morning glories further enlivened the plain brick facade. The block soon became crowded with antique shops, photographers' studios, landscape architects' establishments, and the workrooms or living quarters of artists. A tearoom, patronized periodically by most of the occupants, became a factor of fusion for the community spirit.

Since four of the houses at the Spring Street corner were razed to make way for an oil company, only ten dwellings now remain in the block, and only one of the original families still owns the property here. But Baltimore Block has again become a leading sight of Atlanta, both because its architectural style is unique in the city and because it is the home of persons prominent in Atlanta's artistic life.

18. The GEORGIA SCHOOL OF TECHNOLOGY, North Ave. between Williams and Luckie Sts., occupies a 55-acre campus in a section of Atlanta that is rapidly changing from residential to commercial. Along North Avenue old-fashioned frame dwellings, now serving as lodgings, are interspersed with small shops that cater to student trade. Near the south entrance of the campus the severely modern brick buildings of a housing project replace a former slum region, while to the west is the distant smoke of factories and railroad yards. The entire scene is constantly animated by the life of the students—in blue and khaki uniforms hurrying to the drill field, or with levels, rods, and chains busily absorbed in surveying the campus plots and adjacent streets. Several gayly painted "jalopies" usually stand at the curbs, bearing on their sides lopsided letters spelling out words of the school song "I'm a ramblin' wreck from Georgia Tech."

Grouped compactly within this area, the 32 buildings are dominated by the administration building, conspicuous for its tall spire with the word TECH emblazoned in electric lights on all four faces. The older halls are plain red-brick structures with little adornment, but the newer ones, designed by faculty members of the architectural department, have limestone trim and other decorative details in Collegiate Gothic style.

This institution, maintained by State appropriations, tuition fees, and the income from a $574,000 endowment, is the technological school of the University System of Georgia. Courses leading to bachelors' degrees are offered in aeronautical, ceramic, chemical, civil, electrical, general, mechanical, public health, and textile engineering and also in architecture, chemistry, and industrial management. In addition the college grants masters' degrees in architecture and in aeronautical, ceramic, chemical, civil, electrical, and textile engineering. The graduate department, which was organized in 1922, is still small. During the year 1939-40, the school registered only 41 graduate students but had 3,767 undergraduates, including those in the evening and summer schools. The faculty numbered 165 professors, 37 graduate assistants, and several student assistants.

The Co-operative Plan, introduced in 1912, permits students to co-ordinate theory and practical experience. Those who are accepted in this department spend alternate quarters of five entire years attending school and working in such industrial firms as construction, railroad, and electrical companies and with such manufacturing plants as steel, textile, and paper mills. Degrees are offered in chemical, civil, electrical, mechanical, and textile engineering, and students are fitted for positions in designing, production, and sales departments of industries in these engineering fields.

Extension work is conducted on the campus by the Evening School of Applied Science. This department, organized in 1908, offers two-year courses in various technical fields, including automobile engineering, building construction, heating, ventilating, and radio. Credits are not applicable toward a degree, but certificates are issued upon completion of the requirements.

The State Engineering Experiment Station, the engineering research unit of the university system, is operated on the campus and is affiliated with the various teaching departments. The purposes of this agency, which was founded in 1934, are to aid industry by developing the resources of the State, to integrate agricultural and industrial activities, and to support scientific research, both fundamental and applied, in the numerous university institutions. Here the varied facilities of numerous laboratories and the services of technically trained men are available in an academic atmosphere. The studies are financed by the State in co-operation with private enterprises, government agencies, or technical foundations, and the results are made public through bulletins and circulars. During the school year 1939-40, experiments were conducted on such problems as the more efficient processing of cotton, analysis of the proper types of industry for Georgia and the Southeast, the development of a new kind of aircraft, the finding of new uses for pecan oil, improvements of the properties of rayon, and the processing of domestic flax to suit cotton mill methods.

Both a military and a naval unit of the Reserve Officers' Training Corps are maintained at the Georgia School of Technology. The army unit, established here in 1920, is the successor of the Citizens' Military Training Corps, which was organized as a war measure in 1917. The War Department provides a staff of officers and equipment for instruction in four divisions—infantry, artillery, signal corps, and ordnance; these courses in military science and tactics are more extensive than those offered at any other school in the State. Georgia Tech was among the six colleges selected by the Navy Department in 1926 for the establishment of Naval R.O.T.C. units to train students in navigation, seamanship, naval ordnance and gunnery, and naval engineering. Enrollment in the naval unit is limited, and graduates may receive appointments as Ensign in the Supply Corps of the U.S. Navy or as Second Lieutenant, U.S. Marine Corps.

In addition to the physical equipment of the laboratories and shops, five engineering departments have reading rooms where books and magazines of special technical significance are kept. Writings of a more general nature are housed in the main library. In all, the college possesses 45,000 bound volumes, 5,000 unbound pamphlets, and many periodicals.

An informal collegiate atmosphere prevails in the writing and editing of four publications: the *Technique,* a weekly newspaper; the *Yellow Jacket,* a monthly humorous magazine; the *Georgia Tech Engineer,* a serious magazine published four times during the school year; and the *Blue Print,* the college annual. A more professional attitude, however, predominates at the meetings of such local and Nation-wide technical organizations as the Architectural Society, the American Society of Civil Engineers, the American Institute of Chemical Engineers, and the American Ceramic Society. The college chapters of these associations meet frequently to hear prominent lecturers, to see motion pictures on technical subjects, to make inspection tours of industrial plants, to plan displays, or to entertain practicing engineers.

Sports, under the supervision of the Georgia Tech Athletic Association, occupy a prominent place in student life. Since intramural and intercollegiate contests are scheduled in many sports, including tennis, swimming, fencing, golf, track, rifle shooting, baseball, basketball, and football, more than 50 per cent of the Tech men participate in some form of exercise. The sport best known outside the college halls is football. Tech's football team, the "Yellow Jackets," has steadily increased its popularity since its organization in 1893 by Leonard Wood, student and coach, and has distinguished itself in games throughout the United States. After the successful 1928 season, the Tech team defeated the University of California in the Rose Bowl game at Pasadena on New Year's day. The 1939 season culminated in an invitation to play in the Orange Bowl at Miami, where Tech defeated the University of Missouri in the New Year's Day game.

Georgia Tech was founded in that period when the general cry for industrialization was finding a response in the establishment of engineering schools in all parts of the Nation. A need for such a school in Georgia, first voiced by W.T. Hanson, editor of the Macon *Telegraph and Messenger,* was also ardently advocated by Henry W. Grady in the Atlanta *Constitution.* As a result, N.E. Harris of Macon, later governor of Georgia, introduced before the legislature a resolution to consider the establishment of a technical school in Georgia. This resolution was passed on November 24, 1882, and Governor Alexander H. Stephens immediately appointed a commission of ten men to visit and study the leading engineering schools of the United States. On the recommendation of the committee the general assembly in 1885 appropriated $65,000 for the establishment of the Georgia School of Technology.

One of five competing cities, Atlanta made the high bid of $130,000 in land and money for the site of the new school. Professor M.P. Higgins, of the Worcester Polytechnic Institute, was engaged to supervise the organization, and in 1887 construction of the first buildings was begun on a five-acre tract purchased from the Peters Land Company. Later Richard Peters donated an additional tract of four acres. Dr. Isaac Stiles Hopkins, who had instituted the first technological course in the South at Emory College in 1884, was chosen the first president. School was opened on October 3, 1888, with 84 students, and four days later formal installation services were held at DeGive's Opera House on Marietta Street.

Growth was steady from the beginning. After the first eight years, during which the only degree offered was that of mechanical engineering, other courses were added to the curriculum with the aid of State appropriations, private endowments, and gifts from scientific foundations. When textile engineering was introduced in 1899 and ceramic engineering in 1924, these were the first such courses in the South. A period of rapid expansion followed the Greater Tech Campaign of 1920, when funds were raised for buildings and equpiment. The building program was accelerated during the 1930's by funds from the various Federal public works agencies.

In 1931 the general assembly passed a law requiring the reorganization of the State institutions of higher learning and the creation of the University System of Georgia. During that year the school lost its individual board of trustees and a few courses in business and commerce that were duplicated at the State University. Since January 1, 1932, when the measure became effective, the control of the Georgia School of Technology, like that of all the State colleges, has been vested in a central board of regents, appointed by the governor.

The GUGGENHEIM SCHOOL OF AERONAUTICS BUILDING, corner North Ave. and Cherry St., is constructed of red brick with concrete trim, its facade ornamented with figures of Pegasus, the winged mythological horse, and of the American eagle. In the building are an exhibit room and a drafting room for the designing of model aircraft, a machine and woodworking shop for construction, and laboratories, including two wind tunnels, for testing. The course in aeronautical engineering, the only one in the South, is open only to students who have received a degree in civil, electrical, general, or mechanical engineering. It was added to the curriculum in 1930 with the aid of a grant of $300,000 from the Daniel Guggenheim Fund for the Promotion of Aeronautics. The founding was the result of a previous survey made by Emory Land, a United States naval aeronautics authority, who was the vice president of the foundation. Because of its high scholastic standards, Georgia Tech was chosen from 27 Southern colleges and universities for the location of the school.

BRITTAIN HALL, on Techwood Drive between North Ave. and Third St., was completed in 1928 and dedicated to Marion Luther Brittain, who has been president of the Georgia School of Technology since 1922. With its square central tower and loggia with pointed arches, this structure shows a more marked Gothic influence than the other buildings on the campus. It is set well back on a deep lawn and is flanked by dormitories placed almost flush with the sidewalk. The interior of the dining hall with its high gabled ceiling reflects the architectural style of the exterior. A large four-pointed stained-glass window of Tudor design in the right wing contains 14 panels, symbolizing the various activities of the school. The design, chosen from plans submitted by the graduating class of 1928, was made by Julian Harris, who has since achieved distinction as a sculptor and become a faculty member of the department of architecture. The panels were executed by the J. and R. Lamb Studios of New York.

GRANT FIELD, corner North Ave. and Techwood Drive, is the major athletic arena of the Georgia Tech campus. Here in the fall, the "Yellow Jackets" meet the teams of rival colleges and universities to the accompaniment of frenzied cheering and the music of bands. The games played here every alternate year with the "Bull Dogs" of the University of Georgia are of unusual local interest because of the intense traditional rivalry between these two leading schools of the university system. Here, also, the churches hold Easter sunrise services and the city schools present pageants. Charles Lindbergh spoke here October 11, 1928; Winston Churchill on February 23, 1932; and Franklin Roosevelt on November 29, 1935. The field, 800 feet long and 400 feet wide, is named in honor of Hugh Inman Grant, the son of John W. Grant, who made possible the purchase of the tract. The U-shaped stadium, completed in 1925 at a cost of about $350,000, seats more than 30,000 spectators.

The NAVAL ARMORY (*open daily 9-4 during school term*), SW. corner Techwood Drive and Third St., is headquarters for the R.O.T.C. Naval Unit, the Atlanta Naval Reserve Unit, and the Georgia Tech Athletic Association. The two-story main hall, which is 196 feet long and 60 feet wide, is equipped with a complete ship's bridge for instruction in steering and compass computation and with various instruments for training in seamanship and naval warfare. In the entrance hall hangs a print in low relief of the frigate *Constitution,* which was framed in the woodworking shop with timber from the original boat.

This structure, completed in 1934, is a severely plain rectangular building of two stories, stuccoed to blend with the adjacent stadium. A four-foot bronze eagle in a niche above the entrance once formed a part of the massive figurehead on the bow of the U.S.S. *Georgia,* a battleship built in 1906 and scrapped as a result of the 1921 Washington Disarmament Conference. The grilled doors were designed by Julian Harris and made from the heavy bronze scrollwork originally attached to the eagle. On the lawn, across the driveway to the right of the building, hangs a bell, also from the battleship *Georgia.* Two four-inch cannon that stood for several years on the lawn were removed in 1941, to be used in arming United States merchant ships.

The AUDITORIUM-GYMNASIUM, facing Third St. between Techwood Drive and Fowler St., is constructed of reinforced concrete to harmonize with both stadium and armory. The sharp modern lines of the facade are relieved only by ornamental concrete grilles above the double doors, which open onto a terrace a few steps above the street level. The auditorium is used for commencement exercises and the student lecture series, which is open to the general public. When the removable seats are stored beneath the permanent spectators' galleries along each side, a gymnasium floor is provided for contests in basketball, fencing, and badminton. A wing on the south side contains a large tile swimming pool and also a spectators' gallery.

Laboratory work in process in many of the departments is of interest to the technically trained. In the Ceramics Building are exhibited the various clays native to Georgia and wares that have been made from them.

19. PIEDMONT PARK, embracing 185 acres bounded by Tenth St., Piedmont Ave., Westminster Drive, and the Southern Railway, is Atlanta's largest municipal park. Within this area are a lake, swimming pool, golf course, polo field, baseball diamonds, tennis courts, and a supervised playground for children. The rolling terrain has proved readily adaptable to landscape work, which has resulted in the steep slopes, high terraces, and climbing roadways that give so bold and spacious an aspect to the scene. Throughout the grounds wind asphalt driveways and gravel walks shaded by many trees: oaks, sycamores, elms, beeches, poplars, magnolias, and weeping willows, as well as imported varieties less common to this section. Many of the trees have been classified and marked with identification tags by the WPA.

During all seasons of good weather the park is full of life— bicycling schoolboys, children with their nurses feeding the ducks, elderly ladies with leashed dogs, boys and girls in white tennis clothes, fishermen dangling their lines for black bass. On summer nights lamps glow softly upon the strolling couples and cast reflections of jagged brightness along the lake.

The present area of Piedmont Park was contained in a grant issued to Samuel Walker in 1834. This holding remained intact in the possession of his descendants until 1887, when Walker's large stone house and a 189-acre tract were purchased by the Gentlemen's Driving Club. This smart, newly formed organization bought the land for the forthcoming Piedmont Exposition, for which Henry Grady, the famous orator and journalist and a member of the club, provided publicity in the pages of the *Constitution*.

The exposition was opened on October 10, 1887, with a parade and an address by the handsome, popular Governor John B. Gordon, who had become a Confederate idol for his services on General Robert E. Lee's staff. A week later President Grover Cleveland addressed a crowd of 50,000 here. During the 12 days of the exposition great crowds viewed exhibits demonstrating the advancement of the modern South and derived entertainment from parades, sham battles, bicycling, clay pigeon shooting, and fireworks displays.

In 1889 the Gentlemen's Driving Club sold all but four acres of the tract to the exposition company, which during the following years held small fairs on the grounds. In 1894, after a charter had been drafted for the Cotton States and International Exposition, it was proposed that this land be purchased by the city for this occasion, but the proposal was vetoed by Mayor John B. Goodwin, who declared that the site was too far out in the country. The exposition company went ahead with their plan, however, and the lake was dug and several large buildings erected.

The Cotton States and International Exposition was opened on September 18, 1895, when President Cleveland in the White House pressed a telegraphic key and a 100-gun salute was fired. Many States throughout the Nation had displays here, while European and South American countries were well represented. The most striking State exhibit was Pennsylvania's Liberty Bell brought from Independence Hall in Philadelphia. Music was provided by the bands of Victor Herbert and John Philip Sousa and by Theodore Thomas' orchestra from the Cincinnati Conservatory of Music. The lake was used for aquatic events, the first time such sports had been publicly demonstrated in Atlanta.

Among the celebrated men who attended the exposition were General George W. Schofield, the Federal commander whose troops had invaded Georgia more than 20 years earlier; Jeff Cain, the engineer of the *General* when it was captured by Andrews' Raiders in 1862; and Booker T. Washington, the Negro educator, who made a stirring address on the opportunities of his emancipated race.

During the exposition Atlanta business boomed and the city received world-wide publicity. After its close various proposals were made for future disposition of the land, but all were rejected and on May 23, 1904, the park was purchased by the city for $93,000. All connection was now broken between Piedmont Park and the Gentlemen's Driving Club, which had become the Piedmont Driving Club. The park, becoming constantly more popular, was improved from year to year by additional recreation facilities and scenic beautification.

The most important event here in recent years was the brief address by President Franklin D. Roosevelt during his visit to Atlanta in November 1935. Although the day was chill and sunless, an enthusiastic crowd gathered to pay homage and receive the President's warm words of greeting and encouragement.

The PEACE MONUMENT, centering the driveway at Fourteenth Street entrance, is a massive bronze group depicting a Confederate soldier kneeling with lowered gun while the Goddess of Peace extends an olive branch. This sculpture, the work of Allen Newman of New York, was presented to Atlanta by the Gate City Guard and unveiled before a large crowd on October 10, 1911. In commemoration of peace, blue-coated Union veterans mingled with Confederate veterans in gray uniforms at the ceremony.

20. The HIGH MUSEUM OF ART (*open weekdays 9-5; Mon.,*

Wed., Fri., 7-9 p.m.; Sun. 2-5), 1262 Peachtree St., NE., is housed in
a two-story brick and stucco building, the former residence of Mrs.
Joseph Madison High who, in 1926, presented it to the city for use
as an art gallery.   The lower floor is occupied by the offices of the
Atlanta Art Association, chartered in 1905, and by the museum's large
permanent exhibition of paintings, sculpture, and furniture; on the
upper floors are the classrooms of the High Museum School of Art,
which provides instruction in commercial and fine. arts to approximately
175 pupils.   The school was formed in 1925 by the Atlanta Art
Association.

At frequent intervals the museum arranges for a display of loan
collections both from local artists and from well-known galleries in
other cities.   The permanent collection, which is constantly growing,
now covers a broad range of periods and techniques.   The early Italian
painters are well represented. A large canvas, *Lucretia and Tarquinius,*
remarkable for its dynamic action and for the rich red color characteristic of the Venetian School, has been identified as being probably
the work of the famous Luca Giordano.   This painting contrasts with
the equally large *Offerings of the Matronali* by Giovanni Battista
Tiepolo, with its cooler tones and majestic figures.   Other Italian pictures of note are the *Madonna and Child* of Cristoforo Caselli and a
landscape of Salvatore Rosa.

The paintings by French and English artists are few but excellent.
Maxine E.L. Maufra's *Chateau Gaillard* is a fresh, vivid example of
French post-impressionism, while Catherine Lusurier's *Portrait of a
Little Girl with a White Cat* skillfully demonstrates the manner of a
later French school. *Je Vous Salue, Marie* by Oliver Merson, after
being first exhibited in Atlanta at the Cotton States Exposition in 1895,
was purchased by the Piedmont Driving Club and presented years later
to High Museum.   The two most famous of the English portrait
painters whose work is on exhibition here are Sir Joshua Reynolds and
Sir Henry Raeburn.

The work of distinguished American painters, both past and contemporary, forms a large part of the collection.   The *Portrait of the
Reverend George Houston Woodrough* by Thomas Sully is the earliest
representative of the American school, and *A Glass with the Squire*
by Eastman Johnson is a good example of early nineteenth-century
painting.   Prominent in the modern group are portraits by Wilford
S. Conrow, N.R. Brewer, and Frank Duveneck; etchings, lithographs,
and the painting *Isle of Shoals* by Childe Hassam, a noted exponent
of French impressionism; the fanciful *Moon Magic* by Ralph Blakelock; and two works of striking contrast in subject and method by
Thomas Moran, *Fingals Cave* and *Pueblo of Acoma, New Mexico.*
John McCrady's *Woman Mounting a Horse* has caused much discussion by its vigorous modernistic departure from realism in treatment.
Other pictures showing a strong modern trend in color and execution
are Ernest Lawson's *Harlem River at Highbridge,* Robert Brockman's
The Bathers, and Frederick Carl Frieseke's *Girl in Blue Arranging*

Flowers. *In the Dressing Room* by Louis Kronberg shows the influence of the French painter Degas. *Portrait of Scarlett O'Hara* by Helen Carleton is of particular interest to Atlanta citizens because it was presented to the museum by the Hollywood producer David Selznick after the Atlanta premiere of the motion picture *Gone With the Wind*.

In addition to its many paintings the museum contains sculpture, antique furniture, sketches by Rembrandt and Whistler, and water colors by the Hindu philosopher and poet Rabindranath Tagore.

MEMORY LANE, a gallery constructed on the south side of the museum building in 1941, was the gift of Mrs. Thomas K. Glenn and contains only pictures given as memorials. A biographical plaque of the individual is placed beneath each picture. A number of pieces of fine furniture have also been given to Memory Lane.

21. RHODES MEMORIAL HALL or THE GEORGIA DEPARTMENT OF ARCHIVES AND HISTORY (*open Mon.-Fri., 8 a.m.-4 p.m., Sat. 8 a.m.-12 m.*), 1516 Peachtree St., NW., is the repository for Georgia's official documents and historical collections. A commanding edifice of Stone Mountain granite with massive pillars and pointed turrets, the house was erected in 1900 at a cost of about $1,000,000. Most of the 23 rooms are finished in the ornately handsome manner of the period, each being floored in hardwood with a different design in mahogany. The Rose Room is particularly striking because of its hand-painted ceiling, walls covered with old rose damask, and original draperies and portieres trimmed in handmade lace. Two imported gold-leaf cabinets and three circular glass-topped tables are all part of the original furnishings.

Over the carved mahogany stairway a series of Tiffany stained-glass windows depicts *The Rise and Fall of the Confederacy*. These windows, costing $40,000, were installed when the house was built by its original owner, A.G. Rhodes, who made a great fortune from his furniture store and from early transactions in Atlanta real estate. The story is told that Rhodes, who had served in the Confederate army, sent the submitted design of the windows back several times to be altered. The panel showing General Robert E. Lee's farewell to his troops was rejected because Lee had his hat on "and he was too much of a gentleman to tell anybody good-bye without taking off his hat." The Battle of Manassas panel irritated Rhodes still more because the Federal troops were not retreating fast enough "and we had those Yankees running till their coattails were standing out."

The historical collection, subdivided into State and county records, is composed of approximately 1,000,000 unbound original documents and 50,000 books and pamphlets. Private papers pertaining to the State and its citizens are also kept on file. Pictorial items in Rhodes Memorial Hall include miniatures, daguerreotypes, paintings, and photographs. The museum displays relics that portray Georgia life from its early days, including furniture, china, battle flags, and weapons. Of particular interest are the long "Joe Brown pikes," named for

Georgia's pugnacious wartime governor and used by Confederate troops in battle.

Among the recent additions is an exact reproduction of the shrine of the Declaration of Independence and the Constitution of the United States. The shrine, one of a limited number made in honor of the 150th anniversary of the signing of the Constitution, was presented to the State by the Davison-Paxon Company, in whose large department store it was unveiled and dedicated January 6, 1938.

The Department of Archives and History was created by legislative act, August 20, 1918, to keep the State's official records. Lucian Lamar Knight, author of the popular *Georgia and Georgians* and other historical works, was the first director of the department and first State historian. The department was housed in the State capitol until 1930; at that time it was moved to Rhodes Memorial Hall, which had been presented to the State by the heirs of A.G. Rhodes. Records are now sent from every State department, and rooms in the house are reserved by various historical organizations for display of their collections.

22. WASHINGTON SEMINARY, 1640 Peachtree St., NW., has long been Atlanta's most fashionable school for girls. Facing Peachtree Street from the crest of a broad rolling lawn is the dormitory, a white clapboard building with Corinthian columns extending all the way across the front. An unpretentious building in the rear contains classrooms, administrative offices, and an auditorium with a stage for dramatic presentations. With a faculty of 30 and a student body of 300, Washington Seminary offers courses ranging from the nursery school through high school. The high school pupils, which make up the larger part of the student body, are divided about equally between the general and the college preparatory courses. Most of the enrollment is from Atlanta, but accommodations are provided for 25 boarders, and these are always reserved well in advance by girls from various sections of the United States.

The institution was opened in 1878 by the three Misses Washington, lateral descendants of the famous George. While visiting in Atlanta these aristocratic ladies had been struck by the need of a good private school in the city, which was taking its first difficult steps toward recovery from carpetbagger domination. Having no money for a building or equipment, the sisters borrowed the use of a parlor in a Cain Street home and began with eight children to teach the usual elementary subjects. First as the Misses Washington's School for Girls, later as Washington Seminary, the school flourished through the eighties and nineties, moving several times into larger quarters and adding more advanced courses. On fair days the young ladies could be seen practicing their archery and elegant Delsarte calisthenics, which were added to the childish games of the first pupils. Administration passed from the Washingtons successively to Mrs. Emily Park, Mrs. Alice Chandler, L.D. Scott, and Miss Emma Scott.

The present dormitory building was erected in 1890 as the residence of the affluent, widely traveled General Clifford Anderson, whose wife had collected decorative ideas from Europe, Africa, and Asia before the house was built. W.T. Downing, the architect, succeeded in embodying most of Mrs. Anderson's suggestions on the inside, which belies the "Southern Colonial" exterior. The long reception hall is opulent with Pompeiian red walls and cream-colored woodwork forming a background for the bronze statuary, brass jardinieres, and heavy carved teakwood furniture. The vaulted ceiling, studded with many plaster rosettes, is centered by a goldleaf dome. This room and the adjoining dining room give views of a patio encircled by a pillared arcade in the Spanish style.

Miss Emma Scott, the present (1942) principal, speaks with amusement of a great plaster dragon, resplendent in gold and Chinese red, its claws ending in a cluster of electric bulbs, which adorned the wall of a bedroom. For years the girls delighted in the dragon room, proudly showing it off to visitors and pleading with their principal to leave it intact. Miss Scott complied until she found a Cuban student in tears, looking up at the ceiling and crying in broken English, "I have great fear!" The next day the dragon was removed.

23. The NATIONAL STOCKYARDS, Marietta St. and Brady Ave., NW., an area given over to ten independent dealers and one large commission firm, is the largest mule market in the country. Cows, hogs, and sheep are also important in the business of the market, and three large packing plants are operated near the yard. The rush season is from September through May, but wholesale auctions are held every Monday throughout the year and independent sales are negotiated every day in the week. Average annual sales are about 80,000 animals, representing a value of more than $10,000,000. The market brings more buyers to the city than any other Atlanta industry.

Lining both sides of Brady Avenue are the stables, large rambling structures of brick or frame, occasionally painted outside with pictures of prancing horses. All day trucks rumble in and out with loads of mules being brought in for sale or taken out to new owners. This delivery is supplemented by railroads, which have spur tracks leading into the yards. The auction barn, always filled with the smell of straw and sawdust, is a brick building, whitewashed inside, with a high ceiling broken by many skylights. The main floor is given over to stalls, while upper compartments built along the side walls are loaded with bales of hay and sacks of feed.

The auctions are noisy and exciting. Frisky young mules, led by attendants with long whips, prance into the arena before an auctioneer who stands on a raised platform. Buyers crowd in a semicircle around auctioneer and animals, breaking their ranks only to avoid being trampled by a too lively mule. As an animal is brought in, a ringman checks to see that identification numbers are glued to its halter and flank and announces the mule's age, weight, and other characteristics, as well as calling attention to any defects such as cuts and bruises. The ringmaster states a basic bid; then the auctioneer, beating time on the counter, breaks into a chant that is almost unintelligible to newcomers. Voices are drowned in the chant, the crack of whips, and the stamping of hoofs, as buyers indicate their bids by nods or winks. As they are usually experts who know exactly what they want, the auction proceeds at a rapid pace—about one mule a minute —and as many as 800 mules have been sold in a single day. When a sale is closed, the information is conveyed through a speaking tube to a man who records the deal on a ledger and sends the animal to a specified stall.

At the time Atlanta was founded there was a great demand for mules in Georgia and other sections of the agricultural South, and the town's advantage as a distributing center early established it as a livestock market. Tanyards and slaughter pens were operating as early as 1848, but the first definite record of mule transactions is the listing of three "livery and sales" stables in the city directory of 1859. In 1866 the leading citizens of Marietta persuaded Jeremiah Huff to erect stables and pens around his house just off Marietta Street and to provide for owners and drovers bringing livestock to Atlanta for sale. At that time the mules were not shipped by railroad but were brought down on the hoof from the north Georgia mountains.

One of the most successful dealers of the years after the War between the States was John A. Miller, who set up his stables on Alabama Street and later moved to Marietta Street where he established the Miller Union Stock Yards. After his death in 1903 his associate, T.B. Brady, purchased more than 30 acres of land between Marietta Street and Howell Mill Road. A street was cut and named for Brady, and a large frame hotel was erected to accommodate buyers and drovers. Shortly afterward, J.W. Patterson, prominent in the horse and mule business in Lexington, Kentucky, came to Atlanta and joined the firm.

In 1933 the J.F. Huyton Company moved here from Memphis, Tennessee. This long-established firm had held exclusive contracts to furnish horses and mules to the British Government during the Boer War and to the United States Government during the World War. The coming of this company to Atlanta, in addition to similar concerns already operating here, definitely established the city as the country's largest mule market.

24. The SITE OF JOHNSTON'S HEADQUARTERS, Marietta St. and Lewis Ave., NW., is marked by a pyramid of cannon balls on a concrete base. Here, on July 18, 1864, General Joseph E. Johnston, in compliance with orders from President Jefferson Davis, transferred his command of the Army of Tennessee to General John B. Hood. From the town of Dalton, Georgia, Johnston had made a gradual and orderly retreat before the vastly superior numbers of General Sherman, choosing his positions shrewdly and falling back to avoid costly losses of men in open battle. Dissatisfaction with these tactics increased among the civil authorities, however, until Johnston was relieved of

his command, a move that is generally regarded as a serious military blunder in the Atlanta campaign.

25. The HUFF HOUSE (*private*), 70 Huff Rd., NW., one of Atlanta's oldest buildings, was erected in 1855 upon the foundations of a former dwelling built in 1830. A small clapboard structure with a double front gable and brick end chimneys, the cottage stands inconspicuously upon a hill overlooking the Inman railroad yards. Although the house has caught fire twice, its appearance has remained virtually unchanged.

The house is still (1942) occupied by Miss Sarah Huff, who has lived here all her life except for the four months in 1864 when she was a war refugee. In her booklet *My Eighty Years In Atlanta* she recounts her childhood experiences during that stirring summer when General Sherman's Federal troops were forcing the Confederate defense lines to fall back to Atlanta. At that time her father, Jeremiah Huff, a courier for Stonewall Jackson, was fighting in Virginia, and his wife and children had no protection against Confederate marauders who forcibly took their supplies. At last the family was forced to take flight with other refugees.

While the retreating army was massing for a last stand, the house became headquarters for Major Charles T. Hotchkiss, and the Confederate flag was raised over its roof. When the Union troops advanced, General George H. Thomas, commander of the Army of the Cumberland, established his headquarters here under the United States flag. When Sherman's men began to set fire to the city, George Edwards, a resourceful Scotch neighbor, saved the house by saying it belonged to an Englishwoman and running up the Union Jack. Thus the Huff House became known as the House of Three Flags.

When the family returned just before Christmas of 1864, they found the place abandoned except for hordes of hungry cats howling dolefully. Until the cottage could be made habitable again, Mrs. Huff and her children took shelter in the kitchen, which stood separate from the house. Here the indomitable woman not only set up her own household but dispensed hospitality to itinerant refugees who were trying to reach their own homes.

26. SUTHERLAND, 1940 DeKalb Ave., NE., is the former home of General John B. Gordon, Georgia's celebrated Confederate leader and statesman of the Reconstruction. The present structure was erected in 1899 on the site of an earlier residence built shortly after the War between the States and later destroyed by fire. Set far back from the street in a grove of oaks and superb magnolias, the white clapboard house now (1942) stands vacant, badly dilapidated but still showing in its handsome classical facade some vestige of its former grandeur. Eight massive Ionic columns support the second-story roof and frame the simple palladian doorway with its overhanging balcony. The fine appearance of the interior in its heyday is indicated by the ample proportions of the octagonal dining room, galleried two-story reception hall, and tall French windows. Re-

peated efforts have been made by civic and patriotic organizations to secure the house and restore it as a memorial to the famous Confederate general, but present plans are uncertain.

John B. Gordon (1832-1904) was born in Upson County in central Georgia and attended the State University, from which he was graduated with highest honors in the class of 1853. At the outbreak of the War between the States he was engaged in the promotion of coal mine activities in the mountains of northwestern Georgia. The resourceful young man quickly organized a company of mountain men who, known as the Raccoon Roughs, later caused excited comment in Atlanta when they marched about in their homespun jackets and coonskin caps. This company joined the Sixth Alabama Infantry and took vigorous part in the Virginia campaign. Gordon, moving from one military promotion to another, commanded a wing of General Robert E. Lee's Army at Appomattox and at the end of the war bore the rank of lieutenant-general. Besides Appomattox he took part in the fighting at Malvern Hill, Chancellorsville, Gettysburg, Spotsylvania, and Petersburg. Throughout the war he was closely followed by his courageous wife, who nursed him when he was wounded.

After peace was proclaimed he came to Atlanta, opened a law office, and soon joined the energetic group that became known as the vanguard of the South. With Joseph E. Brown, Henry W. Grady, and other practical progressives he strongly advocated wholehearted return to the Union and development of industrial resources. His handsome and eloquent presence soon became familiar on the political scene; in 1868, in the thick of reconstruction strife, he ran as a Democratic gubernatorial nominee against the carpetbagger candidate, Rufus Bullock, but was defeated because of the disfranchisement of many of his own adherents. Constantly fighting for the end of the Northern military rule in Georgia, he became State head of the original Ku Klux Klan, the secret order that did much to restore white supremacy in the South. He was elected to the United States Senate in 1873 and again in 1879 but resigned the following year to raise funds for the Georgia Pacific Railway. Because of his adherence to the new spirit of conciliation and because of his extensive interest in Northern commercial developments, he sometimes came into conflict with the conservatives, of which Robert Toombs and Alexander H. Stephens were the chief spokesmen, and later with the agrarian group under the leadership of the fiery Thomas E. Watson. Nevertheless, his popularity increased; he became Governor of Georgia in 1886, was reelected in 1888, and again went to the United States Senate in 1890. Declining a second term, he returned to Atlanta to devote himself to his business interests until his death in 1904.

27. OAKLAND CEMETERY, bounded by Oakland Ave., Memorial Drive, Boulevard, and the Georgia Railroad line, lies peaceful and quiet within the brick walls that separate it from a busy industrial section. In this old cemetery, owned and well cared for by the city, the weathered tombs and monuments are crowded close together, the

somber whiteness of their irregular shapes accentuated against the dark green of the shrubbery and the magnificent old magnolia and oak trees.

Atlanta's first cemetery was a small plot at the corner of Peachtree and Baker Streets. As early as October of 1849, however, the little town of Atlanta had grown to such an extent that it became necessary to find a cemetery site farther removed from town and consolidate the public and private burial plots. Several "graveyard committees" were appointed by the city council to find a suitable location, and on June 6, 1850, six acres of wooded land were purchased in what is now the southwest corner of the cemetery. Additional tracts were bought from time to time until the area covered 85 acres.

Promptly after the purchase of the first six acres the bodies were removed from the old plots to the new cemetery. On February 21, 1851, the city council elected a sexton and instructed a surveyor to lay off lots and build a suitable enclosure around the grounds. One of the items listed in the city treasurer's report on January 1, 1853, was a hearse purchased by the city for $129.50. In 1896 the ground was enclosed by a red-brick wall, and the gates were built at the Oakland Avenue and Fair Street (Memorial Drive) entrances. From 1907 until 1932, when Oakland was placed under the direction of the park board, the affairs of the cemetery were regulated by a committee of five lot owners elected by the city council. This committee published a book of rules, among other things prohibiting the burial of animals in the cemetery, the erection of fences around lots, and the decoration of graves with shells and other small ornaments.

Since no more lots are available, the cemetery is considered full and only a few interments are made in spaces reserved in old family lots and mausoleums or where an exhumation has been made. In the northeastern corner, across from the Fulton Bag and Cotton Mills, an apparently vacant grassy area of about two acres is filled with unmarked graves. Now that there is no longer any income from the sale of lots, the maintenance of the cemetery is provided entirely by an annual city appropriation.

Many mausoleums and monuments bear the names of pioneer settlers of Marthasville and Atlanta and citizens who have figured prominently in the history of the State. A large block of native granite marks the grave of Martha Lumpkin Compton, daughter of Governor Wilson Lumpkin, in whose honor Atlanta was once called Marthasville. In the northwest corner is the grave of Julia Carlisle Withers, who was the first baby born in the little settlement, and in another part of the cemetery is buried Benjamin Franklin Bomar, Atlanta's second mayor. Near the sexton's office stands a granite monument erected by the cemetery commission in 1916 as a memorial to Atlanta's first mayor, Moses W. Formwalt, who took office in 1848. Near by is the grave of James Russell Barrick, Atlanta's first poet and first editor of the Atlanta *Constitution*.

Sports and Recreation

GRANT PARK LAKE

SWIMMING, GRANT PARK

TENNIS, PIEDMONT PARK

BASEBALL, PONCE DE LEON PARK

FOOTBALL, GRANT FIELD AT GEORGIA TECH

GOLF, BROOKHAVEN COUNTRY CLUB

PLAYGROUND, WASHINGTON PARK

PARADE OF THE OLD GUARD

BARBECUE, LAKEWOOD PARK

SOUTHEASTERN FAIR, LAKEWOOD PARK

DANCING, RAINBOW ROOF

BOWLING IN A DOWNTOWN ALLEY

MAY DAY AT WASHINGTON SEMINARY

ARCHERY, AGNES SCOTT COLLEGE

Near the geographical center of the cemetery, in a section set aside for Confederate soldiers, rises a 65-foot shaft of granite blocks erected in memory of the Confederate dead in 1873 by the Ladies' Memorial Association. Also prominent among the low headstones is the *Lion of Atlanta,* which was unveiled on April 26, 1894, by the same organization to honor the unknown soldiers who fell fighting. The figure of the dying lion reclining upon broken guns and a furled Confederate flag was inspired by the famous Lion of Lucerne and carved from a single block of Georgia marble by T.M. Brady, of Canton, Georgia.

Not far away from the Confederate shaft are the graves of General Clement A. Evans and General John B. Gordon. Other prominent men buried in Oakland Cemetery include Benjamin H. Hill, William J. Northen, Hoke Smith, General William A. Wright, and Captain William Allen Fuller, who led the party that pursued and overtook the engine *General* when it was stolen by Andrews and his Union raiders. Seven of Andrews' men, who were hanged as spies in Atlanta in June 1863, were first buried in Oakland and later removed to the national cemetery in Chattanooga, Tennessee. Alexander H. Stephens, Vice President of the Confederate States, was interred here in 1883, but his body was later moved to his old home at Crawfordville.

Many of the monuments are interesting because of their eloquent inscriptions or unusual design. Besides the conventional carved pillows and draperies, there are many stone lambs, cherubim, and angelic heralds, and several mausoleums look like miniature cathedrals, with their spires and pointed stained-glass windows. Among the oddities is a statue of Jasper N. Smith seated above the door of his mausoleum. Because he never wore a collar or tie, Smith had these omitted from the statue, which he ordered carved and placed on the mausoleum some time before his death. When a vine grew up and entwined the neck of the statue concealing its bareness, he forthwith ordered it cut. The smallest plot in the cemetery contains the grave of "Tweet," a pet mocking bird that died in 1874. As the stonecutter was unable to carve the figure of a mocking bird, Tweet's mistress had to content herself with a lamb on the tiny monument.

Like most old cemeteries, Oakland has its share of graveyard legends concerning nocturnal phenomena—weird drum beats heard in the Confederate section, sobbing, harsh metallic gratings like vault doors opening, and mysterious knockings. Perhaps some of the stories were inspired by a sensational occurrence at the first burial service held in the cemetery, that of James Nissen in the fall of 1850. Obsessed with the fear of burial alive, Nissen had requested his surgeon friend, Dr. Charles D'Alvigny, to sever his jugular vein just before his body was lowered into the grave, and this service was performed, to the horror of witnesses.

28. GRANT PARK, covering a tract of 144 acres bounded by Cherokee Ave., Atlanta Ave., S. Boulevard, Park Ave., and Sidney St., is the oldest park in the Atlanta park system. Many miles of shady

walks and broad paved driveways wind through this gently rolling land, which still bears traces of the breastworks that were built for the defense of Atlanta in 1864. In winter the park is quiet, its broad spaces peopled only by strollers in the sun; but in summer the scene is animated with sun-blistered boys and girls in white drill, sauntering and gayly swinging tennis rackets or wet bathing suits. Recreational facilities include tennis courts, baseball diamonds, a pony ring, a swimming pool, a lake with rowboats, a picnic ground equipped with a pavilion, and a natural amphitheater for band concerts and plays. Gardens and greenhouses supply all the shrubs and plants for the other parks in the city.

The park is named for Colonel Lemuel P. Grant, who planned the fortifications for Atlanta in the spring of 1863. Grant donated the original hundred acres to the city in 1882, a time when Atlanta had recovered sufficiently from the turmoil of reconstruction to give more attention to civic enterprises. With the aid of a topographical map, development of the natural advantages of the wooded area was begun almost immediately, an expenditure of $3,611.70 being reported for the year 1883 by the first park committee appointed by city council. A natural ravine formed by Willow Brook, which flowed through the center of the area, was used for construction of a small lake in 1886, and the following year the larger Lake Abana was completed and boats placed on it. Since Lake Abana could not utilize all the water of Willow Brook, Lake Loomis was built adjoining it in 1888 and later was merged with it. Constitution Spring, which rose clear and cold from the ground near the lake, was surrounded by a picnic pavilion and became a popular gathering place. The lake was enlarged again in 1901, but soon afterwards the contamination of the water resulted in the abandonment of Constitution Spring and Willow Brook, and since 1906 the lake has been filled with water from the city reservoir.

An extension of the park area was made on April 4, 1890, when the city purchased 44 additional acres of land. The large concrete swimming pool, 500 feet long and 200 feet wide, was constructed in 1917, with a low, curving wall through the center to divide the shallow section from the deep. Extensive improvements have been made in recent years throughout the park by workers of the Work Projects Administration.

The GRANT PARK ZOO (*open daily 7-6*) was begun in March 1889, when G.V. Gress, a wealthy merchant of Atlanta, presented to the city the menagerie of a bankrupt circus which he had bought in order to secure the heavy horse-drawn wagons for use in his lumber business. Gress also erected the first shelter to house the animals and their keeper. To this early collection, which was at first known as the Gress Zoo, additions were made from time to time, the most popular being the elephants Clio and Maude, who as long as they lived remained favorites with Atlanta children.

The addition that made Grant Park Zoo the most outstanding

in the Southeast, however, came in 1935 when Asa G. Candler, Jr., gave his valuable private collection to the city. For three years Candler had been assembling fine species of wild animals and birds for a zoological garden on his estate on Briarcliff Road. But suits and injunctions by neighbors, who objected to having a menagerie so close to their homes, and the heavy taxes demanded by the county made this hobby both excessively expensive and embarrassing. Rejecting a bid by the City of New York as too low, Candler offered his vigorous and well-kept specimens to Atlanta as a gift provided suitable quarters were erected to house them. Volunteer contributions of dimes by school children and other public donations provided the necessary funds for the new quarters, and the following year 84 animals and almost 100 birds were transported to their new home.

The most spectacular of the animals in the zoo is Jimmie Walker, a Royal Bengal tiger reputed to be the largest in captivity, whose ferocious claws tore to death a valuable black leopardess in a fight through the bars of their adjacent cages. Large crowds are always attracted to the bears in the cages along the side of the lake, especially the two friendly Himalayans that constantly go through comical exhibitionist antics. The recent arrival of two trained Canadian brown bears lends further appeal to this colony. Another newcomer owes her domicile here to the defense program, for Alice, an 18-year-old elephant that had been trained to pull the big disc harrow on a South Carolina plantation, was brought to Grant Park when her master was called for military service.

FORT WALKER, on Dabney's Hill near the Boulevard and Atlanta Ave. entrance to Grant Park, is a restoration of the Confederate battery that formed the southeast salient angle of the defenses encircling the city in the summer of 1864. The guns and ammunition wagons have been replaced in their original commanding position at the crest of the hill. The fortification was named in memory of General W.H.T. Walker, who was killed in the Battle of Atlanta on July 22, 1864.

The CYCLORAMA OF THE BATTLE OF ATLANTA (*open daily 8 a.m.-10 p.m.; adults 50¢, children 25¢; lectures according to attendance; no cameras allowed*), is housed in an impressive building near the center of Grant Park. The front section of the building, which is situated on a broad paved terrace, is constructed of white, stone-flecked terra cotta in neoclassic design, its recessed entrance dominated by two-story Ionic columns. The facade is decorated by two long bas-relief panels symbolizing peace and reconstruction. The rear section is of white stucco, especially constructed in a circular design to fit the dimensions of the great canvas.

The approach to the painting is by means of a tunnel, which leads to a platform in the center of the circular section of the building. The position of the platform is above the tracks of the contested Georgia Railroad and consequently between the main bodies of the opposing forces.

The great circular painting portrays the Battle of Atlanta which occurred on July 22, 1864, when General Sherman, with approximately 106,000 Union troops, stormed the defenses of Atlanta in an effort to wrest the city from its 47,000 dogged Confederate defenders. Fighting began in the morning and continued until nightfall, with heavy losses on both sides. The dramatic moment perpetuated in the cyclorama took place at about half past four in the afternoon, when General Benjamin F. Cheatham's Corps broke through the Federal line and the Union forces made a counter attack to retake their positions. Scores of dead and wounded lie scattered over the battlefield, clad in the blue uniform of the Union or in the shabby gray or brown homespun that clothed the weary soldiers of the Confederacy. In the distance lies Atlanta, soon to be leveled to ashes, and in the hazy air far above the exploding shells of the battle, soars Abe, the eagle mascot of Union Company C, who was later memorialized on the silver dollar.

The painting, which is 50 feet high, 400 feet in circumference, and weighs more than 18,000 pounds, was produced in the studios of the American Cyclorama Company of Milwaukee, Wisconsin, under the direction of William Wehner of Austria. The staff that executed the painting included a corps of German artists and many Americans, among them Theodore R. Davis, who had accompanied General Sherman to Atlanta in 1864 to make drawings for *Harper's Weekly Magazine*. So thorough was the research and so accurate the reproduction that veterans of the battle not only recognized the scenes but were able to identify many of the combatants.

In 1887 the cyclorama, completed at a cost of $40,000, was first shown in Detroit, Michigan. From there it was sent to various cities in the country for display until 1891, when Paul Atkinson bought it from the Indianapolis Art Exhibit Company for $2,500 and brought it to Atlanta for exhibition. Later Atkinson sold the painting to H.H. Harrison of Florida, who planned to exhibit it at the Chicago World's Fair in 1893. When this project failed, the great canvas was sold for $1,100 at an auction on August 1, 1893, to the East Atlanta Land Company, owner of the Edgewood Avenue building where the painting had been displayed. Ten days later the newspapers carried a notice that the picture had been sold again for the auction price to George V. Gress, who displayed it at Grant Park to raise funds for the aid of the poor children of the city. In 1898 Gress presented the painting to the City of Atlanta, and it has since remained on permanent exhibit at Grant Park.

Until 1921, when the present fireproof building was erected, the painting was housed in a flimsy wooden structure, where it became badly streaked because of leaks in the roof. This damage was repaired in 1937, when the Works Progress Administration completed a project for the renovation of the painting. Under the direction of Victor Llorens, artists and workmen not only cleaned and retouched the canvas but extended the action of the picture onto the groundwork to give a realistic three-dimensional illusion.

More than 1,500 tons of Georgia clay in various shades of red were hauled in to recreate the irregularity of the battlefield within the circular area between the platform and the painting. Tree trunks were dynamited and treated to produce a shell-torn effect; grass was made with excelsior tinted green; bushes and small trees, some with eight to ten thousand handmade leaves, were built of wire and plaster and embedded in the clay. An irregular concrete siding built close to the canvas was used as a foundation for the plaster modeling that joins the action of the picture to the scene in the foreground. To the legs of a dying man, drawn up in agony at the edge of the picture, the upturned face and shoulders have been added in plaster; an ambulance is partly painted and partly modeled in plaster; and the railroad tracks that appear in the picture have been extended with graded rails across the groundwork to the opposite side. The illusion of reality is heightened further by a special lighting system that gives the appearance of daylight.

The painting of the Battle of Atlanta is now valued at more than $1,000,000. According to an artist on the staff of the American Cyclorama Company, two paintings of this battle were made at the studio, but it is thought that the second one disintegrated in Baltimore in 1897. Two companion pictures, portraying the Battle of Gettysburg and the Battle of Missionary Ridge, were both destroyed, the former by fire and the latter by cyclone.

The RAILROAD ENGINE TEXAS (*admission free*) is kept in the basement of the Cyclorama Building in memory of Andrews' Raid, one of the boldest and most thrilling exploits of the War between the States. At Marietta, on April 11, 1862, James J. Andrews, a Union spy, and 21 volunteers mingled among unsuspecting passengers and boarded a train drawn by the engine *General* and headed for Chattanooga, Tennessee. When Conductor William A. Fuller stopped the train at Big Shanty, now Kennesaw, so that the passengers and crew could get off for breakfast, Andrews' men quickly uncoupled the engine and three cars and made off with them, intending to destroy every railroad bridge they passed over and thus cut a vital supply line between the Confederate armies in Virginia and Mississippi. But Conductor Fuller and his crew started off on foot in hot pursuit of the marauders. At Moon's Station, about a mile up the road, they found a handcar and appropriated it for the chase. Fortune favored the Confederates, for when they reached the bridge over the Etowah River, there on a side track with a full head of steam was the *Yonah,* a switch engine of the Cooper Iron Works. Seizing this, they were able to press the pursuit with more speed until they found themselves blocked at the junction at Kingston by some freight cars, which had delayed Andrews also. Without wasting time in moving the cars, Fuller abandoned the *Yonah* and took the *William R. Smith,* a faster engine; but he was stopped again a short distance north of Kingston by a break in the tracks made by the fleeing raiders. Again the pursuers had to proceed on foot until, near Adairsville, they met the *Texas,* the fastest engine in the Western & Atlantic service, and commandeered it for their purpose. Running in reverse, the *Texas* gained rapidly on the raiders, who had been too hard pressed all the way to destroy bridges and tracks as they had planned. In desperation, Andrews and his men attempted to block the path of the *Texas* by tossing wood onto the tracks, but this only exhausted their fuel without appreciably delaying their pursuers. Finally, within five miles of Chattanooga, the raiders abandoned the stalled *General* and scattered through the woods in an effort to escape.

Within a week Andrews and all of his men were captured and brought to trial before the Confederate authorities in Chattanooga. After their conviction they were sent to Atlanta, where Andrews and seven members of the group were executed by hanging and the others were imprisoned. In October 1862, eight made their escape, and the remaining six were sent to Richmond, Virginia, where they were exchanged on March 18, 1863.

The *Texas,* built by Danforth and Cook, was placed in freight service on the Western & Atlantic Railroad in 1856. After the war it was converted to a coal burner and continued in active service until 1907, when it was sent to the Atlanta railroad yards to be scrapped. The pressure of public opinion, however, caused it to be preserved as a historic relic, and in 1911 the City of Atlanta put it on display in Grant Park. In 1937 it was cleaned and repainted by employes of the Works Progress Administration.

A MUSEUM (*admission free*), left of the foyer in the Cyclorama Building, houses such unrelated objects as Confederate money and weapons, Indian arrowheads, beadwork from Constantinople, paddles from South America, stuffed birds and animals, a swordfish, a vampire bat from Sumatra, a Patagonian shrunken skull, and a Spanish halberd found near Atlanta.

A large room to the right of the foyer contains eight enlarged photographs taken by Sherman's official photographer. Seven are pictures of Federal trenches, breastworks, and artillery, and one is a view of downtown Atlanta after the fall of the city.

29. The McPHERSON MONUMENT, corner Monument and McPherson Aves., NE., a large cannon standing on end, marks the spot where the Union General James Birdseye McPherson lost his life at the hands of Confederate sharpshooters on July 22, 1864. The monument is encircled by an iron railing, and a bronze plaque relates the particulars of the incident.

Shortly after the battle began on the morning of July 22, General McPherson rode from the summit of Copenhill, Sherman's head-quarters, to the Georgia Railroad tracks near what is now Candler Street. He then passed to the rear of his troops along Moreland Avenue en route to the main portion of his army that was stationed at Glenwood and Flat Shoals Avenues. Traversing a road cut through the forest, he galloped into the advancing line of General Cleburne's skirmishers and was shot from his horse. His body was recovered after a Confederate retreat, carried to Sherman's headquarters, and sent under escort to Clyde, Ohio, for burial.

30. The WALKER MONUMENT, on Glenwood Ave. 1¼ miles from Moreland Ave., NE., an upright cannon in a granite base, marks the site where the Confederate General W.H.T. Walker was slain by a Federal picket on the morning of July 22, 1864. General Walker commanded a division of Hardee's Corps, which was moving across the territory in a northwesterly direction to attack the rear of the Federal 17th Corps. While he was reconnoitering to see that his men were in position, his horse mired in a swamp northeast of this point and he risked returning to the main road for faster traveling. Soon after he reached the road, he was shot from his horse by a musket ball. General Walker is buried at Augusta.

31. The ROBERT BURNS COTTAGE (admission free), Alloway Place, SE., maintained by the Atlanta Burns Club, is a reproduction of the famous poet's birthplace in Alloway, Scotland. The low rectangular gray stone structure is surrounded by nine acres of wooded land, which in spring is covered by the white blossoms of dogwood trees. The interior plan of the Alloway cottage has been closely followed except for the addition of a small modern kitchen at the rear. The long cattle room, which adjoins the cottage at a slight angle, serves as an assembly hall for the club, which meets once a month for a dinner and program. The kitchen-bedroom more closely resembles the corresponding room in the original Burns house; here the stone-flagged floor, stone fireplace, and curtained, recessed bed carry an authentic suggestion of an austere Scottish farmhouse. Numerous books, pictures, and documents are other tangible reminders of the poet.

The Atlanta Burns Club, organized in 1896, erected this memorial building in 1911. In 1914 the local organization became a member of the Burns Federation, which functions in almost every country in the world. Although the principal purpose of the meetings is commemoration of Burns and his works, other writers are frequently the subject of conversation, and sometimes topics of current interest take the place of literary discussions.

32. The FEDERAL PENITENTIARY (open only to immediate relatives of prisoners and to those having business to transact), McDonough Rd. and South Boulevard, SE., housing an average population of 3,000 inmates, is one of 30 similar institutions in the United States Prison System. The building, constructed of granite cut from Stone Mountain by prison labor, stands gray and massive behind its fence of tall iron pickets. The central main building was completed for use in 1902, the east and west wings being added in 1915 and 1918. The reservation comprises 28 acres of land enclosed by a wall 4,178 feet long, between 28 and 37 feet high, and varying in thickness from 2 to 4 feet.

Penologists have often praised the excellent equipment of the penitentiary, which includes a hospital, a library of about 20,000. books, and a school with required attendance for prisoners who have not completed the third grade. The prisoners, who occupy four five-tiered cellhouses, work at various occupations. Several hundred are employed in maintenance shops, while more than a thousand work in a textile mill, the only one in the United States that manufactures government mail sacks.

A wide variety of vocational and occupational training is provided in the industries and maintenance shops, ranging from textile manufacture to the various specialized types of construction work. Foremen-instructors, selected from civil service lists on the basis of their ability to provide supervision, guidance, and training for prisoners, are in charge of the shop work. A placement service is operated to find employment for released prisoners who have equipped themselves by training and given evidence of plans to take advantage of job opportunities.

Sixty-nine per cent of the prisoners take part in the program provided by the education department of the institution. The curriculum and general educational program is specially adapted to the training and rehabilitative needs of these men and is co-ordinated with the entire prison program. Illiterates capable of education are required to take elementary courses. Those further advanced are given opportunity to pursue studies which will aid them in their job training and general rehabilitation.

33. LAKEWOOD PARK (*open May to October*), Lakewood Ave., SW., a rolling wooded area of 370.9 acres, is an amusement park and fair ground with permanent exhibit buildings, midway attractions, a race track, and a large artificial lake. Lakewood was formerly the site of the city waterworks, and the lake was a reservoir created by damming the South River. Soon after the present waterworks on the Chattahoochee River was completed in 1893, this site was leased to the Lakewood Park Company and converted into an amusement center. Since 1915 Lakewood has been under lease to the Southeastern Fair Association.

During the summer the midway attracts thousands of pleasure seekers. The Whip and the Shoot-the-Chute afford the more thrilling rides, but the Old Mill and the Merry-Go-Round remain perennial favorites. A dirt track encircling the lake is the scene of exciting automobile, bicycle, and sulky races. Many racing celebrities have established records here in their various mediums. "Lucky Teeter," with his famed "Hell Drivers," frequently stages an auto-hazard show on the track. Motorboat races are held on the lake.

Barbecue pits and picnic tables dot the grounds, and delegates of virtually every convention held in Atlanta are entertained with a barbecue or watermelon cutting here. Band concerts, roller skating, and dances complete the summer program. The park is closed during the winter.

The Southeastern Fair (*first week in October, no fixed admission price*), Atlanta's largest annual event, attracts more visitors from over the entire Southeast than any other city enterprise. In the three permanent buildings, large concrete structures built along mission lines, are displayed exhibits of farm products, agricultural machinery, preserved and canned foods, needlework, and handicrafts. The exhibit of livestock and poultry is one of the most important showings in the South.

During the week of the Fair, when the permanent carnival attractions are augmented by those of a traveling show, the midway is packed with people eating hotdogs and cotton candy and drinking soda pop. Lucky winners at the game booths come away loaded with tinselled dolls, bright "Indian" blankets, gaudy lamps, and other gewgaws, while others purchase balloons, swagger sticks, and various noise-makers.

Special days are designated in honor of various groups, but the farmer who brings his showings of cattle settles down for the entire week with his family in a near-by tourist camp and spends every day on the grounds. The changing program features keep the crowds rushing from grandstand to exhibit buildings to the midway during the day, but at night all wind up again at the grandstand to witness the spectacular fireworks display across the lake.

34. GAMMON THEOLOGICAL SEMINARY, McDonough Rd. and Capitol Ave., SW., occupies four red-brick buildings on a campus of 25 acres. Near by are six frame residences for members of the faculty and ten small cottages for married students. The brick buildings to the left of the driveway, now leased by the Atlanta Board of Education and used by the Federal Government for NYA projects, formerly were occupied by Clark College, which moved to its new site on Chestnut Street in 1941.

Gammon is one of nine theological schools maintained by the Methodist Church and private contributions. With an endowment of $500,000, it is one of two Negro seminaries approved by the American Association of Theological Schools. In 1941 the enrollment of full-time students was 64 and there was a faculty of nine, augmented by visiting lecturers from other schools The curriculum is broad for so small a school, and the students have the further advantage of being permitted to register for special courses at any of the schools affiliated with the Atlanta University System.

A department for training women workers accepts students with two years of college credits and prepares them to become lay leaders, pastors' assistants, religious education directors, and social workers. This course, established through co-operation with the Woman's Home Missionary Society, is particularly popular with the wives of the theological students. The Department of Christian Missions is supported by the Stewart Missionary Foundation for Africa, which was established here in 1894 by the Reverend William Fletcher Stewart with an endowment of $100,000. This corporation also maintains contact with active missionaries and publishes the *Foundation,* a quarterly religious magazine.

The seminary was founded by Bishop Henry White Warren, who made Atlanta his official residence in 1880 and became interested in the welfare of Clark University (now Clark College). Enlisting the aid of Elijah H. Gammon, a retired Methodist clergyman who had become wealthy through his manufacturing interests, Warren induced him to give $200,000 to endow a chair of theology at Clark University and to pledge $5,000 for a theological building. This donation was made on the condition that Warren raise an equal amount for the building. The bishop was quickly successful; a building was constructed on a nineteen-acre campus adjoining the university, and the first classes were held on October 3, 1883.

In order that the department of theology might be expanded to serve all the schools of the Freedmen's Aid Society in Atlanta, Gammon offered to give the Methodist Episcopal Church an endowment of $200,000 to establish a separate theological school. The donation was accepted, and a charter for the Gammon School of Theology was granted on March 24, 1888. The institution was given its present name the following December. Through subsequent years Gammon gave additional help by building the residences for faculty members and frequently by paying their salaries. Upon his death the endowment was more than doubled by provisions of his will.

The GILBERT HAVEN LIBRARY, situated on the left of the campus at the head of the walkway, is a small red-brick structure with a front bay window and an arched entrance portico. Its 26,000 volumes are listed in the Union Catalogue being compiled at Emory University (1942). In the African collection, which relates to Negro slavery and to African history, missions, and languages, are Bibles and hymnbooks in native African dialects. There are also several English Bibles and scriptural tests, some published as early as the seventeenth century. On the walls are framed letters from Harriet Beecher Stowe and John Greenleaf Whittier, as well as several manuscripts of Whittier, who wrote a motto for the library.

The library opened in 1887, when Elijah Gammon purchased many books from H. Bannister, of Garrett Biblical Institute. During the following year, D.P. Kidder, secretary of the Methodist Board of Education, offered to give his personal collection when a library building should be completed. Construction was soon begun and the completed building was dedicated on May 26, 1889. The number of volumes has been increased from time to time by other donors.

35. The STATE FARMERS' MARKET (*open day and night*), occupying a 16-acre plot of State-owned land at the junction of Murphy Ave. and Sylvan Rd., SW., is one of a system of eight markets built and operated by the Georgia Department of Agriculture since 1936. This State-directed marketing is part of a concerted effort to encourage a diversification of Georgia's farm produce, to lower con-

sumer costs, and to solve the problem of distribution. For this reason operations are confined to the wholesale selling of foodstuffs only.

Although the market was established primarily for the distribution of Georgia products, trucks from almost every State in the Union, and even from Mexico, bring vegetables and fruits here for sale. The market has been operated on its present site only since April 1941, having first been set up on a smaller tract at Courtland and Gilmer Streets. Within the market area the streets are named for State officials such as Eugene Talmadge, present (1942) Governor of Georgia, and Thomas E. Linder, Commissioner of Agriculture. Large open sheds are used by the farmers and truckers, who spread their produce in rented stalls on both sides of the long concrete runways. The brokers and wholesale dealers occupy low brick buildings with open fronts, over which hang signs bearing the names of the proprietors. Occasionally there is a name such as "Jardina" or "Cerniglia," and sometimes among the sun-reddened impassive faces there appears a dark, mobile face indicating Greek or Italian ancestry.

Trucks loaded with produce pull in at all hours of the day and night. All activities are directed by a market master who, with the aid of several assistants and a loud-speaker system, keeps the market in smooth operation. Much of the trading is done by barter, one kind of foodstuff being traded for another. Produce so acquired is sold by the truckers on return trips to their home districts. The biggest trading period occurs during the first days of the week, when the lot teems with activity. The piles of vegetables, the net bags stuffed with oranges, and the hanging bunches of green bananas form a colorful background for the shifting figures of the buyers who pass back and forth examining the produce. As buying slackens, the truckers, dressed in clothes which vary from ordinary overalls to near-cowboy outfits, gather in little groups to smoke, play checkers, or discuss the weather and crops. Others shuffle around the lot joking fellow drivers about the quality of their produce while urging buyers to look at their own foodstuffs. A few stretch out in their trucks or on the platform for a brief nap after an all-night drive, leaving a companion or a watchful dog on the alert to give notice of approaching buyers. All, however, keep a listening ear cocked for the raucous instructions and announcements which blare sporadically from the loud-speakers installed throughout the grounds.

The season from Thanksgiving to Christmas and New Year is one of intense activity. The number of trucks roaring in and out is greatly increased and wholesale buyers throng the lot. Foodstuffs are sold quickly and packed in crates, bushel baskets, and gunny sacks to make room for the constantly incoming loads.

More than 200,000 trucks visit the market annually, while the yearly volume of trade amounts to approximately $15,000,000. The venture has proved so successful that the idea has been adopted by several other States.

36. WREN'S NEST (*open weekdays 9-5; 25¢, children 10¢*), 1050

Gordon St., SW., was for many years the home of Joel Chandler
Harris, whose Uncle Remus stories are world famous for their humorous interpretation of Negro folklore.   The two-story frame house,
with many gables and elaborate scrollwork eaves, is now maintained as
a public memorial to the author, and a number of his personal possessions are on exhibition here.

The place was given its name after a wren had built a nest in
the mailbox; Harris refused to have the bird disturbed and let the
broods be hatched there year after year.   The writer, diffident and
retiring at the height of his fame, often wandered off alone to observe
the animals and birds on the surrounding land, which he called Snap
Bean Farm.   After his death in 1908 plans were made to purchase
the house as a memorial, and funds were collected from various con-
tributors including Theodore Roosevelt and Andrew Carnegie, both
friends of Harris.   In 1914 Wren's Nest was formally dedicated· by
the Uncle Remus Memorial Association, its present owners.   A walkway of pink Georgia marble, whose first stones were put down in
1932, has been laid to honor Harris and other Georgians who have
become known for their writings.

Joel Chandler Harris (1848-1908) was born on an old plantation
in Putnam County near Eatonton, Georgia.   He passed his boyhood
in poverty but, with much assistance from kindly neighbors, attended
the local academy and in 1862 became printer's devil on *The Countryman,* a weekly newspaper just established by Joseph Addison Turner
on his plantation.   The 14-year-old boy soon began to slip paragraphs
of his own into the paper, thus winning the interest of Turner, who
began to school him in the writing of sound English prose.   Encouraged by Turner to find his material close to home, the young
writer closely observed the animals and the Negroes in their cabins,
which he later presented in a combination that made him famous.

At the close of the War between the States *The Countryman*
ceased publication and Harris began a wandering career, forming con-
nections with several newspapers.   A co-worker on the Savannah
Morning News describes his first sight of Harris: "... of small stature,
red-haired, freckle-faced, and looked like a typical backwoodsman. . . .
But that night when his copy came out, we knew he was a writer."

In 1876, when he was working on the Atlanta *Constitution,* the
editor, Evan P. Howell, gave him the assignment of writing a daily
story in Negro dialect.   These sketches formed the nucleus of his
first book, *Uncle Remus: His Songs and Sayings,* published in 1880.
Other books followed, and the stories became famous not only for
their dialect and Negro humor but for their permanent contribution
to the study of African folklore.   Thus the memory of Harris is kept
alive both by children and by learned scholars.

37. The ATLANTA UNIVERSITY SYSTEM, occupying three
separate areas between Ella and Hunter Sts., SW., includes Atlanta
University, Morehouse College, Spelman College, and the Atlanta
School of Social Work.   These schools, though occupying virtually

adjoining campuses and doing work of much the same general nature, were originally separate institutions. By an affiliation in 1929 Morehouse became the liberal arts school for men and Spelman for women, while Atlanta University was made the graduate school. In 1938 the Atlanta School of Social Work, the only exclusively Negro institution of its kind, also became an affiliate. The reorganization has voided much duplication of work, reduced administrative and faculty costs, raised the standard of the individual schools, and extended co-operation to other leading Negro colleges in the city.

Each institution in the system has a separate board of trustees, the chairmen of these bodies forming the controlling board of the whole. In addition to the four main institutions, there are a nursery and a laboratory school covering the grades from kindergarten through high school. Thus the system provides a complete education from the nursery through professional and graduate work with a master's degree.

Total enrollment under the Atlanta University System varies between 1,500 and 2,000. The endowments of the several colleges, along with their 31 buildings and 91 acres of land, represent an investment of $10,000,000.

ATLANTA UNIVERSITY, covering two separate blocks on Chestnut St. between Greensferry Ave. and Hunter St., is situated on a campus designed along formal lines with smooth expanses of lawn and angular walkways bordered by straight rows of elms and water oaks. Since Atlanta University is the graduate school of the system, its enrollment is rather small, usually numbering about 100 students.

The institution grew out of a small school established in 1865 for freed slaves, the first quarters being the Jenkins Street Church and the "Car Box," a railroad car purchased in Chattanooga and brought to Atlanta for this purpose. Edmund Asa Ware, who came to Atlanta in 1866 under the auspices of the American Missionary Association, aroused interest in the institution and secured $25,000 from the association for enlarging it. The school was chartered as Atlanta University in 1867 and was moved two years later to a 50-acre tract bounded by Walnut, Tatnall, Hunter, Beckwith, and Chestnut Streets. Under the leadership of Ware, the first president, the school was remarkably successful.

After its affiliation with Morehouse and Spelman in 1929, Atlanta University acquired a portion of the Morehouse grounds for a central campus and erected there a new administration building, opened in 1932. On the western end of the older campus, two dormitories and a dining hall, the million-dollar gift of an anonymous donor, were completed in 1933.

The ATLANTA UNIVERSITY LIBRARY (*open weekdays 9:30-9:30*), corner Chestnut St. and Greensferry Ave., is a red-brick-and-limestone structure in the classic tradition and is surmounted with a graceful cupola. Erected in 1932 through donations of the General Education Board of the Rockefeller Foundation, the library has served as a model for the construction of similar institutions throughout the country. The building was erected on the Atlanta University campus with the stipulation that it was to be used by all other Negro institutions of higher education in the city. The stacks now contain 60,000 volumes with additional space for twice that number.

The ATLANTA UNIVERSITY ADMINISTRATION BUILDING, 223 Chestnut St., is a brick and limestone edifice of Georgian Colonial design. Both the front and rear have columned porticoes, and on the roof is a cupola topped with a gilded dome. The building, completed in 1932, houses seminar rooms, a conference chamber, administration offices, and a commissary.

The ATLANTA SCHOOL OF SOCIAL WORK, Chestnut St. between the library and administration building, is a red-brick structure with a simple, Doric-columned portico surmounted with an ornamental grille balustrade. For several years after its organization in 1920, the school borrowed classrooms and office space, as well as the part-time services of a professor of sociology, from Morehouse College. In 1925 an appropriation from the Laura Spelman Rockefeller Memorial made it possible for the school to function as an independent institution in rented quarters.

In addition to training Negroes for the profession of social work, the school has also become recognized as a promotional agency for welfare work among Negroes throughout the South. Some of this work has developed through the school's extracurricular activities, while other services have been rendered through the medium of studies and surveys made by the students under the supervision of the research department. The faculty is constantly called upon to consult with executives of public and private social agencies on questions involving social planning for the entire community. Special projects in which the school has participated include a tuberculosis institute, a WPA old age survey, a WPA population study, a regional conference of student health workers, and a summer camp for Negro children. Because of its high scholastic standards the institution is today the only Negro member of the American Association of Schools of Social Work. Enrollment numbers about 100 students.

MOREHOUSE COLLEGE, covering 12 acres adjoining the main campus of Atlanta University, is composed of the college of arts and sciences and the school of religion. The two are housed in seven red-brick buildings and have an enrollment of more than 400 students.

Morehouse was organized in Augusta in 1867 as the Augusta Institute by the American Baptist Home Mission Society. In recognition of Atlanta's growing importance as a Negro educational center, the school was moved to the city in 1879 and renamed the Atlanta Baptist Seminary. In 1897 it became known as the Atlanta Baptist College, and in 1913 the name was changed again to Morehouse College in honor of the Reverend Henry L. Morehouse, who was then corresponding secretary of the mission society and a prominent benefactor of the Negro race. From 1906 to 1931 Morehouse had as its president Dr. John Hope, an outstanding Negro educator and leader, who also became president of the entire university system when it was organized in 1929.

SPELMAN COLLEGE, bounded by Ella St., Leonard St., Greensferry Ave., and Culver St., occupies a campus of 25 acres with 14 brick buildings grouped about a quadrangle. The level greensward, densely shadowed by magnolias, is particularly beautiful in spring when the oaks, elms, and weeping willows are in full leaf.

Spelman College was founded in 1881 by two New England women, Sophia B. Packard and Harriett Giles. Miss Packard, sent by the Women's American Baptist Home Mission Society to study the conditions in the South, was impressed by the need for education among Negro women. She solicited the aid of Miss Giles, and, with $100 provided by the Mission Society, the two opened a school in the basement of Friendship Baptist Church, using even the coal bins as classrooms.

Just prior to the opening of the seond term, Miss Packard and Miss Giles went North to secure additional funds for the school. In Cleveland, Ohio, they spoke in a church of which John D. Rockefeller was a member. Rockefeller was present, and, in keeping with his custom, he put every cent he had in his pockets into the collection plate. Then he approached Miss Packard. "Are you going to stick?" he asked the astonished lady. He went on to explain, "You know, there are so many who come here and present their work and get us to give money. Soon they are gone and we don't know where they are or where their work is. Do you mean to stick? If you do, you will hear from me again."

Back in Atlanta, Miss Packard set about looking for a new location for the school. The American Baptist Home Mission Society had secured an option on the present property, which had been used as barracks and drill grounds for Federal troops after the War between the States. This they transferred to Miss Packard on condition that she raise the balance due of $15,000.

With little money but unbounded faith, Miss Packard moved the school to the five frame buildings on the new site in February 1883. Her faith was justified. The enrollment increased rapidly and teachers volunteered their services, while missionary societies and other groups and individuals in the North sent gifts of clothing and supplies. The Negro Baptists of Georgia gave $3,000, and other Negro friends raised $1,300 more. Even after the time for payment had been extended twice, however, less than half the needed funds had been raised.

In April 1884, Mr. and Mrs. John D. Rockefeller, their two children, and Mrs. Rockefeller's mother and sister visited the school. So favorably impressed were they with the work of the institution that Rockefeller immediately gave enough money to clear the title to the property and to provide additional facilities. Miss Packard thereupon changed the name of the school from the Atlanta Baptist Female

Seminary to Spelman Seminary in honor of Mrs. Lucy Henry Spelman, the mother of Mrs. Rockefeller.

With the aid of Rockefeller and other individuals and groups, Spelman expanded greatly. At the time of Miss Packard's death in 1891, the school had 800 pupils. As the city system of public education for Negroes grew, however, Spelman gradually eliminated its elementary classes in order that the resources of the institution might be concentrated on college work. The student enrollment of Spelman College today is about 375.

ROCKEFELLER HALL, on the east side of the quadrangle, the first permanent building of the school, was erected in 1886 from funds donated by Rockefeller during his visit in 1884. Formerly a chapel and dormitory, the building is now used for administrative purposes. The assembly room on the second floor has been converted into a theater for the school of dramatics. This building is probably better known to the white people of Atlanta than any other on the campus for many plays, ranging from Greek tragedy to modern high comedy, are presented to the public here.

SISTERS' CHAPEL, near the Ella St. entrance, is a red-brick building patterned along classic lines. Six large Doric columns support a massive entablature and a severely plain pediment. Erected in 1926 and named in honor of the mother of John D. Rockefeller and her sister, the building has a seating capacity of 1,500 and is used for concerts, commencement exercises, and daily chapel services.

The SPELMAN NURSERY SCHOOL, occupying a half-timbered brick structure on a triangular block east of the Ella St. campus entrance, provides modern training for approximately 100 children of preschool age. The youngest children, from 18 months to 3 years, have separate facilities for games, lunches, and naps. The older children are furnished with equipment for such constructive work as modeling, block-building, drawing, painting, paper-cutting, and woodworking. Adequate indoor play rooms are available for use in inclement weather, and there are spacious, well-ventilated sleeping rooms as well as large porches for sun-bathing. The older children have access to a well-equipped library and are given special training in language, music, story-telling, and dancing.

The parent education program operated in conjunction with the work of the school gives parents the opportunity of co-ordinating training techniques used in the school with those used in the home.

MORRIS BROWN COLLEGE, Tatnall and Hunter Sts., NW., occupies four of the old red-brick buildings and a portion of the campus that formerly were used by Atlanta University. Essentially a liberal arts college, it is controlled by the African Methodist Episcopal Church and has a strong theological department called the Turner Theological Seminary. Approximately 500 Negro men and women are annually enrolled at the institution.

Morris Brown is not a unit of the Atlanta University System but is one of three institutions that co-operate with the larger organization, the other two being Clark College and Gammon Theological Seminary. The colleges have a plan of mutual assistance, whereby the Atlanta University Library is open to all their students, a combined summer session is held, and teachers are exchanged. Junior and senior students of one college may register for courses at the other institutions.

The movement to found Morris Brown was begun at Big Bethel Church in 1881, when the North Georgia Annual Conference of the African Methodist Episcopal Church passed a resolution to establish a school in Atlanta. It was not until 1885, however, that a charter was secured and that the institution was opened on a lot at the corner of Houston Street and Boulevard. The school was named to honor Morris Brown, a bishop of the African Methodist Episcopal Church. Only high school courses were offered for several years, but in 1894 the trustees organized the liberal arts college and established the department of theology. The institution has since maintained a continuous growth. In 1932 the preparatory school was abolished, the Williams Business College was made the commercial department, and the school was moved to its present location.

CLARK COLLEGE, 240 Chestnut St., SW., occupies four modern red-brick buildings with limestone trim. The school, a member of the Association of American Colleges and the American Council on Education, has been rated Class A by the Southern Association. It is authorized to confer on Negro men and women the Bachelor of Arts and Bachelor of Science degrees. An endowment of $550,000 enables the college to maintain low tuition charges and to extend opportunities to deserving students. For the school year of 1940-41 the enrollment was more than 400, including the students registered in evening classes. With courses in literature, languages, natural sciences, mathematics, social sciences, and the arts, the curriculum lays emphasis on both academic and practical aspects of liberal arts training. The department of business administration places particular stress on adaptation of the student to employment in Southern commercial enterprises, while the department of home economics, aided by the Woman's Home Missionary Society, provides courses in all aspects of domestic science. The department of music presents choral performances for public entertainments as well as for the regular chapel exercises.

Like many other such institutions, Clark first opened as the result of the enthusiasm for Negro improvement felt by Northern educators and philanthropists in the years following emancipation. The college is the outgrowth of a primary school for Negro children opened early in 1869 by the Reverend J.W. Lee and his wife in Clark Chapel on Fraser Street. In the following year this small institution was acquired by the Freedmen's Aid Society of the Methodist Episcopal Church, which was doing extensive missionary work among the Southern Negroes. Then began a period of rapid development. In 1872 better quarters were secured at Whitehall and McDaniel Streets, and in 1877 a charter was granted to elevate the school to the status of a university. The enlarged institution was named in honor of Bishop D.W. Clark, who had been a strong friend of the Negro race during his period of service in the South. Bishop Gilbert Haven, an abolitionist clergyman who had become interested in the school during his official residence in Atlanta, worked energetically to raise subscriptions throughout the United States and purchased between 400 and 500 acres for a new site at McDonough Road and Capitol Avenue. The first building was erected in 1880 and in the following year was used both as recitation hall and dormitory. In 1883 Elijah H. Gammon endowed a chair of theology at Clark, and five years later this department was chartered as the Gammon Theological Seminary, a separate institution occupying an adjacent campus and co-operating closely with the older school.

Through the generosity of various benefactors the institution continued to grow. For many years emphasis was placed on the teaching of trades, but gradually this work was supplanted by courses in the liberal arts. The academic work was further strengthened in 1941 when the school was moved to the education center that has developed around Atlanta University.

The name was changed to Clark College in 1940. Removal to its present site was made possible by donations from the General Education Board, the Rosenwald Foundation, and Mrs. Henry Pfeiffer of New York. These changes have not affected the separate status of the institution. In its new location the school can more easily share in the combined facilities of all the Negro colleges grouped around Atlanta University. Through co-operative arrangement Clark offers courses in physics to students of all the colleges in this center, and, in turn, Clark students register for the courses emphasized in the other colleges.

38. The BOOKER T. WASHINGTON MONUMENT, before the main entrance of Booker T. Washington High School, SW. corner Hunter and C Sts., SW., is a vigorously executed bronze group showing the renowned Negro educator lifting a veil from the eyes of a laborer, who is seated on an anvil with a plow at his side. On the marble base is inscribed, "He lifted the veil of ignorance from his people, and pointed the way to progress through education and industry," and Washington's own words delivered in Atlanta, "We shall prosper in proportion as we learn dignity and glorify labor and put brains and skill into the common occupations of life." This memorial, a replica of a monument designed by Charles Keck of New York and now standing on the campus of Tuskegee Institute at Tuskegee, Alabama, was erected in 1925 through contributions of white and Negro citizens and of students and teachers of the Booker T. Washington High School.

Booker T. Washington devoted his life to building Tuskegee Institute, where he served as principal for 34 years, but so great was his contribution to the general betterment of the Negro race that he exerted a vital influence on widespread educational enterprises. In the spring of 1895 he was invited to accompany a group of Atlanta citizens to the National Capital in order to secure a subsidy from the Congressional Committee on Appropriations for the Cotton States and International Exposition, which was to be opened in Atlanta the following September. Making his plea after the white speakers had been heard, Washington spoke eloquently in praise of the exposition as a means of improving interracial relations. The appropriation was made.

Washington was the only Negro invited to speak at the opening of the exposition. In Atlanta he and his family were met at the station by a group of Negro citizens, and on the following day he marched in the parade to the exposition grounds at the present Piedmont Park. There Rufus Bullock, who had been governor of Georgia during Reconstruction, introduced him to a varied audience of Northerners and Southerners, white people and Negroes. An arresting and dignified figure, the tall, tawny-skinned educator then made an address so stirring that the audience was aroused to wild acclamation. Washington, refusing generous offers for professional lectures, remained in Atlanta about a month longer as judge of awards for educational exhibits, then quietly returned to his duties at Tuskegee.

39. The SAMUEL SPENCER MONUMENT, facing the plaza of the Terminal Station, NW. corner Spring and Mitchell Sts., was erected on May 21, 1910. The seated bronze figure is the work of the renowned sculptor Daniel Chester French.

Spencer, who was born in 1847 in Columbus, Georgia, received a degree in civil engineering from the University of Virginia in 1869 and immediately entered the field of railroading. His first position was with the Savannah & Memphis Railroad, and within ten years he had become president of the Baltimore & Ohio Railroad. In 1894, when the Southern Railway System was organized, he became its first president and was consequently a vital influence in the economic development of the South. Throughout his career Spencer was a leading spokesman for all American railroads and he was noted for his fiery opposition to legislative rate regulation. He was killed in 1906 in a collision of two trains on his own railroad. The monument was erected through funds contributed by employees of the Southern Railway System.

Part Three

POINTS OF INTEREST IN ENVIRONS

Points of Interest in Environs

(Numbers coincide with those on maps on inside back cover.)

40. FORT McPHERSON (*no visitors*), a few miles southwest of Atlanta, is a permanent cantonment maintained by the United States Army. From the highway only a few of the red-brick barracks are visible through the iron picket fence; other rows of buildings can be seen only by entering the grounds. In addition to the 236 acres of this reservation, 1,500 acres in Clayton County are to be utilized by the Quartermaster Corps Regional Supply Depot, designated in September 1940.

This post was first established in 1867 on the present site of Spelman College and named McPherson Barracks for General James Birdseye McPherson, a Union commander who was killed in the Battle of Atlanta. The land had then been used intermittently as a drill ground for more than 30 years. A cartridge factory and barracks, established there by the Confederate Government after the secession acts, was destroyed by retreating soldiers when General Sherman captured Atlanta. After the war the difficulty of enforcing Union regulations upon the conquered people led to the establishment of the Third Military District in Atlanta. It was shortly afterward that McPherson Barracks was set up as a ten-company garrison.

In 1875 an unfavorable inspection report of housing conditions led to consideration of a new site for the post. During the 1880's the land and buildings were sold to the American Baptist Home Mission Society for the use of the Atlanta Baptist Female Seminary, which later became Spelman College. Some of the barracks were repaired and used for a time as dormitories. In 1885 the present site was selected and construction work was begun. Four years later the post was first garrisoned by the Fourth Artillery.

When the United States declared war on Spain in 1898, Fort McPherson was designated as a depot to train recruits for the field. A general hospital also was established on the grounds and in its year of operation handled 1,342 cases. When the hospital was dismantled in 1900, the frame buildings were moved intact on rollers and placed in various new locations throughout the post.

At the outbreak of the Spanish-American War, Leonard Wood, then a lieutenant stationed here, joined Colonel Theodore Roosevelt's

"Rough Riders" to fight in Cuba. Later he became a major general
under President Theodore Roosevelt's administration and served with
distinction during the first World War. Stanley D. Embick, who in
1899 was stationed at the post as a second lieutenant, returned here
in 1938 as its commanding general. In 1940 Lieutenant General
Embick was appointed by President Franklin D. Roosevelt as representative of the army on the joint defense board of the United States and
Canada.

From 1914 to 1917 the reservation was abandoned except for a
small detachment of quartermaster, hospital, and civil service corps
that served as caretakers. In 1917, however, a succession of events
quickened activities at the fort. The Federal Government set up a
base hospital and later an officers' training camp in which 2,500 civilians were given 90 days' instruction and commissioned in the army.
During the summer of that year a war internment barracks was built
west of the fort. The first 800 German prisoners were men taken
from vessels interned in United States ports when war was declared.
A barbed wire enclosure was placed about the yard, and during the
summer Atlanta people often used to drive by and see the prisoners,
in sleeveless shirts and white drill trousers, walking aimlessly about
the grounds. At one time 1,411 men were interned here.

During the first World War and afterward a motor transport
general depot functioned at Camp Jessup, adjacent to the post and now
a part of it. In 1921 all Fort McPherson's available buildings were
cleared for use by the base hospital. Rehabilitation shops were set up
for instructing the disabled soldiers in useful trades, and it became a
common sight to see rows of khaki-clad men, crutches leaning against
the wall, applying themselves to the mastery of various trades and
handicrafts.

The decade of the 1930's was uneventful. Since the beginning of
the national defense program, however, the post has been in full action.

41. EAST POINT (1,046 alt., 12,403 pop.), in Fulton County, six
miles southwest of Atlanta on US 29, is a separate municipality that
has become the leading industrial center of the vicinity. On the east
side of the principal street, which is paralleled by the Atlanta & West
Point Railroad tracks, rises an uneven line of industrial buildings with
their high tanks and smoking chimneys. Opposite this line of structures, on the western side of the street, is a row of stores beyond which
is a residential area with small parks, brick and frame cottages, and the
handsome red-brick city hall with tall white columns.

In the summer of 1864, the site of the town was important in the
defense of the Confederate supply lines to the besieged city of Atlanta.
The town, incorporated in 1887, was given its name because it was
at that time the eastern terminus of the Atlanta & West Point Railroad. A buggy works and a wagon factory formed its industrial
nucleus, which has grown to include cotton mills, saw works, machine
shops, and chemical companies.

In 1940 East Point came into national prominence as the scene of a series of night-rider floggings, one of which caused the death of a victim. Although the men charged with implication in the outrages were tried merely as individuals and no formal charges were made against any organized body, the publicity resulted in a ruling by the Ku Klux Klan that none of its members could appear in public masked.

42. COLLEGE PARK (1,060 alt., 8,213 pop.), in Fulton County, eight miles southwest of Atlanta on US 29, is a suburb from which many residents set forth each morning to work in Atlanta and the factories of near-by East Point. College Park itself has no industries, maintaining a pleasing residential character in its neatly kept, unpretentious houses and in the plantings of grass and shrubbery along the tracks of the Atlanta & West Point Railroad, which parallel the highway.

The town, incorporated in 1891 as Manchester, received its present name four years later when Cox College (formerly Southern Female College) was moved here from LaGrange, Georgia. At that time the academic note was further carried out by giving the avenues such names as Oxford, Rugby, Harvard, and Princeton. In 1900 the Georgia Military Academy was established here.

College Park continued to be the home of the two institutions until 1938, when Cox College ceased to function and its building was razed. On the Cox College site a civic center and park have been planned, and an auditorium and a high school are under construction. Now the only college town atmosphere is given by the students of Georgia Military Academy.

43. GEORGIA MILITARY ACADEMY, E. Rugby Ave., College Park, is a boys' preparatory school with a standard of military training that has earned it a high rating by the United States War Department. The 12 red-brick buildings are grouped about a landscaped campus of 30 acres with athletic fields and a large parade ground. Each Sunday afternoon a parade is held and the public gathers to watch the lines of cadets, smart in their dress uniforms of blue-gray coats and white trousers, marching to the music of the band.

The enrollment of more than 300 students includes boarders from various States in the Union and foreign countries as well as day students from the Atlanta vicinity. Four courses are offered: classical or college preparatory, scientific or engineering, commercial, and special preparatory for West Point or Annapolis. Only one period of 45 minutes a day is given to drill, the greater part of the school hours being used for academic studies. Teams are coached in all the major sports, and each student is required to take part in some athletic activity.

The school was founded in 1900 after a number of College Park citizens had initiated a movement to establish a military academy in this vicinity. With only one assistant, Colonel James Woodward opened his school to 40 students in the first building, the present Founders Hall. Despite small beginnings, the school rapidly grew and became popular. An inspection made in 1908, by order of the President of the United States, revealed so high a standard of proficiency that an army officer was detailed here as military instructor. The War Department placed at the school a Junior Reserve Officers' Training Corps unit in 1916 and added a second instructor to the faculty; three years later other officers were assigned here and a quantity of military equipment was provided. From that time on, the school has grown steadily in the favor of the War Department, which has designated it for the past 15 years as one of the honor military schools in the United States.

44. HAPEVILLE (1,027 alt., 5,059 pop.), 6 miles south of Atlanta on US 19 and US 41, was incorporated in 1891 when the Central of Georgia Railway laid additional tracks in this vicinity and built a depot here. One hundred and fifty people were then living within the area of slightly more than two square miles about which the town limits were set, and a school and a Baptist church had been established during the previous decade. Since the citizens meant to keep Hapeville a home community, they incorporated into their charter an explicit prohibition of manufacturing enterprises.

As Atlanta business and industry spread southward, the town experienced a normal growth as the residential center for employees of these establishments, and many citizens went to work in the factories of near-by East Point. This growth was sharply accelerated in 1925, when plans were under discussion for the establishment of an Atlanta airport in this vicinity. By 1929, when the airport was built, more paved streets had been laid and many compact modern cottages erected among the more commodious, old-fashioned houses that made up the older Hapeville.

In the same year the restriction on industrial establishments was removed by special act of the legislature, and soon afterward a lumber mill and a textile plant were set up on the outskirts of the town. Since then other small manufactories have found a place here, but Hapeville has remained principally what its founders wished it to be—a city of substantial homes.

45. The ATLANTA MUNICIPAL AIRPORT, Virginia Ave., about one-half mile east of Hapeville, one of the largest of such stations in the United States, provides mail and passenger service for the Eastern and Delta air lines. This property, formerly known as Candler Field, was first developed as a flying field through private funds in 1925 and was purchased by the city in 1929. Later the work was completed through municipal, county, and Federal appropriations.

Partly encircled by shops and hangars stands the severely simple stucco administration building, which houses not only the executive offices but mail and weather services, flight surgeon's headquarters, and the inspection division of the United States Department of Commerce. Ticket offices are maintained on the lower floor. When the large airplanes land on the paved runways, the space in front of this building becomes suddenly crowded with passengers, spectators, uniformed attendants, and newspaper reporters. The Atlanta *Journal* broadcasts daily a radio program, in which alighting or embarking passengers are interviewed in regard to their businesses and their impressions of the city.

46. DECATUR (1,049 alt., 16,561 pop.), 6.5 miles east of Atlanta on US 29, is a residential town of shady streets and many small, attractive modern houses. Although the city limits of Decatur and Atlanta almost touch in places, the older town has stoutly held its separate character and withstood absorption into the metropolis where many of its citizens are employed. Because it is the seat of DeKalb County, Decatur has a strong flavor of local politics. The business section is dominated by the dignified granite courthouse with its massive columns, and this square is often filled with farmers, white and Negro, who have driven in from the surrounding county lands. Here, side by side with the town residents, they purchase supplies, discuss current political issues, and exchange news of their own affairs.

DeKalb County covers an area of 272 square miles and has a population of 86,942. Within its boundaries are eight incorporated towns (Avondale Estates, Chamblee, Clarkston, Decatur, Lithonia, North Atlanta, Pine Lake, and Stone Mountain), several unincorporated villages, a section of Atlanta, and several residential suburbs of that city. Because of this proximity to the large Atlanta markets, numerous truck farms, poultry farms, and dairies are operated throughout the rural section of the county. More extensive farm tracts are cultivated in cotton, corn, and hay-producing crops. Although DeKalb County is primarily an agricultural section, there are several well-developed industrial enterprises, of which the principal ones are textile manufacturing and granite quarrying.

The land now included in DeKalb County was ceded by the Creek Indians to the United States through a treaty signed at Indian Springs on January 8, 1821. The area was made a part of Henry County during the latter part of the same year and was subsequently opened to settlement by a land lottery. Small farmers poured into the region from North Carolina, South Carolina, and Virginia. Settlement was so rapid that within a year the legislature deemed it necessary to create a new county from a part of Henry. By an act approved on December 9, 1822, DeKalb was created and named for Baron Johann DeKalb, a Bavarian-born officer of the French army who had come to America with LaFayette and had died fighting for the cause of American independence. In establishing the boundaries of the new county, it was found necessary to include small portions of Gwinnett and Fayette.

Fourteen days after the creation of DeKalb, the legislature named William Jackson's house on what is now McDonough Road as a temporary site for the election of officers and the holding of court sessions. The county commissioners who were appointed by the legislature purchased Land Lot 246 near the center of the county, and on July 28, 1823, the inferior court issued an order declaring that a county seat would be permanently established on this site. The town was named in honor of Stephen Decatur, a distinguished naval officer of the War of 1812.

The county commissioners were also authorized to purchase land for the site of a courthouse and a jail. Accordingly, a log cabin was erected on the north side of the public square to serve as a temporary courthouse. Another log structure served as the first jail; the entrance to this building was a flight of stairs that led to the second floor, the first floor being a sort of dungeon that could be reached only through a trap door. Both these log buildings continued in use for several years until better quarters could be established. A brick courthouse, built at the seemingly enormous cost of $5,100, was erected in 1829 on the site of the present courthouse, where it stood until it was destroyed by fire in 1842. A granite jail was erected in 1849.

Strict laws and customs governed the conduct of all public officers. A sheriff upon taking oath of office was required to swear that he "had not since the 1st day of January, 1819, been engaged in a duel . . . in this state." One justice, Walter T. Colquitt, opened every sitting of his superior court with a prayer as he knelt on the judge's bench. But, despite the strong influence of religion and the customary strict rules for daily conduct, there were some who enjoyed their grog. Among the first commercial houses was a grocery store where spirituous liquors were also sold, chiefly corn liquor and brandy made of apples or peaches.

Having formed their government and built their dwellings, DeKalb and Decatur citizens set about the establishment of schools and churches. The first school was the DeKalb County Academy, established under a resolution of the general assembly approved on November 10, 1823. Since all county academies at the time were considered members of the State university system, the legislature provided financial assistance. On December 26, 1823, a lottery was authorized by this body to raise $3,000 for the academy, which was opened in Decatur during 1825. Further aid from the State was limited, and the school was forced to charge tuition and to function to some extent as a private institution. Other academies were opened in the outlying sections of the county during the 1830's.

As the county increased in population, many private schools were opened, often by teachers and ministers in their own homes, but financial difficulties made most of these short-lived. Tuition fees were low; one statement submitted to a patron shows that the total amount due was based on a charge of 5½¢ a day for each pupil. It was not until after the middle of the nineteenth century that efforts were made to provide more advanced courses. The Hannah Moore Female Collegiate Institute was chartered on December 22, 1857, and was opened soon afterward under the direction of the Reverend John S. Wilson, first pastor of the Decatur Presbyterian Church.

The land had hardly been opened to settlement before missionaries and evangelists began to organize congregations throughout the county. The first Presbyterian congregation in Decatur was that of the Westminster Church, which was formed on October 29, 1825, by a pastor from Gwinnett County and incorporated by legislative action two years later, when its name was changed to the Decatur Presbyterian Church. The Decatur Methodist Church, now the First Methodist Church, was organized at about the same time. The Baptists worshipped at the rural churches except for a short time following December 7, 1839, when a few members of the Hardman Church, two miles north of Decatur, seceded and formed the Decatur Baptist Church. The church in town apparently proved unsatisfactory, for two years later the meeting place was moved three miles east of the city and the name was changed to the Indian Creek Church. The Decatur Baptists continued to worship at the Indian Creek Church or with the other denominations until the present Decatur Baptist Church, now the First Baptist Church, was formed in 1861.

The congregations of the early churches were not long in erecting houses of worship. The Decatur Methodist Church was built in 1826. In order to hasten the construction of other religious edifices, the general assembly in 1832 passed an act authorizing the inferior court to grant lots to the Presbyterian and Baptist congregations. The Presbyterians soon availed themselves of this offer, but the Baptists did not build their church until 1871.

The galleries of several early churches were set aside for the use of Negro slaves, and contemporary sources show that many masters gave them religious instruction. Although DeKalb was never a section of large slave-holders, the 1850 census listed 2,942 Negro slaves, about 20 per cent of the total population.

Evidences of another form of servitude are found in the minutes of the inferior court, which indicate that custom permitted the leasing at public outcry of anyone dependent on the county for support. In 1846, Old Suck or Sookey, a female pauper, was obtained in this manner for a salary of $5.87 a month, the bidder being required to give her care and food. Sookey apparently became more decrepit, for three years later the bid was only $3.75 a month.

In 1845 Decatur was selected, alternately with Macon, as a meeting place for the third district sessions of the State supreme court, which had been established during that year. After ten years this honor was bestowed upon Atlanta, which had grown rapidly about the terminus of the railroad. For a time Atlanta's sudden development as a railroad center caused DeKalb to lose much valuable land and many citizens, for Fulton County was created from its area in 1853 with Atlanta as its seat. Federal census reports show that the number of citizens decreased from 14,328 in 1850 to 7,806 in 1860—a loss of almost half the population in the county.

As a whole the citizens of this area were in favor of preserving the Union, but with the secession of Georgia sentiment changed and the entire county cast its lot with the Confederacy. Prior to this time there had been only one military organization, the Volunteer Light Infantry Company, formed in 1835. With the outbreak of the war, however, extensive activity began. During the four years of conflict the county produced ten companies with such names as the Murphey Guards, the McCullough Rifles, and the Bartow Avengers. In all, 136 officers and 1,220 men marched off to battle from Decatur, and many men joined companies from other sections of the State. The county was away from the line of battle until 1864, when the western portion along the Georgia Railroad was devastated during the Battle of Atlanta. Two major generals, W.H.T. Walker of the Confederacy and James B. McPherson of the Union, were killed within the boundaries of DeKalb on July 22 during the progress of that battle.

After the war more farmers began to settle on the DeKalb County lands, and by the end of the century the county had more than regained the population lost as a result of the creation of Fulton. The courthouse that had been completed in 1847 was too small to house the increased number of county officers and the accumulation of records. Consequently this building was torn down in 1898 and replaced by another two years later. This courthouse served the county until 1916, when it was destroyed by fire. The present granite edifice, the fifth in Decatur, was erected 1917-18 at a cost of $110,000.

Although the county was getting back its lost population, the town grew very little until after the first decade of the new century. In 1900 Decatur, overshadowed by Atlanta, had a population of only 1,418. The only public school was the poorly equipped DeKalb County Academy, which had become a grammar school called the Decatur Male and Female Academy. During the following year Decatur citizens voted to tax themselves for educational purposes. In organizing their public school system they took over the old academy and began its operation under their own board of trustees in January 1902.

Since Decatur had no public high school, pupils in the upper grades were dependent upon such private institutions as Agnes Scott Institute and the Hillyer School. They also sent their sons to the Donald Fraser School, which had been opened in 1889 by Donald Fraser, pastor of the Decatur Presbyterian Church, and operated as a prominent boarding and day academy for boys of all ages. In 1909, when the owners saw that many of the younger pupils were attending the public school, they decided to close their academy; but upon the request of patrons they promised to continue operation until a public high school could be opened. It was not until 1912, however, that the city board of education consented to maintain a high school, and this was upon the condition that 64 boys and girls attend and pay a fee of $6 a month. The required patronage was quickly secured, and the public high school was opened in September of that year in the Donald Fraser building.

Even as late as 1907 the streets of Decatur were unpaved, the stores were of the old-fashioned general-merchandise type, and the school system possessed only one building. The town was lighted with electricity, but it was not until that year that water works were constructed. The period of greatest civic improvement started in 1911,

Around Atlanta

DOGWOOD BLOSSOMS—ATLANTA'S SPRING SNOWFALL

STONE MOUNTAIN

MIMOSA HALL, ROSWELL

EAST LAKE

THE CHATTAHOOCHEE RIVER

COVERED BRIDGE AT SOAP CREEK

DAIRY FARM NEAR ATLANTA

BACK-YARD GARDEN, DECATUR

CYCLORAMA BUILDING

DECATUR FROM COURTHOUSE SQUARE

DRESS PARADE INSPECTION AT THE GEORGIA MILITARY ACADEMY, COLLEGE
PARK

INSPECTION AT FORT MC PHERSON

ATLANTA AIRPORT, HAPEVILLE

when 35 citizens organized the Decatur Board of Trade, now supplanted by the DeKalb County Chamber of Agriculture and Commerce. That body immediately undertook the modernization which soon made Decatur desirable as a residential town. As a result, the population began to increase rapidly and rose to 6,150 in 1920.

In order to further their civic enterprises the Decatur citizens voted on November 17, 1920, to change their established system of political administration by electing five commissioners, who in turn would choose a city manager. This meant a reversion to the original commission form of government which had been superseded in 1882 by the mayor and council type. On January 3, 1921, the commissioners held their first meeting and elected P. P. Pilcher as city manager. The continued growth of Decatur and the consequent improvement in financial conditions soon enabled the commissioners to build a new city hall, construction of which was begun in 1925 and completed in 1926.

In 1922 the DeKalb County Centennial Association was organized to commemorate the founding of the county. During the celebration on November 9 great crowds in Decatur watched the presentation of an historical pageant and listened to an address of Charles Murphey Candler, a prominent citizen. The Decatur Public Library Association was formed on February 6, 1925. Its members immediately set about acquiring books through gifts and subscriptions and opened a small library on April 13. The number of volumes has increased from a few hundred on the opening date to 17,000 at the present time. The association maintains not only the main library on the second floor of the city hall but four branches, two in the county and two in town including the one in the high school auditorium building. A traveling librarian, in an automobile fitted out for carrying books, extends the service of the association to remote sections of the county.

Since 1938, the DeKalb County Chamber of Agriculture and Commerce has sponsored an annual Harvest Festival, held near Decatur. Each fall pageants, addresses, produce exhibits, and livestock shows attract citizens, farmers and business men, from all sections of the county.

47. AGNES SCOTT COLLEGE, W. College Ave., Decatur, one of the most highly rated Southern colleges for women, is housed in more than 30 buildings on a well-wooded campus. In accordance with the tradition of school architecture of the 1890's, the older buildings are substantial red-brick structures with broad white-banistered porches. The newer buildings follow the more modern Collegiate Gothic trend of brick construction with limestone trim. The library, costing $230,000, is notable for its modern facilities, which include cubicles for individual research, a room for art exhibitions, a projection room for motion pictures, and a terrace equipped with weather-proof furniture and gayly colored umbrellas for outdoor study. Presser Hall, completed in 1940 at a cost of $285,000, is used for instruction in music, and has a well-equipped auditorium and a chapel that may be used both for religious services and dramatic performances.

The school was established as the Decatur Female Seminary by members of the Decatur Presbyterian Church, with their pastor, Dr. F.H. Gaines, as its head. In order to finance the undertaking, the trustees had provided in the charter for selling shares at $50 par value to raise a minimum capital of $5,000, and the stock was quickly subscribed. Classes met for the first time on September 24, 1889, in an old rented residence, the work covering only elementary and grammar school grades. The first enrollment numbered 60 day students and 3 boarders.

The following year Colonel George F. Scott, a wealthy manufacturer who had bought $2,000 worth of the capital stock, offered to erect a building provided the school should bear the name of his mother, and the name was changed by charter amendment to Agnes Scott Institute. This building, equipped with all the latest conveniences and completely furnished, cost $82,000 and attracted wide attention because it represented the largest individual gift that had been made in Georgia for the cause of education. Later Scott bought all the outstanding stock and cancelled it. At the time of his death in 1903, his contributions to the institution totaled $175,000.

In 1906 the first college degrees were conferred and the preparatory school was given the name of Agnes Scott Academy. In 1913 the academy was discontinued and Agnes Scott became an institution solely for college work. In 1920 the Association of American Universities rendered recognition, and in 1921 graduates became eligible to the Association of Collegiate Alumnae. The college was invited in 1922 to make application for membership to Phi Beta Kappa and received the Beta Chapter of this honorary fraternity. ·

Liberal endowments were made from time to time by the Carnegie Foundation, the General Education Board, and various well-known philanthropic organizations, and total assets and endowments are now valued at more than $3,500,000. Although the school is not under ecclesiastical control, the charter provides that only members of the Presbyterian Church are eligible for election to the self-perpetuating board of trustees. From the first enrollment of 63 the student body has now increased to approximately 500, while the early elementary studies have been replaced by excellently conducted courses in the liberal arts. The four student publications are popular, and Agnes Scott is widely known for the performances of its Blackfriars Dramatic Club and also its glee club, which in 1940 combined with the Emory Glee Club to render a highly successful presentation of the Gilbert and Sullivan opera *Iolanthe*. A large number of Atlanta and Decatur people attend lectures by famous writers and commentators that are given at frequent intervals in the Agnes Scott auditorium. Athletic activities among the students include golf, swimming, and archery.

48. COLUMBIA THEOLOGICAL SEMINARY, 701 Columbia Drive, Decatur, is a historic Presbyterian institution housed in two handsome, modern brick buildings. Entirely controlled by the synods of Georgia, South Carolina, Florida, Alabama, and Mississippi, the

school in 1940-41 had an enrollment of 77, the largest in its history. Courses in biblical, historical, systematic, and practical theology lead to the degree of bachelor of divinity, and the master's and doctor's theological degrees are also conferred. In the study of practical theology, a recording machine is used, enabling the students to discover and overcome faults in the delivery of sermons. The library, it is said, contains the largest and most extensive collection of theological literature in the South.

Chartered in 1828, the institution first opened at Lexington, Georgia, as the Theological Seminary of the Synod of South Carolina and Georgia. Only five students were registered for the first courses, and the only instructor was the learned Dr. Thomas Goulding, pastor of the Presbyterian Church. Two years later, Goulding, with his family, his slaves, and a few of his students, moved to the First Presbyterian Church Manse at Columbia, South Carolina. On January 25, 1831, the school was transferred to the plant acquired for the seminary.

In the commodious, white-columned buildings the institution soon began to spread its influence widely, while the problem of financial insecurity was met by larger endowments and increased enrollment. The school has been closed for several brief periods: once during the War between the States; again in the early 1880's; and a third time, 1886-87, because of the loss of patronage resulting from the well-known controversy which ensued when a seminary teacher, Dr. James Woodrow, frankly expressed his views on evolution. The seminary carried on its work at Columbia for almost a century. During the earlier years of this period Francis Goulding, son of the minister and later a popular novelist, passed part of his boyhood there, and in later years young Woodrow Wilson made his first profession of faith at a devotional service in the chapel. Later, as President of the United States, he said: "I have heard much eloquent speaking but on the whole the best speaking I ever heard in my life was in the little chapel."

As the years passed, other Southeastern synods joined in control of the seminary. In 1924 a plan was advanced for moving the school to Decatur, and a campaign for $500,000 for endowment and equipment was launched. The charter was amended in 1925 increasing the board of directors to 21 and officially giving the school its present name. Two years later the first classes were held on the present site—a rolling, wooded campus of 57 acres.

49. AVONDALE ESTATES (1,025 alt., 535 pop.), 8½ miles east of Atlanta on US 78, is a subdivision of trim parkways and well-kept houses, the prevailing type of which is the steep-gabled, brick and half-timber structure characteristic of Tudor Gothic architecture. Even the stores, all fronting together along one block, follow this style, with sharply sloping roof and second-story overhang. As the highway passes this commercial section it widens to include a broad central parkway, on the opposite side of which are the residences with their shrubbery and well-clipped lawns.

This suburb, for which the land was purchased by G.F. Willis in 1924, offers its residents many advantages of modern community life. Adult recreation is provided by a clubhouse with tennis courts, a golf course, a swimming pool, and an 80-acre lake with rowboats, and the children of the community are accommodated by three large playgrounds distributed over the several hundred acres that make up Avondale Estates. A fireproof grade school is operated municipally, while the high school is part of the DeKalb County system. Although the houses are characterized by certain uniform structural and decorative details, they range in size from six-room bungalows to spacious two-story dwellings.

50. STONE MOUNTAIN, 16 miles east of Atlanta on US 78, is known to geologists as the largest granite monadnock in North America and to the general public for the partly completed Confederate monument carved on its sheer northeastern wall. From the highway the mountain appears bare except for a few dark spots of scrubby pine growth. The gray color of the stone is faintly tinged with the green of moss and lichen that covers it, and the surface is broken by deep cracks that run in long jagged lines down the slopes. Here and there are darker streaks formed by iron oxide and organic matter washed down from the summit.

Stone Mountain is elliptical in shape, with an axis 2 miles long. It rises 1,686 feet above sea level and 650 feet above the surrounding piedmont plain, measures more than 7 miles around the base, and has an estimated weight of 1,250,000,000 tons, although it is believed that the exposed section is only a small part of the entire mass. The mountain was formed perhaps two hundred million years ago as a molten mass underground. Further scientific research indicates that it appeared above the surface of the earth not by upheaval but by the gradual erosion of the soil and softer rocks that once overlaid the granite. The mass slowly cooled, its surface breaking into crevices with contraction, and a few hardy shrubs began to take root.

The sheer side on which the carving is shown is almost 900 feet high. The scope of the original plan for the sculpture is scarcely indicated by the work that has been begun. Actually, the memorial gives the appearance of a gigantic sketch, with Augustus Lukeman's projected figures showing barely in outline. The heads of Jefferson Davis, President of the Confederacy, and General Stonewall Jackson are only faintly suggested, but the majestic form of General Robert E. Lee on his horse Traveller emerges more definitely. From the crown of the general's hat to the horse's hoof the distance is 130 feet, the height of an average 10-story building. The granite chips scraped out by the stonecutters form a scattered pile on the ground below the monument.

A clearer conception of the finished memorial can be had from the photographs and plaster molds on exhibition at the museum across the highway. These working models provide an interesting study of the problems that confronted the sculptors while working, for the great figures had to be rendered with a proportionate change of scale from head to foot, as the feet are so much nearer the view of spectators below. In order to give a just illusion, Lee's aquiline nose was shown as upturned.

The southern slope of the mountain can be climbed; although there is no road, the ascent is not difficult for a reasonably active climber. From the flat summit is a clear panoramic view of the surrounding countryside with its wooded slopes, green pastures, and clusters of houses.

The mountain was probably used by prehistoric Indians as a refuge from the gigantic animals that were forced south by glaciers. When the first white settlers came to this region in the latter part of the eighteenth century, they found Indians using the mountain as a vantage point for sending smoke signals. A number of boulders laid in regular formation were probably the remains of a fortress or a sacrificial altar. These rocks were not moved until work was begun on the Confederate monument.

In 1790 Alexander McGillivray, a half-breed chieftain of the Creeks, met here with a band of tribesmen to discuss plans for selling the mountain to the Federal Government. Shortly after this conference he went with a selected group to New York, and the entire mountain was sold for a pony and a gun. Nor did the early white owners set an inordinate value on their mammoth acquisition, for it is recorded that E.V. Sanford, a plantation proprietor who later purchased it, was annoyed because the mountain stood in the path of his plowing and sold it for a five-foot flintlock rifle.

In due course the property, after passing successively into the hands of several private owners, was developed as a popular summer resort. By 1825 there were a stagecoach terminus and a hotel at the base of the mountain. A long observation tower, 175 feet high, built on a 40-foot base and having a winding interior stairway, was erected on the summit in 1836. Three years later the village of New Gibraltar, later Stone Mountain, was established. During the 1850's the town came into considerable local prominence when the Southern Central Agricultural Society, which later grew into the State Department of Agriculture, held its first four fairs here.

Although the mountain itself had no part in the War between the States, important troop movements were effected in the vicinity during the summer of 1864, when Atlanta was under siege. Here the Federal troops, bent on destroying Confederate communications, took up the iron rails of the Georgia Railroad and rendered them useless by heating them and bending them around trees.

Between 1845 and 1850 some efforts were made to quarry the stone from the partly disintegrated ledges, but these enterprises had little success. The first systematic effort at quarrying the granite was made in 1869, when John T. Glenn, S.M. Inman, and J.A. Alexander, of Atlanta, chartered the Stone Mountain Granite and Railway Company. Their output was small, however, and the property was purchased in 1880 by Samuel Venable, who for many years quarried the granite for use in bridges, buildings, and roadways.

The huge mass of solid granite was a remarkable enough sight to attract many tourists even before 1914, when William Terrell, an Atlanta lawyer, suggested the plan of carving a Confederate monument on the perpendicular side. In the following year the United Daughters of the Confederacy invited the well-known sculptor Gutzon Borglum to submit a design, which was accepted. The northeastern side of the mountain was donated by Venable, his sister Mrs. Frank T. Mason, and his nieces Mrs. Priestly Orme and Mrs. Walter G. Roper, a gift valued at approximately $1,000,000. The site was dedicated on May 20, 1916. Although no sculptural work was done before the end of the World War, Borglum aroused considerable excitement throughout the country by his lectures on the memorial plan.

During the early years of the 1920's, public enthusiasm mounted high. The carving was begun, much of it done by Borglum himself suspended by cables over the mountainside. The outlines for the figures were set forth by a projection an acre in size cast from a two-inch stereopticon slide by means of a specially prepared triple-lens projection lamp. General Lee's sculptured head was unveiled on his birthday, January 19, 1924. During this time the Stone Mountain Memorial Association raised funds by the sale of memorial 50¢ coins at $1 each.

Soon after the Lee head was unveiled, a dispute over the proper distribution of these coins caused the association to break into bitter factions. Borglum left the project after destroying his working models except for the completed figure of Jefferson Davis, giving as his reason his unwillingness to have his work completed by a successor. Another sculptor, Augustus Lukeman, was engaged. Borglum's head of Lee was blasted away, and Lukeman began directing the carving of another memorial. Funds were soon exhausted, however, and public approval had been chilled by the acrimonious controversy. The work was suspended in 1930. Plans were advanced in 1941 for completing the memorial, and Julian Harris, an Atlanta sculptor, has been selected for this work.

51. The main campus of EMORY UNIVERSITY, bounded principally by Oxford, North Decatur, Clifton, and Briarcliff Rds., NE., covers more than 400 acres in the wooded, rolling residential section of Druid Hills. The 17 university buildings, constructed of varicolored Georgia marble in a simplified Italian Renaissance design, are grouped about the cleanly landscaped lawns of the main quadrangle and other cleared plots. On Fraternity Row, a circular drive west of these, are the handsome red-brick and white-brick houses of the 12 Greek letter fraternal organizations at Emory. Encircling these areas is a dense natural growth of pine and hardwood trees, brightened in spring by dogwood and flowering shrubs.

Although Emory is owned by the General Conference of the Methodist Church, it is nonsectarian in its administration. The university is made up of Emory College (the college of arts and sciences), the

School of Business Administration, the Graduate School, the Candler School of Theology, the School of Medicine, the Lamar School of Law, the Library School, and the School of Nursing. The curriculum of the liberal arts college includes courses in journalism, education, fine arts, and chemical and electrical engineering. Except for the School of Nursing, the institution is primarily for men, but women are admitted to the graduate, theological, law, and library schools. The only women students in the undergraduate college of Emory are enrolled from Agnes Scott College in Decatur through a system permitting approved junior and senior students of either institution to register for courses given at the other. In addition to the schools on the Druid Hills campus, the university maintains the clinical division of the medical school in connection with Grady Hospital in downtown Atlanta, the Emory Junior Colleges in Valdosta and Oxford, Georgia, and the Emory University Academy, operated in conjunction with the Oxford institution.

As a whole, the institution has a faculty of more than 350, a student enrollment of more than 2,000, and an endowment and trust funds exceeding $6,000,000. Among the large donors have been Asa G. Candler, Sr., Samuel Candler Dobbs, and other members of the Candler family. In 1939 the institution was offered a $2,000,000 grant by the General Education Board of the Rockefeller Foundation with the provision that double that amount be raised by Emory. The purpose of the grant is to further co-operation with other institutions in the State and to develop a comprehensive program of higher education, especially on professional and graduate levels, and the completion of this program will strengthen the school materially.

Many extracurricular activities are carried on under the control of the Student Activities Council. The *Emory Wheel* provides weekly news of undergraduate enterprises, while the more literary *Emory Phoenix* presents articles and short stories by the students. The Emory Players produce each year a number of standard and original plays. Interscholastic debates are an important feature of university life, and in years past student debating teams have met others from the leading universities of the United States and England. Emory men do not participate in intercollegiate athletics. In accordance with an extensive program of physical training, the university emphasizes intramural sports and schedules contests between classes, schools, fraternities, and other groups.

The student organization that is best known off the campus is the Emory University Glee Club. Under the direction of Malcolm H. Dewey, who has been in charge since 1920, the mandolin clubs and jazz bands of former days have been superseded by a standard choral organization, which has attained a widespread reputation by making annual concert tours to the larger cities of the Eastern States. The singers have also appeared in Cuba (1923) and have made two European tours (1926 and 1928), including performances in English cities and in Amsterdam, Holland. President Calvin Coolidge attended the concert in Washington in 1925, and eight years later President Franklin D. Roosevelt heard the club sing on a program dedicating Georgia Hall at Warm Springs. The glee club is especially well known for its rendition of Negro spirituals and for its annual Christmas carol program, presented at Glenn Memorial Church in the dim light of burning tapers.

Two other important groups are the Emory University Orchestra and the Student Lecture Association. The orchestra, organized in 1921 and called the Little Symphony, annually presents several Sunday afternoon concerts of classical music. The lecture association offers to both the student body and the general public a series of lectures by celebrated men and women. The association occasionally sponsors a musical program, a monologuist, or a group of players.

At a session in Washington, Georgia, in 1834, the Georgia Methodist Conference was asked to aid Randolph-Macon College in Virginia. The only dissent came from "Uncle Allen" Turner, who stoutly insisted that Georgia Methodists needed a college of their own. Turner's suggestion was overruled, but the conference decided to establish an academy in which literary instruction would be supplemented by manual labor. As a result the Georgia Conference Manual Labor School was chartered on December 18, 1834, and was opened the following March on a large tract west of Covington. Students worked three hours a day on the farm, their pay, usually four cents an hour, being applied on their tuition. But the institution was burdened by constantly increasing indebtedness.

Meanwhile Ignatius Few, chairman of the board of trustees, was seriously considering a plan for expanding the manual labor school into an institution of higher learning. On January 18, 1836, he induced the conference to apply to the legislature for an extension of the charter for this purpose. Although a new charter was granted on December 19, 1836, the trustees of the academy became the trustees of the college, and some of the faculty members were later transferred. Emory College, named for Bishop John Emory of the Methodist Church, was opened with Ignatius Few as president in the fall of 1838 on land donated by the academy and for a time was conducted along the manual labor plan. Soon the institution owned 1,452 acres, on which both the farm and the town of Oxford were laid out. Two years after the college was opened, its board of trustees closed the manual labor school and assumed its assets and liabilities.

Until 1914 Emory College was owned by the Georgia Methodists alone, but in that year it was taken over by the General Conference of the Methodist Episcopal Church, South, which was seeking to establish two universities, one west and one east of the Mississippi River. The educational commission appointed by that body then decided to accept the offer of $500,000 from the Atlanta Chamber of Commerce and a $1,000,000 endowment from Asa G. Candler, Sr., and to establish a university in Atlanta with Emory College as the school of liberal arts. The charter of Emory College was consequently extended to care for its functioning as a university. Bishop Warren A. Candler, a former president, became chancellor of the enlarged institution and directed its organization until his retirement in 1922. The office was then discontinued and authority vested in the president.

The first division to be opened in Atlanta was the Candler School of Theology, named for Bishop Candler who had begun a preachers' training course at Oxford in 1894. Hastily organized to receive students in the fall of 1914, this school held classes in the Wesley Memorial Church on Auburn Avenue until the first building on the campus was completed in 1916.

The subsequent development of the university was rapid. On June 28, 1915, the Druid Hills campus was acquired, and on the same day the trustees of the Atlanta Medical College deeded its property to Emory University to serve as a medical division. The Lamar School of Law, opened on the campus during the fall of the following year, introduced into Georgia the case study method of instruction and held a practice court twice a week. In 1919 the entire college was moved up from Oxford, and both the School of Business Administration and the Graduate School were founded. The School of Nursing, which had been established in Atlanta with Wesley Memorial Hospital in 1905, was moved with the hospital to the Emory campus in 1922, and three years later it too became a part of the university.

The youngest of the university divisions is the Library School, an outgrowth of an apprentice class formed in 1889 by Anne Wallace to train assistants to help her in the management of the newly organized Carnegie Library of Atlanta. The school, officially organized in 1905, when Andrew Carnegie provided $4,000 a year for its maintenance, offered a one-year course patterned after that of the Pratt Institute School of Library Science, and, since there were few library commissions in the South and no other library school in the State, the institution was an important factor in training assistants and planning buildings for many libraries throughout Georgia. The larger cities of several other Southern States also called upon its services. At first the institution was called the Southern Library School, but in 1907 it was incorporated as the Carnegie Library Training School of Atlanta. Although it became affiliated with Emory in 1925, it remained in the Carnegie Library in Atlanta until 1930, when it was transferred to the university campus. A college degree is required for admission.

The complicated story of the School of Medicine includes the histories of the Atlanta Medical College, the Southern Medical College, the Atlanta College of Physicians and Surgeons, and the Atlanta School of Medicine. The parent institution was the Atlanta Medical College, chartered in 1854 and opened the following year under the guidance of Dr. John G. Westmoreland. Dr. Alexander Means, a professor of chemistry at Emory College, Oxford, also taught at the medical school, and his merciless satire was influential in freeing Georgia medicine from superstition. A summer session held classes from May 1 to September 1 and continued to do so for many years. Students listened to five lectures daily and attended several clinics each week but failed to get adequate practical experience because bedside instruction was prohibited by the hospitals of the city. Since there was no law permitting medical schools to have unclaimed corpses, students and teachers alike had many exciting experiences obtaining cadavers. One professor who had robbed a grave was overtaken by daylight before he could deposit his burden in the college building. Undaunted, he placed the body in a sitting position between himself and the driver of his vehicle and boldly rode along the street until he reached his destination.

Beginning with the term of 1862, the college was closed for three years, its building being used as a Confederate Army hospital. Dr. N. D'Alvigny, one of the medical instructors, was placed in charge of the hospital on the day when Atlanta was evacuated. As soon as he learned that this building was on the list of those to be burned by General Sherman's order, he formulated a plan to save the structure and plied his hospital attendants with liquor. On the night of the burning he approached a Union officer and angrily demanded if the hospital was to be burned before its inmates were removed. The official curtly replied that the wounded soldiers had been taken away and that the building would be destroyed immediately. The doctor thereupon led the way to the hospital, threw open the doors, and revealed the room where his attendants lay groaning amidst straw and kindling. He was given until morning to care for the men, but by that time the invading army had started southward and the period of danger had passed.

Although much of the equipment had been ruined during the war, the Atlanta Medical College continued as formerly from 1865 until 1878, when a group of doctors withdrew to form the Southern Medical College. This second institution advanced the quality of medical instruction by establishing the Providence Infirmary for clinical work, but after a period of 20 years it became evident that one institution would be stronger than two rival colleges. Committees worked out plans and on November 9, 1898, a charter was granted for the combined institution under the name of the Atlanta College of Physicians and Surgeons. The school prospered and strengthened its dental and pharmaceutical department, but it was not long before another group became dissatisfied with its administration. The result was a second offspring, opened in 1905 and called the Atlanta School of Medicine. Soon this college had its own hospital and offered increased facilities for practical demonstrations. During the ensuing year both institutions struggled hard to meet the rising standards of medical education and in 1913 decided to unite. The single institution, again called the Atlanta Medical College, functioned as such until 1915, when its trustees sought affiliation with Emory and decided to accept the university's offer to appropriate a $250,000 endowment and to build a hospital for more adequate teaching facilities. Since then the medical college has been the Emory University School of Medicine.

The WILBUR FISK GLENN MEMORIAL CHURCH, intersection of Oxford and North Decatur Roads, is a cream-colored stucco building of Georgian Colonial design, a departure from the characteristic Renaissance style of the other Emory buildings. Standing on the landscaped elevation at the entrance to the campus, this well-proportioned church has a tall spire that springs from an Ionic portico and rises by means of setback tiers to a delicately fashioned cupola. The Colonial motif is emphasized inside by a row of Corinthian columns in each of the side aisles and by the clear glass windows. The light ivory coloring of the walls is offset by dark red draperies, which are suspended behind columns arranged in a Palladian design to form a background for the choir. The church is so constructed that it can be transformed from a religious edifice into a public auditorium. The columns of the choir gallery when swung back on large hinges reveal a stage, and the pulpit platform when rolled upon a steel track beneath the stage leaves an orchestra pit. The hall is used for services by members of the congregation, who come from the entire Druid Hills area, for chapel exercises by the university, and for lectures, concerts, and plays presented by the student organizations. Designed by the Atlanta firm of Hentz, Adler, and Shutze and erected in 1931, the building was given to the university by Mrs. Charles Howard Candler and Thomas K. Glenn in memory of their father Dr. Wilbur Fisk Glenn, a well-known Methodist minister.

At the rear of Glenn Memorial is the CHURCH SCHOOL BUILDING, designed by the same architects and completed in 1940. In addition to well-appointed classrooms, offices, assembly halls, and lounges, there is a small chapel inspired by the church of Saint Stephen Walbrook, London, designed by Christopher Wren. The room is given its decided character by the plaster ornamentation of the domed ceiling and the delicate carving of the oak doorway and altar. The chapel has become popular with Emory alumni and others for small weddings. The left side of the Church School Building forms the background of an amphitheater with sodded terraces and a rostrum for outdoor services. The bright green of the terrace is emphasized by the dark boxwood borders.

The LAMAR SCHOOL OF LAW BUILDING, east side of quadrangle, is a two-story pink-marble edifice with recessed arched entrances rising almost to its red-tiled roof. The structure is one of the first buildings erected on the campus in 1916 from the designs of Henry Hornbostel of New York. In the white marble lobby is a bronze bust of Judge John S. Candler, benefactor of the school. Winding upward from the lobby past the large arched window is a marble stairway of such remarkable beauty that it is a favorite subject for photographers. The School of Law was named for Lucius Q.C. Lamar, an Emory alumnus of 1845 who pioneered in the case study method of instruction at the University of Mississippi in 1867 and who later served as United States Senator and as Associate Justice of the United States Supreme Court.

The CANDLER SCHOOL OF THEOLOGY BUILDING, west side of

quadrangle, similar in style to the law building, was also designed by
Henry Hornbostel and constructed in 1916. In the white marble
foyer is a bust of Bishop Warren A. Candler, for whom the School of
Theology was named, and at the rear are glass doors, which open into
a pink-marble chapel with a high red-pine wainscot. This small room,
used for daily religious worship, is given an appearance of spaciousness
by its high ceiling. The wall sconces are shaded by pink-marble plaques
bearing bronze reproductions of early Christian symbols.

The WESLEY MUSEUM (*open Mon.-Fri. 8-9 and Sat. 8-12 upon
application to the librarian of the theological reading room*), right of
the theological school lobby, contains 2,615 books, a variety of documents, and many articles of historic interest to the Methodist Church.
The museum takes its name from the numerous books and objects that
concern John and Charles Wesley, the founders of Methodism. This
Wesleyan collection, secured by Bishop Warren A. Candler, former
chancellor of the university, and supplemented by Charles Howard
Candler, is one of the most extensive and important in either America
or England. Two of the most treasured possessions are a portrait of
John Wesley, painted by Henry Eldridge when the noted divine was
88, and a prayer desk, made about 1740 and used by John Wesley
while he was preaching to the miners of Wales. Among the objects of
interest outside the Wesleyana are a roll of the Pentateuch, a collection
of letters of early Methodist ministers in the United States, and a
chair used by Bishop Francis Asbury when he held conference in
Chester, South Carolina.

The ASA GRIGGS CANDLER LIBRARY (*open Mon.-Fri. 8-9; Sat.
8-12*), north end of quadrangle, is a white-marble building designed by
Edward L. Tilton, of New York, in the characteristic architectural
style of the campus. The structure, erected in 1926, houses more
than 100,000 bound volumes and 60,000 unbound pamphlets, the principal part of the university collection. The books in the departmental
reading rooms of the Schools of Law, Theology, and Medicine bring
the total number of bound volumes up to 170,000. Among the excellent bibliographical resources in the main library is the card catalogue
of the Library of Congress, and among the special collections are the
Tracy W. McGregor Americana and the Keith M. Read Confederate
manuscripts and printed sources. The JOEL CHANDLER HARRIS
MEMORIAL ROOM contains the greater part of the manuscripts of the
noted author of the Uncle Remus stories together with first editions
and other literary relics.

The EMORY UNIVERSITY MUSEUM, a large room on the main floor
of the Candler Library, contains several varied collections ranging
from present-day natural history specimens to ancient coins, ornaments,
and artifacts. The objects are displayed to emphasize the curios from
Egypt, Babylon, and Palestine, including three mummies and reproductions of ancient monuments. This collection was begun in 1921
by the Reverend William A. Shelton, then a member of the Emory

faculty, while he was on an archeological expedition with men from Chicago and Yale Universities.

52. The STATE GAME FARM (*open 10-5*), Briarcliff Rd. about 12 miles northeast of downtown Atlanta, is devoted at present to rearing quail for distribution in Georgia areas where the native stock has been depleted either by over-shooting or by lack of food. On the 35-acre tract of wooded land the loud, clear bobwhite call rings like a frequently repeated echo. From the entrance gate a driveway leads past caretakers' cottages to the breeding pens, incubators, and brooder houses. Here 650 hens lay about 2,700 eggs a week during the season.

Domesticated quail are used for breeding. Because they are not allowed to set, they lay an average of about 80 eggs a season; wild birds under the same conditions lay only an average of from 35 to 40. One domesticated hen laid 121 eggs in a single season. When the birds are from 10 to 12 weeks old, they are released to individuals and groups who promise that no hunting will be permitted on restocked land for at least 12 months. Plans have been made to give the excess eggs to 4-H Clubs, the Future Farmers of America, and similar organizations, the eggs to be hatched under bantam hens and the young to be placed in depleted areas. The young club members will be given instructions in the conservation of wild life, and, if the program is successful, only eggs will be distributed in the future. About 7,000 quail and 16,000 eggs were released in 1940.

Experiments have been conducted with the chukar, an Asiatic partridge that is faster, hardier, and four times as large as the Georgia quail. From an original stock of three pairs, many chukars were reared and distributed throughout the state, but these birds did not prove to be adaptable to conditions in Georgia, since they were unable to protect themselves from predators. The few remaining chukars are displayed in pens.

The game farm was established in 1936 by the Georgia Game and Fish Department, a part of the Department of Natural Resources. The quail brood-stock was built up from an initial purchase of Tennessee birds and from native Georgia quail. Plans are being made to establish a fish hatchery here and also to enclose acreage for the rearing of deer.

53. OGLETHORPE UNIVERSITY, on Peachtree Rd. about 12 miles north of downtown Atlanta, is a coeducational institution which offers courses leading to the degrees of B.A., B.S., and M.A. Experimental work in courses other than those usually included in a standard liberal arts curriculum has earned for the school the title "The Unique University." The enrollment for the year 1939-40 was about 600, and the faculty numbered 35.

The extensive campus of the university covers more than 600 acres of meadow and woodland, including 80-acre Phoebe Lake, which is used by the students for swimming, boating, and fishing. On the well-landscaped quadrangle near the entrance are grouped the three main buildings, the Administration Building, Lupton Hall, and Lowry Hall,

all constructed of Georgia blue granite and white limestone in a Gothic style. In the tower of Lupton Hall are an illuminated clock and chimes on which concerts are given. Lowry Hall is a copy of old Corpus Christi College at Oxford, England, the alma mater of General James Edward Oglethorpe, founder of Georgia. Hermance Stadium, not yet completed, is also being constructed of blue granite, trimmed with carved limestone. The finished section seats about 5,000, only one-ninth of the total seating capacity planned.

A complete radio broadcasting station, WJTL, was installed and began operation at Oglethorpe on May 24, 1931, for the purpose of offering college courses to people who were unable to attend classes on the campus. The expense of offering free lecture courses, however, proved to be too great, and the station was sold in 1935 to a private commercial organization which operates it as WATL in downtown Atlanta.

The Oglethorpe University Press owns a printing shop equipped with a Babcock optimus press, linotype machine, and two job presses, which are operated entirely by student labor. Besides college publications, the press has published novels and volumes of poetry.

A medical school was opened October 1, 1941, and now has a freshman class of about 75 students instructed by eight full-time faculty members. Plans have been made to add more advanced work as the present class proceeds and additional students are enrolled.

Oglethorpe University traces its history back to 1823, when at a meeting of the Hopewell Presbytery a movement was begun to found a manual training school. In 1835 this school became Oglethorpe College, and a handsome building was erected for it on the outskirts of Milledgeville, then the capital of the State. Among the distinguished men who served on the faculty of the old college were Joseph LeConte, a noted geologist, James Woodrow, a brilliant scientist, and Samuel K. Talmage, an able minister and teacher. Its most famous graduate was the poet Sidney Lanier, who received his degree in 1860 and acted as tutor until the following spring, when he enlisted in the Confederate Army with the Oglethorpe cadets. In 1862 the college was closed and its buildings were used as barracks and a hospital until they were destroyed by fire during the Federal occupation of Milledgeville.

Although Oglethorpe's endowment had been lost with the failure of Confederate bonds, an effort was made in 1870 to reopen the college in Atlanta, but after a few sessions it was forced to close again for lack of funds. It was not until 1912 that a movement was begun for the present institution by Thornwell Jacobs, who toured the South lecturing to raise funds for the enterprise. The charter was granted in May 1913, and Jacobs was named president of Oglethorpe on January 21, 1915, when the cornerstone of the first building was laid. Classes met the following fall.

The CRYPT OF CIVILIZATION is a vault beneath the Administration Building containing records and materials of twentieth-century civilization collected and stored with the hope of preserving them intact for 6,000 years. Four years were spent in assembling and preparing the articles, which were treated in accordance with the methods of preservation recommended by the United States Bureau of Standards. Included in the collection are hundreds of books transferred to microfilm, recorded music and speeches, motion picture films, a projector, a phonograph, a typewriter, a radio, an electric generator, a sewing machine, and a microphone, as well as miniature models of mechanical inventions and numerous articles of every-day use.

The crypt is 20 feet long, 10 feet wide, and 10 feet high, built upon a ledge of granite near the surface of the ground. The granite walls and ceilings are lined with vitreous porcelain enamel, and metal shelves hold the receptacles containing the various articles. The door to the chamber is of stainless steel.

On May 26, 1940, the vault was closed and the steel door welded into place. A complete description of the crypt, giving its exact location, has been translated into every known language and sent to libraries in every country in the world. The date fixed for the opening is the year 8113 A.D.

54. FLOWERLAND (*admission free*), Chamblee-Dunwoody Rd. approximately 13 miles northwest of Atlanta, is the 138-acre estate of Dr. L.C. Fischer, who bought the land in 1931 and immediately began to cultivate it as the most spectacular rose garden of the Atlanta vicinity. For two miles along the highway, fences and trellises are covered with the climbing talisman, Paul's scarlet red, and Dr. Van Fleet pink roses.

To the right of the entrance a path leads through a long arbor covered with Paul's scarlet roses to the beds, where more than 600 varieties of bush roses are planted between terraced pathways. The red, white, cream, yellow, and pale pink blooms glow brightly against the clay-red waters of Nancy's Creek, which has been turned so that it circles through the gardens.

Steps between the rose beds lead down to a path at the edge of the creek that is bordered with lavender and purple rhododendron, flame azalea, and pink and white mountain laurel. The path affords a view of the opposite slope, which is covered with more roses, and winds a short distance through cool woods fragrant with sweet shrub. Banked around a long lily pond near by is a rock garden, where grow forget-me-nots and other small flowers and plants. Flowering vines, including the large blue clematis, climb the trees, and on tree trunks throughout the garden are framed verses appropriate to the setting, such as "Shared" by the Georgia poet Agnes Kendrick Gray:

> Some things there be that are better shared—
> A cottage fire, a table spread;
> A country road in the evening hush,
> And gardens trellised and garlanded.

A bridge with hanging baskets of petunias, geraniums, and coleuses crosses to a path at the foot of a steep embankment, planted in rhododendron and mountain laurel. At the end of this path another bridge crosses the creek where the sluggish waters suddenly come to life in their rapid fall over a dam. Across the bridge is a large rock garden colorful with the velvety hues of innumerable pansies.

On a high eminence overlooking the grounds is the Doric-columned, red-brick residence of Dr. Fischer. Beyond the main entrance to the gardens a long drive leads from the highway to the rear of the house. Along this winding driveway are vivid plantings of multicolored roses, poppies, irises, narcissi, and tulips. A clipped-privet dog and doghouse in the plot just back of the house are popular with children who visit the gardens.

55. UNITED STATES NAVAL RESERVE AVIATION BASE (*main roads only open to visitors: those with business to transact may obtain permission to enter buildings by addressing the aide to the executive officer*), at Chamblee, occupies a 300-acre reservation.

56. The LAWSON GENERAL HOSPITAL (*principal streets only open to visitors; those with business to transact may obtain permission to enter buildings from the adjutant*), on Carroll Ave. between Hood Ave. and US 23 (Buford Highway), is situated on a 140-acre reservation adjoining the naval base.

The hospital was named for Thomas Lawson, Surgeon General of the United States Army before the War between the States. Construction, begun on December 19, 1940, was completed the following May at a cost of $3,500,000. About 900,000 cubic yards of dirt were removed in leveling 4 red-clay hills before the building program was completed.

The naval base and hospital are on the SITE OF CAMP GORDON, one of the 35 cantonments established in the United States during the first World War. At this camp, consisting of 1,200 buildings on 3,000 acres of land, it is estimated that 80,000 soldiers were quartered at one time. The two most prominent units to be trained in the cantonment were the 82d Division and the Base Hospital (Emory University Medical) Unit 43. After leaving Camp Gordon in April 1918, the men of each of these units served as a body with the American Expeditionary Forces in France for the duration of the war. The cantonment, established on July 18, 1917, and named for General John B. Gordon of the War between the States, was abandoned officially on December 13, 1919. After the government sold the land, the area was given over to forests and farmland, but the section has continued to be known locally as Camp Gordon.

57. The RUINS OF SOAP CREEK PAPER MILLS (*ask directions at Sandy Springs on Roswell Rd.*) lie along Soap Creek, a small branch of the Chattahoochee River, 16 miles northwest of Atlanta. The tranquil beauty of the spot has made it popular with picnickers in spring and summer. Pine-covered hills slope down to the stream, which flows rapidly over its shallow bed, its yellowish waters foaming over many rocks. The ruins, extending along both sides, are high granite walls, roofless and with bushes and small trees growing inside.

Spanning the creek on massive foundations of rubble stone is an old covered bridge, one of the few remaining in the South. This structure, probably built in the late 1850's, is a heavy lattice of hand-hewn timbers secured by wooden pegs, enclosed by vertical planks, and covered with a tin gable roof.

The creek was named for Old Sope, a Cherokee chief who remained in this vicinity after his fellow tribesmen were driven out in 1838. Kindly and peaceable, the old man was beloved by the children of this section, who gathered eagerly to hear his stories. Afterward the name was corrupted to Soap Creek.

When the factory was incorporated as the Marietta Paper Mills in 1859, Cobb County was rapidly developing as an industrial section with saddleries, shoemaking shops, printing establishments, grist-mills, and factories for cotton and woolen goods. In this mill, probably the first paper manufacturing plant in the South, "tissue paper, writing, printing, and wrapping paper were made . . . from cotton stalks, wood, and rags." But industrial development was sharply interrupted by the advance of Federal troops upon Atlanta in the summer of 1864. On the night of July 8 General George Schofield's men, having marched to the Soap Creek neighborhood from near-by Smyrna, carried boats down the tree-covered slopes, loaded them with soldiers, and launched them downstream under protection of heavy artillery fire. The Confederates were unable to block this bold maneuver, which brought the invaders nearer their goal. The buildings of the factory were then burned by the fleeing Confederate troops.

Soon after the war the mills were rebuilt and again put into operation, but a succession of disasters followed. Partly destroyed by fire in 1870, they were rebuilt in the following year, but the factory operated only a short time before the national panic of 1873 made collections impossible. The buildings were bought at public sale by James R. Brown, who organized two companies, one to operate the paper mill and the other to establish a cotton goods factory here.

For a number of years the paper manufacturing plant successfully produced books, newsprint, and wrapping paper. In 1886 Saxon A. Anderson, part owner of the establishment, built a wood-pulp mill in addition to the rag paper mill. Three years later a paper twine factory was begun. As there was only one other such concern in the United States, prospects seemed bright for a profitable undertaking, but Anderson found that the machinery was patented and could not be purchased. Undaunted, he and Jeff Land, the mill superintendent, perfected their own machinery.

By 1890 the mills were manufacturing the first blotting paper made south of Richmond. For years the Soap Creek region provided a busy scene, and the work of paper manufacturing was carried on into the twentieth century. The buildings were abandoned when the establishment was moved to Marietta, where it was operated successfully for a number of years.

58. ROSWELL (1,000 alt., 1,432 pop.), 21 miles north of Atlanta

on US 19, one of the earliest Southern manufacturing towns, has lost much of its industrial activity but has kept its tradition of old-fashioned aristocracy intact in several fine historic houses. Though small in population, the town stretches for two miles along the highway, its rows of inconspicuous dwellings broken briefly by two small commercial centers. A broad parkway centers the highway at the southern end of the town. The environs fall away into cotton patches, corn fields, orchards, and woodland stretches that in fall are tinted with the rich hues of turning leaves. The most colorful season, however, is early summer, when lawns are bright with the fluffy golden-pink blossoms of many mimosa trees.

Settlement began here in 1837, the same year in which the first railroad builders came to the near-by Atlanta area. Roswell King, a wealthy planter and banker, stopped here while on a business trip to the United States mint at Dahlonega, Georgia, and was much impressed by the beauty of these rolling hills. Finding the climate more bracing than that of his home at Darien on the Georgia coast, he purchased a considerable land tract and made gifts of ten acres each to seven of his friends from the Sea Island region. A Connecticut artist, Willis Ball, brought here to plan their homes, designed Barrington Hall, Mimosa Hall, Bulloch Hall, Great Oaks, and the Presbyterian Church. The experiment was successful, and the village was soon a center for several prosperous plantations. It was King's aspiration, however, to establish industry as well as agriculture, and with his son Barrington he set up the Roswell Mills for the manufacture of cotton cloth. Soon afterward a woolen-goods factory and a flour mill began operations, more settlers came, and the town was incorporated under the first name of its founder in 1854.

In 1864, as General Sherman's army drew nearer to Atlanta, many of the inhabitants of Roswell fled to points farther south for safety. The mills were burned by the Union soldiers in order to destroy Confederate sources of supply, but most of the houses were spared, the most commodious being used as billets for the troops awaiting the capitulation of Atlanta. When the owners returned after the surrender, they found their homes packed by refugees from the surrounding countryside.

After the war, factories were rebuilt, but Roswell was unable to compete successfully with the richer industrial communities of the new South. Only a few small industries now operate here, and the town is preponderantly residential, chiefly noted for the architectural excellence and historic interest of a few fine old houses.

BARRINGTON HALL (*private*), across the street from the southern end of the park, is notable for its fine proportions and for the excellence of its classical details of architecture. Set well back from the street on a high hill, the two-story frame house is shadowed by a grove of oaks, cedars, and fruit trees. A walkway leading to the front porch is bordered by a low boxwood hedge, and more irregular plantings of boxwood crowd the eastern side of the house. The old

Residential

THE EDWARD INMAN HOUSE, ON ANDREWS DRIVE, IS OF THE GEORGIAN
STYLE WITH EGYPTIAN INFLUENCE SHOWING IN THE TWO OBELISKS ON
THE LAWN

THE HUGH NUNNALLY HOUSE, ON BLACKLAND ROAD, IS A FINE EXAMPLE
OF THE NEOCLASSIC STYLE

THE ABREU HOUSE, PACE'S FERRY ROAD, IS NOTABLE FOR ITS BOXWOOD
BORDERED WALK LEADING TO A BALCONIED REGENCY ENTRANCE

THE JOHN M. OGDEN HOUSE, PACE'S FERRY ROAD, SHOWS A STRONG
NORMAN INFLUENCE

ALL SAINTS EPISCOPAL CHURCH

GLENN MEMORIAL METHODIST CHURCH AND SECOND-PONCE DE LEON
BAPTIST (SPIRE ABOVE) ARE TWO OF THE MANY CHURCHES OF THE
RESIDENTIAL SECTIONS

THE HOME OF MRS. SAMUEL M. INMAN IS A GOOD EXAMPLE OF THE
RICHARDSONIAN-ROMANESQUE ARCHITECTURE

THE OLDER PEACHTREE STREET RESIDENCES, MANY NOW BOARDING HOUSES,
SHOW AN ELABORATE COMBINATION OF DIVERSE ARCHITECTURAL DETAILS

TECHWOOD IS ONE OF SEVERAL WELL-EQUIPPED FEDERAL HOUSING PROJECTS

THE MODERN APARTMENT HOUSE OF FUNCTIONAL ARCHITECTURE AND
WITH PENTHOUSE GARDEN IS STILL RARE IN ATLANTA

MANY ATLANTA PEOPLE LIVE IN MODERN SUBDIVISIONS

A LARGE CROSS SECTION OF ATLANTA LIVES IN TWO-FAMILY HOUSES IN
THE OLD SECTION NEAR THE CAPITOL

NEGRO SLUM AREAS ARE BEING REPLACED BY SUCH FEDERAL HOUSING
PROJECTS AS THE HENRY GRADY HOMES

NEGRO FAMILIES LIVE IN CROWDED SECTIONS THROUGHOUT THE CITY

mansion is encircled on three sides by a Doric colonnade with a pediment placed not at the front in the usual Greek Revival design but on each side. The banistered "captain's walk" in the center of the roof is a feature seldom incorporated in Southern houses, being more characteristic of the New England coast where sea captains watched their clipper ships from such eminences.

Barrington Hall was named for its first occupant, Barrington King, son of the founder of Roswell. During the long period of construction from 1839 to 1842, the family made its home in a small structure in the rear; on the day of completion Mrs. King, carrying her baby and followed by her small daughter with a little chair, walked ceremoniously around to the front door and entered for the first time as mistress of the mansion.

Until the War between the States Barrington King assisted his father in the management of the Roswell Mills and maintained his home in the luxurious and hospitable manner characteristic of plantation days. After the war he returned and resumed his occupancy of Barrington Hall until his death in 1866.

The house has always been occupied by descendants of the original owner. One of these, Evelyn King, was a bridesmaid at the wedding of Mittie Bulloch and Theodore Roosevelt in 1853, and in 1905, as Mrs. W.E. Baker she entertained their son, the famous "Teddy," then President of the United States. In possession of the present owner are many family pieces of china, silver, and furniture. Among the manuscripts are a diplomatic document signed by President Millard Fillmore and Daniel Webster and a letter from Henry Wadsworth Longfellow praising the verses of a young man of the Baker family.

MIMOSA HALL (*private*), on an unpaved street extending west of Roswell Park, has become nationally known as an outstanding example of the neoclassic style that was prevalent early in the 1840's when it was erected. Pictures of the two-story portico, with Doric columns supporting a high pediment, have appeared in the leading architectural publications. Built for Major John Dunwody, one of the original settlers of Roswell, it has changed hands several times; one of the more recent owners, Neel Reid, the well-known architect, acquired the property in 1916 and immediately began extensive restorations. After Reid's death his mother operated a tearoom on the lower floor.

From the street the facade is partly obscured by a dense growth of oaks, mimosas, wisteria vines, and circular plantings of boxwood. In other parts of the grounds the somber foliage of old cedars contrasts with the delicate blooms of roses and of valley lilies that were planted by the original owner.

Like many of the residential structures of its period, Mimosa Hall is fashioned of bricks covered with stucco marked off to simulate stone blocks. The interior has been extensively altered from time to time. The long drawing room with fireplaces at each end was created by Neel Reid by removing the partitions of two smaller rooms. The creamy yellow marble fireplace of the library was acquired from an old house in Macon when it was razed. In the dining room old paintings show effectively against paneled walls of a pale green color. An unusual interior feature is the small stage in the attic, used by some of the earlier occupants for amateur theatricals.

BULLOCH HALL (*private*), beyond Mimosa Hall and closing the western end of the street, was built by James Bulloch in 1842. Although the old plantation outhouses have long been razed, the main house has retained the dignity which characterized it from the first. The front portico is unusually massive, with four Doric columns supporting an attic gable. The rooms on the lower floor are 24 feet square and 12 feet high.

In one of these spacious rooms, Mittie Bulloch was married to Theodore Roosevelt on December 22, 1853. On this occasion the house was ablaze with the light of candles in candelabra of brass and silver, while fragrant cedar logs snapped in the fireplace. Holly and mistletoe were placed against the walls, and vines were twisted about the stair-rail. The bride, in white satin and long veil, descended the stairs preceded by her bridesmaids in full-skirted, tight-basqued white muslin dresses. Although Dr. Nathaniel Pratt performed the ceremony, he apparently considered these costumes worldly, for he would not permit his daughter to be a bridesmaid. After the ceremony the guests were served a bountiful hot supper ending with ice cream made with ice hauled from Savannah.

The son of this couple was Theodore Roosevelt who became President of the United States. Another son, Elliott, was the father of Eleanor Roosevelt, wife of President Franklin D. Roosevelt.

The OLD PRESBYTERIAN CHURCH, east side of US 19 approximately in the center of town, is a small, severely plain white clapboard structure with a Doric portico and a low, square bell tower. Simplicity also characterizes the interior with its slave gallery and double-staired pulpit, but the dead whiteness of walls and ceiling is relieved by the warm red tone of the aisle carpet. Stained glass has been used in all the windows.

The church, which recently celebrated its hundredth anniversary, was erected in 1840 under the supervision of its first minister, Nathaniel Pratt, who had come from Darien with his wife, a daughter of Roswell King. Dr. Pratt served as pastor for almost 40 years, as is attested by a memorial tablet under the pulpit. After his death he was succeeded by the Reverend W.E. Baker, who was married to a daughter of Barrington King. The service of the Bakers is also recognized by memorial inscriptions.

When Roswell was occupied by Federal troops in 1864, the church was commandeered as a hospital. This occupancy is shown by a cabinet door in the rear which was taken down and used as a checkerboard by the patients. Members of the congregation saved the communion silver from the invading army by concealing it in a basket of oats and taking it to the home of Olney Eldredge. Later, when the search for articles of value became more strenuous, it was decided to hide the silver in the residence of Miss Fannie Whitmire, which was less likely to be searched because of the illness of her mother. Each day baskets of dainties were sent to the invalid, inspected by the guard, and allowed to pass. Apprehensively, the custodians of the communion ware tried slipping a piece of silver under the food in the basket; this passed the guard successfully and another was secreted the following day. At last the entire service was smuggled into the Whitmire house.

When word was received that this place was also to be searched, the pieces were hastily put into a large dry-goods box filled with quilt scraps which were being pieced by a group of girls. When the soldiers came to search, Miss Whitmire held up some scraps and defiantly advised them not to overlook this box. A cursory inspection failed to discover the silver, which was then buried until the end of the war. Later the congregation presented Miss Whitmire with a silver cup for her bravery in hiding the communion service.

GREAT OAKS (private), across the street from the church, a red-brick house showing Georgian influence, was built for the Reverend Nathaniel Pratt soon after he came to Roswell in 1840 as pastor of the Presbyterian Church. The young minister, at first planning to have a columned Greek Revival dwelling in the prevailing plantation style, had lumber and other material brought from Augusta at considerable expense, but it was destroyed by fire before construction of the house was begun. Pratt, who had already noted the abundance of red clay in the Roswell vicinity, then decided to have a brick dwelling and set about the building of Great Oaks. Although the front has been remodeled, the house, with its mortised girders, heavy hand-hewn beams, and walls of eighteen-inch thickness, is a fine example of the enduring structural work of its day.

COLONIAL PLACE (private), end of Goulding St., was built in 1857 by the Reverend Francis R. Goulding, author of several well-known adventure books for boys. In this high, angular house of red-painted brick with white-trimmed windows and Palladian doorway, Goulding wrote his sermons, planned his eventful stories, and let his mind range hopefully over the inventions with which he was determined to make his fortune. His bold imagination, however, did not readily adapt itself to practical details. Although he designed a sewing machine some years before Elias Howe's invention was placed on the market, he failed with his model because he did not place the eye of the needle sufficiently near to its point. Barely missing eminence in the mechanical field, he is now remembered for his writings, especially for that adventurous tale of shipwreck and resourceful boyhood *Young Marooners*.

Part Four

APPENDICES

1813 Lieutenant George R. Gilmer establishes fort near The Standing Peachtree.

1821 January. By treaty at Indian Springs, Creeks cede territory later included in DeKalb and Fulton Counties.

April-May. Henry and Fayette Counties (mother counties of DeKalb and Fulton) created.

1822 December 7. DeKalb County created.

1823 December 10. Decatur incorporated and made seat of DeKalb County.

1826 Wilson Lumpkin and Hamilton Fulton survey railroad route through section.

1836 Hardy Ivy builds cabin on Land Lot 51.

December 21. State legislature charters Western & Atlantic Railroad.

1837 Roswell King founds town of Roswell.

Abbott Hall Brisbane drives stake marking southeastern terminus of Western & Atlantic Railroad.

1842 December 24. First train makes trial trip from the terminus to Marietta on Western & Atlantic Railroad track.

1843 December 23. The terminus incorporated as Town of Marthasville under commission form of government.

1845 Summer. Union School and Church erected.

September 15. First train from Augusta over Georgia Railroad reaches Marthasville.

December 26. Town charter amended to change name to Atlanta.

1846 August 18. Macon & Western Railroad reaches Atlanta.

1847 December 29. Atlanta reincorporated as city under mayor and council form of government.

1849 Western & Atlantic Railroad completed to Chattanooga, Tennessee.

1850 Population 2,572 (U.S. Census).

June 6. City buys tract of land for Oakland Cemetery.

1852 Atlanta & West Point Railroad completed to Atlanta.

1853 December 20. Fulton County formed from DeKalb, and Atlanta made the county seat.

1854 City limits extended.

City Hall completed.

Atlanta Medical College chartered.

1855 December 25. City lighted by gas.

1860   Population 9,554 (U.S. Census).
        Chamber of Commerce organized.
1861   January 2. Fulton County delegates to Georgia Secession Con-
        vention elected.
        July 5. Governor Joseph E. Brown designates Atlanta as tem-
        porary headquarters for Georgia State Military Affairs.
1862   June 1. Atlanta made military post under command of Major A.
        Leyden.
        June 7. James J. Andrews, Union spy, hanged in Atlanta.
        August 11. General Braxton Bragg places Atlanta under martial
        law.
1864   May 23. Mayor James M. Calhoun orders all male citizens to
        form home defense companies.
        July 17. General John B. Hood replaces General Joseph E. John-
        ston in command of Army of Tennessee.
        July 20. Battle of Peachtree Creek.
        July 22. Battle of Atlanta.
        July 28. Battle of Ezra Church.
        August 29. Federal forces cut vital supply line by wrecking Atlanta
        & West Point Railroad at Red Oak and Fairburn.
        August 31. Confederate forces defeated in Battle of Jonesboro
        and Macon & Western Railroad line cut.
        September 2. Atlanta surrendered.
        September 7. General William T. Sherman orders evacuation of
        citizens.
        November 14. Sherman burns Atlanta.
        December. Confederates reoccupy city.
1865   May 4. Confederate Colonel Luther J. Glenn turns over com-
        mand of Atlanta Military Post to Federal Colonel B.B. Eggleston.
        July 14. All ordinances differentiating between Negroes and white
        people repealed.
1866   March 3. City limits extended to include territory within 1½-mile
        radius of terminus stake.
        Miller Union Stock Yards established on Marietta Street.
1867   April 11. General John Pope, commander of Third Military Dis-
        trict, establishes headquarters in Atlanta.
        October. Atlanta University (Negro) incorporated.
        December 9. State Constitutional Convention meets in city hall.
        McPherson Barracks established.
1868   January 7. General George Gordon Meade replaces General Pope.
        April 20-23. New constitution ratified. Atlanta made State capital.
        June 16. Atlanta *Constitution* established by Colonel Carey W.
        Styles.
        July 22. Governor Rufus Bullock inaugurated and military govern-
        ment removed next day.
        July 23. Bush Arbor Meeting opens fight against carpetbagger
        rule.
        City leases Kimball's Opera House for State capitol.

1869   December 22. Military rule re-established, with General Alfred H. Terry in command.

Clark University (Negro) opened as elementary school.

1870   Population 21,789 (U.S. Census).

1871   September. Street railway service begins.

October 23. Rufus Bullock flees from Georgia.

1872   January. City opens public schools.

1873   September 28. Atlanta & Charlotte Air Line Railroad completed through efforts of Jonathan Norcross.

1874   City waterworks system built at Lakewood.

New city charter provides for bicameral council.

1876   All Federal troops removed from Atlanta.

November 28. Joel Chandler Harris begins writing Uncle Remus stories in Atlanta *Constitution.*

1878   Washington Seminary opened.

1879   Augusta Institute (Morehouse College—Negro) moved to Atlanta and opened as Atlanta Baptist Seminary.

First telephone system installed.

1880   Population 37,409 (U.S. Census).

1881   Spelman College (Negro) founded as Atlanta Baptist Female Seminary.

October 5-December 31. World's Fair and Great International Exposition held at Oglethorpe Park.

1882   July 1. First paid fire department established.

Colonel L.P. Grant donates 100 acres to city for public park.

1883   Atlanta *Journal* established by Colonel E.F. Hoge.

May 17. First Fulton County Courthouse dedicated.

Gammon Theological Seminary (Negro) opened as department of Clark University.

November. Georgia Western, under control of Richmond & Danville Railroad, completed to Birmingham, Alabama.

1885   City limits extended to include Grant Park.

Morris Brown College (Negro) opened.

1886   May. J.S. Pemberton perfects formula for Coca-Cola.

1887   Southern Dental College established.

October 10-17. Piedmont Exposition held.

East Point incorporated.

1888   October 7. Georgia School of Technology opened.

City drills $50,000 well at Five Points.

1889   March. G.V. Gress presents zoo to city.

March 20. New State capitol opened.

May 4. Fort McPherson established near East Point as permanent post.

September 24. Agnes Scott College opened in Decatur as Decatur Female Seminary.

1890   Population 65,533 (U.S. Census).

1891   October 21. Unveiling of Henry Grady Monument attracts visitors from all over the country.

1891   Hapeville incorporated.
        College Park incorporated as Manchester.

1892   January.   West End included within city limits.
        April 24.   Georgia, Carolina & Northern Railroad reaches Atlanta.
        May 25.   Grady Hospital dedicated.

1893   City waterworks on Chattahoochee River begins operation.

1895   September 18-December 31.   Cotton States and International Ex-
        position held at Piedmont Park.
        Peacock School for Boys established.

1898   G.V. Gress presents Cyclorama of the Battle of Atlanta to city.
        December 14-15.   Peace Jubilee held to celebrate end of Spanish-
        American War.

1900   Population 89,872 (U.S. Census).
        Georgia Military Academy founded at College Park.

1901   June 3.   Confederate Soldiers' Home opened.
        October 10.   City purchases Chamber of Commerce Building for
        use as city hall.
        Marist College opened.

1902   Federal Penitentiary completed.
        Carnegie Library opened.

1903   Southern College of Pharmacy established.

1904   May 23.   Piedmont Park purchased by city.
        City limits extended to include Piedmont Park.

1906   September.   Race riot occurs.

1909   Municipal auditorium-armory completed.
        Atlanta Music Festival Association organized.
        September.   North Avenue Presbyterian School founded.

1910   Population 154,839 (U.S. Census).
        May.   Metropolitan Opera Company gives first Atlanta per-
        formances.

1911   Southern Commercial Congress is addressed by President William
        Howard Taft, Theodore Roosevelt, and Woodrow Wilson.
        October 10.   Peace Monument unveiled at Piedmont Park.

1913   City charter revised.

1914   Sixth District Federal Reserve Bank established in Atlanta.
        Emory University established.
        Fulton County Courthouse completed.

1915   June 22.   Martial law declared to protect Governor John M.
        Slaton after he commuted death sentence of Leo Frank.
        Oglethorpe University opened.
        First Southeastern Fair held at Lakewood Park.

1916   May 20.   Northeastern side of Stone Mountain dedicated for
        carving Confederate memorial.
        Georgia Power Company strike causes widespread disorder and
        violence.

1917   Camp Gordon established as temporary war cantonment.
        May.   Great fire causes property loss of $5,000,000.

1919 September. Atlanta women vote for first time in city election.
Commission on Inter-racial Co-operation formed.
1920 Population 200,616 (U.S. Census).
Atlanta School of Social Work (Negro) opened.
1922 March 15. WSB begins broadcasting.
March 17. WGST begins broadcasting.
1923 Fourth Corps Area headquarters established in Atlanta.
1924 Municipal market opened.
Avondale Estates developed.
1925 City leases Candler Field for municipal airport.
Chamber of Commerce sponsors million-dollar campaign advertising Atlanta.
1926 High Museum of Art opened.
1927 Columbia Theological Seminary moved to Decatur from Columbia, South Carolina.
1928 Atlanta *World* (Negro) founded as weekly.
January 1. East Lake included within city limits.
1929 Twelve city officials and three private citizens convicted of graft.
Candler Field bought by city for municipal airport.
Rhodes Memorial Hall presented to State to house Department of Archives.
Million-dollar City Hall completed.
1930 Population 270,366 (U.S. Census).
Order of Black Shirts organized in Atlanta to replace Negro laborers with unemployed white workers.
Bobby Jones wins four golf championships—the American Amateur, American Open, British Amateur, and British Open.
1931 Atlanta *Constitution* awarded Pulitzer Prize for exposing graft ring.
Evelyn Jackson establishes MacDowell Festival.
May 24. WJTL (WATL) established by Oglethorpe University.
1932 July. Angelo Herndon leads mass demonstrations protesting inadequacy of relief.
Campbell and Milton Counties and the Roswell area merged with Fulton County.
1935 Asa G. Candler, Jr., offers private collection to Grant Park Zoo.
December 29. Ice storm does $2,000,000 damage.
1936 April. Annual dogwood festival inaugurated.
November. Employees of Fisher Body Company stage sit-down strike.
1937 August 1. WAGA established by Atlanta *Journal.*
1939 December 15. World premiere of *Gone With the Wind.*
1940 Population 302,288 (U.S. Census).

Bibliography

Allen, Ivan. *Atlanta from the Ashes.* Atlanta, Ruralist Press, 1928. 144 p. illus., diagr.

American Illustrating Company, comp. *Greater Atlanta Illustrated: the Most Progressive Metropolis in the South.* Atlanta, American Illustrating Company. 160 p. illus., port.

Archer, W. P. *History of the Battle of Atlanta: also Confederate Songs and Poems.* Knoxville, Ga., C.B.H. Moncrief, 1940. 35 p., incl. front. (port.), plates, port.

Atlanta. Fire Department. *History of the Atlanta Fire Department.* Atlanta, Byrd Printing Company, 1917. 38 p. illus., port.

—— Public Forum. *An Introduction to Social Service Agencies in Atlanta.* Atlanta, pub. by the forum, 1938, 62 p.

—— Public Schools. *My Brother's Keeper: the Story of the Welfare Agencies Sharing in the Community Fund.* Atlanta, n.p., 1936. 106 p. Material prepared for distribution by the Atlanta Public Forum staff under the direction of Ethel S. Albion.

—— Social Planning Council. *Directory of Social and Health Agencies. DeKalb and Fulton Counties, Georgia.* Atlanta, pub. by the Council, 1940. 68 p.

Atlanta Centennial Year Book, 1837-1937. Atlanta, pub. by Gregg Murphy, 1937. 170 p. illus., port.

Avary, Myrta Lockett. *Dixie after the War* . . . New York, Double-day, Page & Company, 1906. 435 p. illus., from old paintings, daguerreotypes, and rare photographs.

Avery, Isaac Wheeler, and others. *City of Atlanta: A Descriptive, Historical and Industrial Review of the Gateway City of the South.* Louisville, Ky. The Inter-State Publishing Company, 1892-93. 165 p. illus., port. (World's Fair Series on Great American Cities.)

Bowman, S.M. and R.B. Irwin. *Sherman and his Campaigns: A Military Biography.* New York, Charles B. Richardson, 1865. 512 p. port., maps.

Bullock, Henry Morton. *A History of Emory University.* Nashville, Tenn., Parthenon Press, c. 1936. 391 p. illus., front. (port.), port.

Cable, G.W. *The Silent South* . . . New York, Charles Scribner's Sons, 1907. 213 p. (Includes The Freedman's Case in Equity and the Convict Lease System).

Candler, Charles Murphey. *Historical Address: DeKalb County, Georgia, Centennial Celebration at Decatur, Georgia.* November 9, 1922. Decatur, Ga., pub. by the centennial association. 32 p.

Carter, E.R. *The Black Side: a Partial History of the Business, Religious, and Educational Side of the Negro in Atlanta, Georgia.* Atlanta, 1894. 323 p. illus., port.

Cate, Wirt Armistead, ed. *Two Soldiers: the Campaign Diaries of Thomas J. Key, C.S.A. December 7, 1863-May 17, 1865 and Robert J. Campbell, U.S.A. January 1, 1864-July 21, 1864* . . . Chapel Hill, N.C., University of North Carolina Press. 1938. 277 p. with introduction, notes, and maps.

The *Christian Index,* comp. *History of the Baptist Denomination in Georgia: with Biographical Compendium and Portrait Gallery of Baptist Ministers and other Georgia Baptists.* Atlanta, Jas. P. Harrison & Company, 1881. 613 p. illus., maps, port.

Clarke, Edwin Young. *Atlanta Illustrated: Containing Glances at its Population, Business, Manufacture, Industries, Institutions, Society, Healthfulness, Architecture, and Advantages Generally* . . . Atlanta, Jas. P. Harrison & Company, 1881. 224 p. illus., maps, (3rd edition. 1st pub. about 1877).

Cooney, Loraine M., comp. *Garden History of Georgia, 1733-1933.* Atlanta, Peachtree Garden Club, 1933. 458 p. illus.

Cooper, Walter G. *The Cotton States and International Exposition and South, Illustrated, Including the Official History of the Exposition.* Atlanta, The Illustrator Company, 1896. 504 p. illus., port.

────── *Official History of Fulton County* . . . Atlanta, Walter W. Brown Publishing Company, c. 1934. 912 p. illus., port., maps.

Cox, Jacob Dolson. *Military Reminiscences of the Civil War* . . . New York, C. Scribner's Sons, 1900. 2 v. fronts. (ports.), illus. (maps).

────── *The March to the Sea* . . . New York, C. Scribner's Sons, 1882. 265 p., incl. maps. (*Campaigns of the Civil War* series.)

Cunningham, Cornelia. *Atlanta, City of Today: A Sketch-Book.* Atlanta, Darby Printing Company, c. 1933. 25 p.

Detroit Cyclorama Company. *Atlanta: Battle of July 22, 1864* . . . A résumé of situations shown in the panorama with map of diagram. Detroit, Mich., pub. by the company, 1887. 21 p.

Dugat, Gentry. *Life of Henry W. Grady* . . . Edinburg, Tex., The Valley Printery, 1927. 150 p. front. (port.), plates.

Dyer, Frederick Henry. *A Compendium of the War of the Rebellion* . . . *from Official Records* . . . *Reports of the Army Registers and other Documents and Sources.* Des Moines, Iowa, The Dyer Publishing Company, 1908. 1796 p.

Enslow, J.D. and Geo. A. MacDonald, comp. *Atlanta Illustrated: A Story of Success.* Atlanta, published by the compilers, 1900. 96 p. illustrated.

Evans, Clement A., ed. *Confederate Military History.* Atlanta, Confederate Publishing Company, 1899. 12 v. port., maps. (Chapter XVI of Vol. 6 treats the Atlanta Campaign.)

Fairman, Henry Clay. *Chronicles of the Old Guard of the Gate City Guard, Atlanta, Georgia, 1858-1915.* Atlanta, Byrd Printing Company, 1915. 359 p. illus., port.

Felton, Rebecca Latimer. *Country Life in Georgia in the Days of My Youth.* Atlanta, Index Printing Company, c. 1919. 299 p., front. (port.). Contains addresses by Mrs. Felton before Georgia Legislature and various women's organizations.

Fulton County Medical Society. *Report of the Delegate of the Fulton County Medical Society* . . . Contains a history of the controversy between the Atlanta Medical College and the Fulton County Medical Society. Atlanta, 1939. 149 p.

Georgia: A Guide to Its Towns and Countryside. Compiled and written by workers of the W.P.A. Writers' Program in Georgia. Athens, Ga., The University of Georgia Press, 1940. 559 p. illus., maps.

Georgia. General Assembly. *Acts of the State of Georgia.* Pub. by the State.

Gordon, Asa H. *The Georgia Negro* . . . Ann Arbor, Mich., Edwards Brothers, Inc., 1937. 426 p. illus., ports.

Harris, Joel Chandler, ed. *Life of Henry W. Grady, Including his Writings and Speeches* . . . New York, 1890. 628 p. illus.

Harris, Julia Florida (Collier). *The Life and Letters of Joel Chandler Harris.* Boston and New York, Houghton Mifflin Company, 1918. 620 p. col. front., plates, ports., facsims.

Hart, Bertha Sheppard. *Introduction to Georgia Writers.* Macon, Ga., J.W. Burke Company, 1929. 322 p.

Hood, John Bell. *Advance and Retreat: Personal Experiences in the United States and Confederate States Armies.* New Orleans, privately printed, 1880. 358 p. port., maps.

Hornady, John R. *Atlanta, Yesterday, Today and Tomorrow.* American Cities Book Company, 1922. 442 p. illus., plates.

Huff, Sarah. *My 80 Years in Atlanta.* Atlanta, 1927. 100 p. illus.

Johnson, Gerald White. *The Undefeated.* New York, Minton, Balch & Company, 1927. 120 p. front. (A history of the Stone Mountain Confederate Memorial).

Johnston, James Houstoun, comp. *Western and Atlantic Railroad of the State of Georgia.* Atlanta, Stein Printing Company, 1931. 364 p. front., plates, ports., fold. map, facsim., diagr.

Jones, Charles Edgeworth. *Education in Georgia.* Washington, Government Printing Office, 1889. 154 p. plates. U.S. Bureau of Education Circular of Information. 1888, no. 4.

Knight, Lucian Lamar. *History of Fulton County, Georgia: Narrative and Biographical.* Atlanta, A.H. Cawston, 1930. 514 p. port.

————*Souvenir Book of the General Assemblies, Atlanta, Georgia, May 14-25, 1913.* Atlanta, Byrd Printing Company, 1913. 112 p. illus. (Compiled by Committee on Souvenir Book for the general assemblies of three Presbyterian religious bodies).

Kurtz, Wilbur G. *Historic Atlanta: A Brief Story of Atlanta and its Landmarks.* Atlanta, Conger Printing Company, c. 1929. 33 p. illus.

Kurtz, Wilbur G. *Locations and Descriptions of 117 Historic Places in Atlanta, Georgia, and Vicinity.* Atlanta, Chamber of Commerce, 1937. 23 p. mimeographed.

McBride, R.B. and R.S. McDonald. *Atlanta of Today.* Atlanta, Review Publishing Company, 1897. 62 p. illus.

Martin, T.H. *Atlanta and its Builders: A Comprehensive History of the Gate City of the South.* Century Memorial Publishing Company, 1902. 2 v., illus., port.

Mitchell, Margaret. *Gone With the Wind.* New York, The Macmillan Company, 1936. 1037 p.

National Negro Business League Convention. *1937 Directory and Souvenir Program of the National Negro Business League Convention.* Sponsored by the Atlanta Negro Chamber of Commerce. Atlanta, Arnett G. Lindsay, 1937. 102 p. illus.

Newman, Frances. *Frances Newman's Letters.* Edited by Hansell Baugh, with a prefatory note by James Branch Cabell. New York, H. Liveright, 1929. 372 p. front., (port.).

Northen, William J., ed. *Men of Mark in Georgia.* A complete and elaborate history of the state from its settlement to the present time, chiefly told in biographies and autobiographies of the most eminent men of each period of Georgia's progress and development. Atlanta, A.B. Caldwell, 1907-12. 7 v., ports.

Notable Men of Atlanta and Georgia. Atlanta, Foote & Davies Company, 1913. 156 p. port.

Phillips, Ulrich Bonnell. *A History of Transportation in the Eastern Cotton Belt to 1860.* New York, Columbia University Press, 1908. 405 p. illus., maps, tables, bibl.

Pioneer Citizen's Society of Atlanta. *Pioneer Citizens' History of Atlanta 1833-1902.* Atlanta, Byrd Printing Company, 1902. 400 p.

Ragsdale, B.D. *Story of Georgia Baptists* . . . Atlanta, published under the Auspices Executive Committee of the Georgia Baptist Convention, c. 1938. 3 v.

Reed, T.H., comp. *The Governments of Atlanta and Fulton County, Georgia.* A report of a complete administrative and financial survey of the several departments and activities of the City of Atlanta and Fulton County. Atlanta, Chamber of Commerce, 1938. 2 v. maps, table, diagr. (A summary, also pub. in 1938, contains 161 p.)

Reed, Wallace Putnam, ed. *History of Atlanta, Georgia: With Illustrations and Biographical Sketches of Some of its Prominent Men and Pioneers.* Syracuse, N.Y., D. Mason & Company, 1889. 491 p. of narrative, 211 p. of biography, port.

Sherman, William Tecumseh. *Memoirs.* New York, D. Appleton & Company, 1875. 2 v.

Smith, George G. *The History of Georgia Methodism from 1786 to 1866.* Atlanta, A.B. Caldwell, 1913. 430 p. illus.

Southern Israelite, comp. *One Hundred Years Accomplishments of Southern Jewry.* Atlanta, Southern Newspaper Enterprises, Inc., c. 1934. 72 p. ports.

Stacy, James. *A History of the Presbyterian Church in Georgia.* Elberton, Ga., Press of the Star, 1912. 404 p. front. (port.).

Stokes, Thomas Lunsford. *Chip Off My Shoulder.* Princeton, N.J., Princeton University Press, 1940. 561 p.

Suddeth, Ruth Elgin, ed. *An Atlanta Argosy: An Anthology of Atlanta Poetry.* Atlanta, Franklin Printing Corporation, c. 1938. 175 p.

Thompson, C. Mildred. *Reconstruction in Georgia, Economic, Social, Political, 1865-1872.* New York, Columbia University Press, 1915. 418 p.

Tucker, Nana. *The Atlanta Music Club Silver Anniversary: History and Record.* Atlanta, John T. Hancock, c. 1940. 105 p. illus., port.

United States. Record and Pension Office, War Department. *War of the Rebellion: A Compilation of the Official Records of the Union and Confederate Armies.* Washington, D.C., pub. by the department, 1880-1901. 130 v. and atlas, illus., maps.

White, George. *Statistics of the State of Georgia* . . . Savannah, Ga., W. Thorne Williams, 1849. 617 p.

Wiggins, Robert Lemuel. *The Life of Joel Chandler Harris* . . . *with Short Stories and Other Early Literary Work* . . . Nashville, Tenn., Dallas, Tex., publishing house Methodist Episcopal Church, South, Smith & Lamar, Agents, 1918. 447 p. front. (port.), plates.

Wilheit, Herbert Sayle. *A Few of the Highlights of the History of College Park, Ga.* College Park, dist. by the Community Service League, 1937. 12 p.

Woodward, Comer Vann. *Tom Watson: Agrarian Rebel.* New York, The Macmillan Company, 1938. 518 p. illus., ports.

Works Progress Administration of Georgia. *A Statistical Study of Certain Aspects of the Social and Economic Pattern of the City of Atlanta, Georgia.* Sponsored by the Planning Commission of Atlanta, 1939. 187 p. maps, tables.

NEWSPAPERS AND PERIODICALS

Atlanta Constitution, 1868-1941.

Atlanta Historical Society. *The Atlanta Historical Bulletin.* Atlanta, pub. by the society, 1927-41.

Atlanta Journal, 1883-1941.

Calhoun, F. Phinizy. "The Founding and the Early History of the Atlanta Medical College, 1854-1875." *The Georgia Historical Quarterly.* V. 9, No. 1, March, 1925, p. 35-54.

Hay, T.R. "The Atlanta Campaign," *The Georgia Historical Quarterly.* V. 7, No. 1, March, 1923, p. 18-43 and V. 7, No. 2, June, 1923, p. 99-118.

Ingersoll, Ernest. "The City of Atlanta," *Harper's New Monthly Magazine.* Vol. LX, Dec. 1879, p. 30-43. illus.

Lowry, E.G. "Reconstruction, or Atlanta, for Instance." *The Saturday Evening Post,* V. 192, June 19, 1920, p. 18-19, 113-22.

Index

Index

(In case of titled essays and points of interest, the first number is the principal reference)